ALBERT SLOSMAN

THE ORIGINS TRILOGY
II
THE SURVIVORS OF ATLANTIS

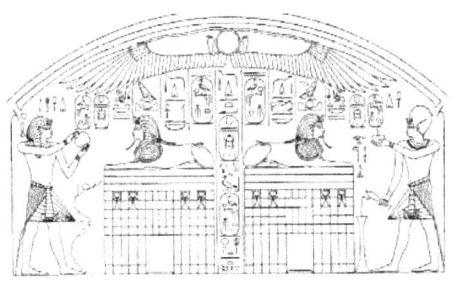

ΩMNIA VERITAS.

ALBERT SLOSMAN (1925-1981)

THE ORIGINS TRILOGY II
THE SURVIVORS OF ATLANTIS

LA TRILOGIE DES ORIGINES II

Les survivants de l'Atlantide

First edition Robert Laffont, Paris, 1978

Translated and published by

OMNIA VERITAS LTD

www.omnia-veritas.com

© Omnia Veritas Limited – 2025

All rights reserved. No part of this publication may be reproduced by any means without the prior permission of the publisher. The intellectual property code prohibits copies or reproductions for collective use. Any representation or reproduction in whole or in part by any means whatsoever, without the consent of the publisher, the author or their successors, is unlawful and constitutes an infringement punishable by articles of the Code of Intellectual Property.

... BY WAY OF PROLEGOMENA	9
ALBERT SLOSMAN	11
INTRODUCTION	13
CHAPTER ONE	37
TA MANA!	37
(Sunset-place)	37
CHAPTER TWO	57
LIFE RESUMES	57
CHAPTER THREE	77
OUSIR THE RISEN	77
CHAPTER FOUR	97
HORUS-LE-PUR	97
CHAPTER FIVE	118
THE COVENANT WITH GOD	118
CHAPTER SIX	136
THE PARABOLIC OF NUMBERS	136
CHAPTER SEVEN	157
THE RA-SIT-OU	157
(The Sit-Soleil rebels)	157
CHAPTER EIGHT	176
"TA OUZ"	176
(The 'Abode' of Usir)	176
CHAPTER NINE	193
THE GREAT MOURNING	193
CHAPTER TEN	208
"THE BLACKSMITHS OF HORUS"	208
(The masnitiou-hor)	208
CHAPTER ELEVEN	223
SA-AHA-RA	223
(The "Burnt-by-the-Sun-Ancient" land)	223
CHAPTER TWELVE	242
THE TRÉPANEURS	242
(The school of "serk-kers")	242
CHAPTER THIRTEEN	262

CHRONOLOGY OF THE "FOUR STAGES" 262
CHAPTER FOURTEEN.. **283**
    THE AGE OF GEMINI 283
    (... OR THE PREDYNASTIC STRUGGLE OF THE "TWO BROTHERS") 283
NOTES AND BIBLIOGRAPHY... **303**
    NOTE A: *ABOUT PLATO'S TIMAEUS* 303
    NOTE B: ON THE ANTIQUITY OF THE DENDERAH ZODIAC 305
BIBLIOGRAPHY... **309**
OTHER TITLES **313**

... BY WAY OF PROLEGOMENA

By transforming the translational movement into a rotational movement, as Heraclitus, Plato's disciple, had predicted, Hycetas did not solve the problem. In the end, it was Aristarchus of Samos who affirmed both movements. He was accused of impiety for daring to move Vesta!

PLUTARCH
(De fac. in orb. Lun.)

The theory according to which the Sun is at the centre of the world and remains immobile is false and absurd, formally heretical, and opposed to the Holy Scriptures. As for saying that the Earth moves and is not at the centre of the world, animated by a daily revolution, this doctrine is as false as it is absurd from a philosophical point of view, and at the very least erroneous in theology.

(Extract from the judgment of the
theologians who, in 1616, judged
COPERNICUS' Astronomical Realities).

And yet Plato begins his account with the story of the island of Atlantis, which was certainly not in Egypt. This association of foreign facts with those specific to Egypt is positive proof of what I have just established, and is at the same time a formal admission that the Egyptians drew their common origin from this island.

LETTER ABOUT ATLANTIS
(from M. Bailly to M. de Voltaire)

But another perhaps fanciful, but by the same token seductive, supposition associates the Berbers with Atlantis, which would imply a push from West to East, and not the other way round!

E.F. GAUTIER
(The past of North Africa)

> Human reason
> does not possess any reasonable reasoning
> in its conception of God!
>
> A. S.

ALBERT SLOSMAN

Passionate about ancient Egypt and Atlantis. Professor of mathematics and expert in computer analysis was involved in NASA's programmes to launch Pioneer to Jupiter and Saturn.

His intention was to rediscover the source of monotheism and write its history.

His search for the origins of everyone and everything led him, by curious and unexpected paths, to fix his attention on the ancient Egyptian civilisation, whose formation and development were approached with an open and independent mind throughout his short life.

Albert was a member of the Resistance during the 2nd World War, was tortured by the Gestapo and later suffered an accident that left him in a coma for 3 years.

Slosman was a person of extremely fragile appearance and health, but animated by an intense inner strength that kept him alive, motivated by the desire to complete a work in 10 volumes that was intended as an immense framework of the permanence of monotheism through time, and which his premature death did not allow him to conclude.

A minor accident, a fractured neck of the femur, following a fall on the premises of the Maison de la Radio in Paris, took his life, perhaps because his body (his human carcass, as he liked to say), already well shaken, could not withstand another assault, however insignificant it may have been.

ALBERT SLOSMAN

Introduction

> *Who doesn't know that you are the accomplices of those whom God caused to die in the Cataclysm? You are of the race of the pharaohs who were kings of Egypt! You are of the race of Sodom and Gomorrah and of all those who fought against God in unbelief from the beginning!*
>
> SENUTI THE PROPHET
> (Demotic papyrus from the 6th century)

> *The extraordinary antiquity of Egyptian civilisation is still too new an opinion, and one that upsets too many opposing opinions for it to be established without contradiction, and there is no lack of contradiction!*
>
> CHAMPOLLION-FIGEAC
> (Ancient Egypt, page 95 b)

The uninformed reader may be surprised to find humanity emerging from the most remote times, defying the millennia, in an attempt to create a second homeland for themselves, their "First Heart", Ahâ-Men-Ptah, having been wiped out by the Great Cataclysm[1]. However, it should not be forgotten that our current knowledge dates the first hominid back three million years! So there's nothing unusual in ethnic evolution for a people who had lived in peace and constant progress for five hundred centuries to have ended up disappearing when their continent sank, and for the survivors to have succeeded in founding a 'Second Heart'.

---

[1] See *The Great Cataclysm*, by the same author, published by Omnia Veritas; www.omnia-veritas.com.

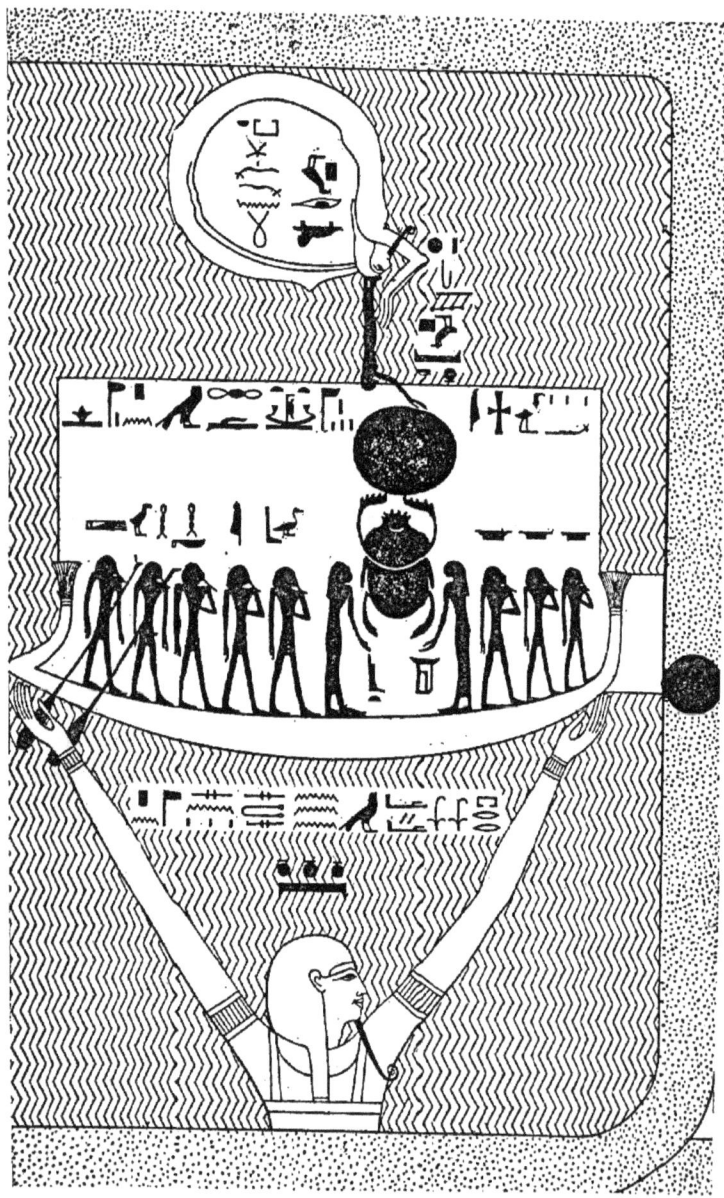

Praise be to these generations, descended from the "Descendants, the survivors of Ahâ-Men-Ptah" "Book of the Beyond of Life" (chapter XVII - V. 47).

My aim is to recount the history of monotheism from its origins, as described in the Sacred Texts in hieroglyphic. For in the mists of time, among the most primitive of men, a "chosen" tribe was instructed in the Divine Law of Creation through the birth of an "Elder", the Ahâ. It was for this reason that all the Kings of the Egyptian dynasties took the name of *Pêr-Ahâ* ("Descendant of the Elder"), which the Greeks phonetised as *Pharaoh*. These Elders therefore knew that they were the image of the Creator, and that it was vital for them, the Creatures, to rely on celestial legislation for their lives. Harmony reigned thanks to a constant Alliance.

But the incredulity brought on by forgetfulness and the wear and tear of time eventually turned into unawareness, then into impiety. Man took himself for God and was rudely awakened with a punishment commensurate with the crime. The survivors vowed to prevent such an abomination from ever happening again, and to this end they engraved all the details in imperishable stone as soon as they could. It is now possible, after twelve millennia, to retrace the events and the epic that followed, both in the light of hieroglyphic texts and by recapturing the meaning of the countless rock engravings that line the route of this exodus. From Morocco to Egypt, this Sacred Way stretches its wide ribbon in a clear west-east direction. It ends at the place where Menes, the founder of the Pharaonic dynasties, built the first temple to the glory of God, in thanks for his safe arrival in this second land, on the banks of the Nile. The most ancient annals sing the praises of the magnificent religious edifice, whose hieroglyphic name, "ATH-KA-PTAH", later encompassed the city that grew up around it, and then the entire country. This patronymic, phonetised by the Greeks as "AE-GUY-PTOS", and "EGYPT" by the French, is significant in its precision: "THE SECOND HEART OF GOD".

The long and arduous journey to this promised land lasted several millennia and stretched over thousands of kilometres. This exhausting and tragic period, which defies contemporary imagination, is ap pelle, in the original texts, "The Great Mourning". Its end is the conclusion of this second volume. The hatred between the two fratricidal clans descended from Seth and Horus, which borders on a battle of the Giants in terms of both the time it encompasses and the space it covers, subsequently gave credence to a delusional mythology among the Hellenes that transformed Egyptian monotheism into a Zoolean barbarism.

All the Pharaohs venerated the symbol of Isis giving birth under the sycamore tree, thus allowing themselves to be penetrated by the Holy Spirit (as was the case with Ramses II, represented here for his establishment as "Son of God", eternally).

This Greek 'elite' unabashedly trampled ancient spirituality underfoot in order to replace it with a certain iconography, although it is possible to attribute a certain degree of fabrication to it. The personification of this behaviour is undoubtedly the pseudo-Plutarch. Since he understood nothing of the Sacred Texts, he made a point of inventing meanings for what remained incomprehensible to him.

And so it was with the very free interpretation of the holy story of Isis and Osiris, which developed nothing but obscenities and absurdities, accumulated with the sole aim of demonstrating the superiority of Greek intelligence. This did not prevent Plutarch from being taken seriously by scholars the world over for the next two millennia, perhaps to keep a clear conscience vis-à-vis the ethics of their time, by sparing themselves an abyss of questions about why monumental constructions were erected to the glory of a single God in such remote times.

The proliferation of hieroglyphic writing on these religious edifices was not the least of their enigmas, especially when they realised that at the same time, their ancestors were living in smoke-filled caves, barely clad in animal skins. But how could they have imagined that this script preserved Knowledge? The new hieroglyphic combination was designed to reproduce the original story of Creation as easily and as protectively as possible. Monotheism, which had peacefully governed the lives of the Ancestors in Ahâ-MenPtah, was no more than an illusion when, in order to serve the rest of the Earth in his grief and anger, God had had to annihilate the continent that Plato called Atlantis, which became 'Amenta', or the 'Land of the Blessed in the Beyond'.

When the "Elder Heart" was swallowed up by the great Cataclysm, unforgettable to those who survived it, which took place on 27 July 9792 BC, the position of the "Second Heart" was already defined, on a distant but accessible land. This is confirmed in various rooms of the Temple of the Lady of Heaven at Denderah, by the explanation that follows the engraving of the circular planisphere near the great terrace, and by the rectangular zodiac in the hypostyle hall.

It was the mortal hatred separating the enemy brothers, the "Followers of Horus" and the "Rebels of Set", that triggered the condemnation of the chosen race. In vying for supremacy of the land, they both forgot their duties, thus encouraging the development of barbaric idolatry. This is why, on the day when the cup of bitterness overflowed into the sky, the celestial floodgates opened, covering Ahâ-Men-Ptah... A liquid immensity covered, like a shroud, the tens of millions of human beings who had been favoured by the Creator, only to be so terribly punished.

For the dazed survivors who crash-landed on another land, an immeasurable fear of God was the first and most lasting reaction. No one should make fun of the Almighty, either openly or in their hearts. The survivors thus relied first of all on his clemency, and then, through their repentance, on a new benevolence. Their main concern, from the very first days, was to try to have their faults forgiven by a solid union between Heaven and Earth. This would be a new Covenant between God and mankind, which this time would be indestructible despite all subsequent attempts, so that Eternal Peace would reign alone on Earth.

It was a fine philosophical and ritualistic concern, but one that failed to take account of a factor foreign to the human soul: oblivion. Dozens of centuries after the Great Cataclysm, a thick veil had covered the event in the consciences of the generations that followed! And over the millennia that followed, the imagination of the masses took it upon itself to transform the Truth into "Hero Myths", then "Allegorical Legends", before culminating in "Affabulatory Tales". History repeats itself over and over again, and monotheism was no exception.

The periods that successively marked the oldest of the chosen peoples, in a constant predestination for a spectator of our time who meditates with sufficient hindsight, can be summarised as follows:

> - The Era of the "Descendant": Ahâ or the Elder. His progeny reigned for the duration of a long divine dynasty, which integrated the nascent multitude into a people whose land was called the Elder-of-God, *Ahâ-Men-Ptah* ;

> - The Era of the descendants of the "demigods". These were the sons of Horus (Hor) and those of Seth (Sit). They guided the survivors of the engulfment, trying to destroy each other, towards the second country promised to them;

> - The Era of the descendants called "Heroes". These were the ones who instituted the governmental unit of the "Second Heart-of-God", *Ath-KaPtah*. They preached a

return to the original monotheism, and were overthrown by the idols of the enemy clan;

- The Era of the only human descendants. They were the usurpers of the Pêr-Ahâ. The ancient pharaohs, of divine essence, gave way to Zolaitan tyrants who made the ram Ammon the new god. This was the prelude to the decadence and loss of civilisation, of which nothing remained when the Persians invaded in 525 BC.

Those who taught during the first era, in times so remote as to seem inconceivable to us, undeniably benefited from what is known as the Light. It was the only possible origin, and it projected the splendour of its thousands of facets onto all the "Cadets", making Wisdom penetrate them luminously.

When they gave way to the first humanised families, at the right time and place in the great spiraloid of Space allied to Time, nothing could change Creation more than the Creator himself. Thus all contact with the Divine Breath that generated Souls was gradually lost. Man took himself for a god! The story of the birth of the world, so much sung by the Elders of Ahâ Men-Ptah and so venerated by the Priests, was from then on no more than a fact touted ironically to lull cowardly consciences to sleep. And recklessness persuaded the strong-minded that they alone were the masters of their own destinies!

The advance of civilisation, with the resulting increase in well-being, shows in every illogicality its ruthless destructive power, and it is with this precise fact that the duality between good and evil was instituted. The Origin could only end in destruction, in order to begin a new origin in another form, to show and demonstrate that Eternity belongs only to God.

The transitional period of Hor's descent, which provided the link between the Elders of Ahâ-Men Ptah and the Cadets of Ath-Ka-Ptah, needs no comment here, since it will be followed step by step throughout the chapters that follow. It was easily and faithfully retraced, having been preserved orally for generations and generations, until it was possible to engrave it on the walls of the temples of the first Egyptian dynasties. Even later, the Greeks took hold of the texts and turned them into epic fantasy writings that reflected their own way of life. It was in these legends that the gods of Olympus were transferred, where they quarrelled, were jealous and committed the worst abuses, contrary to the divine nature of the Elders. So it was only natural that the rumours of a destructive arrival should spread from this strictly human and culpable behaviour.

Hesiod, Homer and Virgil, to name but a few of the poets who are universally known and appreciated, made extensive use of stories they had heard and already distorted during their time in Egypt, turning them into new "heroic" themes. Such was their success that it is still going strong after two thousand years, and rightly so. We all know that these subjects were treated in their own way in order to interest us. This was not the case with Plutarch, who included his Isis and Osiris in his *Moral Works* (sic!).

What is fascinating for a researcher is to try to pinpoint the truth behind the narration of these authors, the origin of the idols they describe, and to compare them, after removing the faint veneer of authenticity, with the original still engraved in hieroglyphic. The many abominable adventures thus find their hereditary entity, the object of a very distant but unique veneration: the One and Only God and Almighty Creator, PTAH.

The monumental iconography, on a scale of unimaginable gigantism, not only recounts the great civilising events of a very ancient and little-known past, but the chronological events that disrupted and ultimately destroyed this people who had been "God's beloved". The same hieroglyphs that make up the texts of the Sacred Language were faithfully reproduced during each reconstruction of a religious building, at the time scheduled by the High Priests to ensure that the Temple remained in the beneficial axis of the "Divine-Mathematical Combinations", right up to the time of the Ptolemies.

The same was true of the Temple of Denderah. It was Evergetes II who ordered its *sixth* reconstruction! This made it possible to reread all the previous annals, using those engraved in the 12 crypts uncovered and in the interior staircases leading to the basement rooms, which were as large as those in the Upper Temple of the Lady of Heaven.

But the Divine meaning that had been lost and buried under the desert sands was not even partially rediscovered. The peaceful Hellenic invaders who moved in after the Persians had left unearthed only gigantic monuments. The illegible hieroglyphs were falsely interpreted, and the key understanding the Covenant between man and God remained in their "abominable" graphics. The ravages caused by this loss became the slow but effective promoters of the total oblivion of the sacred content of the Texts, even among those who had been entrusted with perpetuating the Dogma.

Some temples, freed from their gradual sinking, once again stand proudly near the banks of the Great River; but their symbolism is now limited to Kabbalistic signs, good only for inspiring delirious fables from the minds of travellers overwhelmed by the obvious immoderation of these masses dating back to an era before biblical times.

"Civilised" writing came much later, developing during the time of the Phoenicians, Chaldeans and Greeks. Other mythological stories adapted from more ancient traditions or purely invented from hieroglyphics supplanted the Sacred Texts. From the seventh century BC, the Egyptian priests learned the languages spoken across the Nile in order to compensate for the fact that they themselves had forgotten the original Knowledge.

With a certain humorous humanism, these clerics intoxicated those who came to visit them, with sole aim of extracting from them bits of science that could be monetised. That's why they didn't give in to this temptation, especially as they themselves didn't know much about it any more. And these rapacious tourists no choice but to content themselves with muddled explanations, in order to invent a storyline more in keeping with their contemporaries' conception of the world. The result was the fantasies we know today.

After that, century after century, from distorted interpretations to erroneous juxtapositions; from biliteral approximations drawn from Coptic to justifications based on Hebrew and Arabic similarities, there remained no valid, let alone legible, oral tradition on Knowledge and Wisdom. And yet, at the time of the revival of Egyptological science, simple logic should have shown that trying to understand a language that had been dead for several millennia with the help of contemporary alphabetic letters would be to cause it to die a second time.

Nevertheless, reading our ancient narrators is most instructive. If we are to believe Porphyry, Solinus, Proclus and so many other 'specialists' of this period of the scientific renaissance, we are given a very bizarre picture of the Egyptian cosmogony, which was as precise as ours can be today.

The most striking example of this senility of the mind, typical of all writers returning from the banks of the Nile, was that "the Egyptians placed the rising of the Canicule as having presided over the creation of the Earth and the formation of the first human beings".

Although this is an aberration for our intelligence, it does allow us to see that the 'Fixed One', the *Sep'ti* star we know as *Sirius*, which the Greeks called the Canicular star or *the Dog*, was of real importance in the ancient astronomical system. In fact, for the Egyptians, Sirius determined the beginning of a 'Year of God' that lasted 1,461 years of our annual solar revolutions.

From the depths of the ages, from the most remote past described, the Pontiffs who succeeded one another at the head of the "Double House of Life" teaching "Divine Mathematics" at Denderah, the celestial configurations with the geometric combinations that harmonised them, had as their reference points veritable *fixed points:* luminous points in space with very special properties. And Sirius was one of them.

Even today, it's easy to make sense of the celestial representations engraved here and there over several millennia, and above all to date them with great precision, thanks to the Earth's precessional retreat through space. Each "Fixed:" has its own mathematical day in relation to a human observer on Earth. This is the day when it appears in the night sky *before* the Sun, in other words when it shines in all its splendour *before* daylight arrives, at dawn, on the eastern horizon. Astronomers refer to this phenomenon as the *heliacal rising of a star.*

Now Sirius was the 'Fixed' star par excellence, as far back as the reign of the Pêr-Ahâ, a long way from Egypt. These Ancestors had observed the anomaly of this star, which made it a divine sign to be used in the various divisions that were to punctuate the passage of Time. After meticulously observing it and noting all its particular characteristics, they added qualifications that experience had confirmed. Their distant descendants, having realised that the opposite direction taken by the "Mathematical Combinations" in no way altered the course of the days or their meaning, then decided to re-establish the true calendar, starting from the year willed by God, in such a way that the instructions had to be followed very scrupulously. Thus, with the advent of Athothis, the son of Menes, in the year 4241 before the birth of Christ, the Sothiac calendar, that of Sep'ti the "Guiding Star", was reborn.

As this subject will be dealt with in detail in the next volume, which will be devoted solely to the history of the Temples of Denderah and their "Divine-Mathematical Combinations", there is no point in beginning here the explanatory process of celestial movements and their relationship with our humanity. But the Exodus decided upon by the surviving Elders of Ahâ-Men-Ptah, towards Ath-Ka-Ptah, favourable to the development of a second Alliance promised by God at a beneficial moment in the configurations of the "Fixed Ones", was well and truly inscribed in the future sky at a date that could be calculated in advance. As was the location of this second homeland, the "Second Heart", in perfect harmony with the heavens.

This is why, over these millennia, the path followed by each of the two enemy clans, with all its stages and their duration, was meticulously calculated and ordered in Time from the Moroccan coast to the location ideally determined to be the "Second Heart of God". Whether they were the 'Followers of Hor' or the 'Rebels of Sit', these descendants of the same original ethnic group remained linked in parallel searches for a cosmic accord.

There is, however, one remarkable fact that can be understood here, and which cannot be the result of mere coincidence. From Morocco onwards, during the thousands of kilometres that the multitude travelled to the banks of the Nile, the exhausting epic that lasted for millennia *always* took place *at the same latitude*. It was the same latitude under which the first observatory for celestial combinations was built at Ath-Mer, the capital of the sunken continent , and it was exactly the same latitude under which the observatory at Denderah was built: the imaginary line that we now call the *Tropic of Cancer*.

There can be no doubt that Sep'ti was the landmark star that served as a fixed point along the way. Denderah was the end of the road, and the priests knew there that they had finally reached the end of their expiatory journey. In fact, at this point, the only one of its long course, the Nile makes an enormous loop, leaving a large fertile valley available before being closed off by a long chain of mountains on one side, and the desert on the other bank of the river.

All that remained for Sep'ti to do was to begin again to mark out the beating of Time with a calendar that would regulate the time of mankind. The sky would thus be united with the earth: it would be the "Year of God". It wasn't until almost 5000 years later that the Greeks claimed to have invented astronomy. They were surprised by this very bright star of the first magnitude, which taunted them with obvious connivance with the High Priests, deliberately pointing at the appointed time and place, just like many others at various times, which implied perfect knowledge of their movements in the sky. However, as the Egyptians based a certain cycle on Sirius, Hellenic travellers turned this 'Fixed One' into a vigilant and highly obedient watchdog, also monitoring the movement of the floods, which inspired great respect.

The length of this rhythmic time was beyond their comprehension, and did not allow them to clearly delineate the suppositions arising from the complex calculations of their ancient predecessors on Earth. The cyclical return of a very precisely defined heliacal sunrise only took place after 1,460 solar years, i.e. at the start of *the 1,461th annual revolution* of our fiery star.

The most ancient Pêr-Ahâ had already noted that Sep'ti, i.e. Sirius, rose heliacally at the start of the flood, *six hours later* than the previous year. At the end of four years, it was therefore appropriate to count back the clock by one day. Mathematically, this meant that twenty-four hours were added every four years to ensure that the harmony between Heaven and Earth was not disrupted. In other words, a leap year complex with no use of the Sun as a timekeeper.

This Sothian year, known as the "Year of God", comprised 365 cycles of four years plus one day, or 1,460 Sirius heliacal years or 1,461 solar heliacal years. For each cyclic return, therefore, there was a joint rising of the two stars, an astral conjunction that was the divine sign of an eternal celestial harmonic recommencement of the Covenant accepted by God.

A mixture of several legends, following on from these calculations, many of which postdate these ancient events, associated Sirius with Thoth, "inventor of the calendar". Thoth is the abbreviation of Athothis, the son of Menes, who, in 4241 BC, re-established the Sothian calendar on the very day of the Sun-Sirius conjunction, i.e. the 27th of July at that time.

At this memorable hour, which re-established all the institutions of a reunited Egypt, the Nile began to flood, inundating all the arable land with fertile silt. Sirius was clearly visible for as long as it lasted, after which it ceased to appear until the next beginning of

Thoth. This is why the Greeks retained only the image of a bright point in the sky, "Fixed", faithfully watching like a dog, hence *canis* and caniculaire, which became synonymous with torrid for our month of August, which was the Thoth of that time.

Plutarch's 'mythologists', who had also seen everywhere on the walls of temples and tombs the representation of an enormous black dog with proudly erect ears and wide-open eyes, did not stick to the explanations given to them, namely that it was the companion of Anepou; they preferred to make it the earthly representation of Sirius, whom they called Anubis. Hence the complexity of the fables they invented, with Sirius becoming the guardian of the Beyond, and the unifying 'Fix' of Death and Life, beyond the ether.

Anepou will be much in evidence in this book, as will his faithful black dog, who was far from "prowling the cemeteries" as our imaginative Plutarch claimed. He had been a faithful protector and friend to this High Priest who reinvented the principles of mummification of bodies, thus facilitating the passage of Souls from their carnal envelopes to the "Kingdom of the Blessed". Everyone will be able to judge for themselves what this affabulation is, born of the strong minds of the so-called writers of our own antiquity.

The year of Sirius, by virtue of its astronomical duration, allowed the first survivors a constantly planned ascension in time. They became a multitude and, at the end of their labours, reached the outskirts of the promised territory, which would be the Second Heart. Every move of these wanderers was thought out and prepared, as was the profile and length of each stage of this exhausting Exodus, which was thus able to faithfully follow the course of the celestial "Mathematical Combinations" thanks to the "fixed" point of the "Dog" star.

For this star of the first magnitude had not suffered any of the disturbances felt by the Earth. Its exceptional celestial navigation had in no way been affected by the Great Cataclysm, a fact that the High Priests of the first days of renewal had perfectly recognised.

They saw this as a clear Divine sign of appeasement, the prelude to forgiveness for the survivors.

In this way, the Denderah planisphere rediscovers its very clear and primordial meaning through six successive reconstructions. There is no doubt about them, despite the scepticism of some. Numerous ancient writings attest to this. From the time of King Khufu, the famous Khufu of the Greeks, during the 4th dynasty, a document written by the Royal Scribe confirms this. Preserved in the Museum of Boulaq, in Egypt, the papyrus reads: "The Temple of the Lady of Heaven, of Tentyris, (Denderah) must be renovated by order of His Majesty Khufu, with the Just Voice. This will be the third reconstruction; it will be carried out according to the very ancient primitive plans of the "Followers of Hor", which are drawn on gazelle skins and which we preserve in the Archive Room."

It has been formally established that the origins of the temples of Denderah are lost in the mists of Predynastic time, even if it is true that the last reconstruction dates back only to the reign of Ptolemy in the ninth century BC. Exploring the many excavations that have already been uncovered in the basements, as well as in the twelve underground crypts, it is easy to see that the engravings, identical *down to the smallest detail*, nevertheless differ very clearly in the style of the reproductions on the stone. The further underground you go in the oldest rooms, the coarser the overall workmanship becomes. This is understandable if we accept that the tools used were no more than rudimentary.

The same was true of this zodiac, which indicated the exact date of the Great Cataclysm through the position of the "Fixes" and the constellations reproduced on it, identical in every detail to the first original engraving. On this "map of the heavens", Leo leads the cohort of the "Twelve", standing on his boat and unwinding the spiral of Creation in its eternal swirling motion. In this way, he directs the various "Mathematical Combinations" thanks to the Breath pulsing through the Earth from God himself. On this very day, the beginning of a new cycle, the brand new road was the opposite of the one that had preceded it, as demonstrated by a second lion, seated below, turning its head towards the western horizon and resting its front paws on the hieroglyph meaning "Flood".

This finely engraved imagery hardly needs to be explained to be understood, as it clearly depicts the catastrophic event that forever changed the history of a people who believed themselves to be chosen. Punished for their impiety, their savagery and their thoughtlessness, the surviving men wanted to preserve an imperishable souvenir so that their descendants would remember and not repeat such a crime.

It was thanks to this precaution that it was possible to carry out our contemporary research with the help of a computer. The precise programming of the astronomical and mathematical data required to obtain the result resulted in one date, printed on a tape terminal: 27 July 11,767, i.e. 9792 BC.

This date represents, without any possible error, that of a terrible plague. On the ceiling of the initiation room where it is engraved, this planisphere is surrounded on two sides by six broken lines, forming a kind of raging wave, a hieroglyphic representation of a super-flood: the Great Cataclysm that engulfed AhâMen-Ptah.

At first sight, this seems too fantastic to be true. Our narrow mind defends itself against the possibility of such a resurgence. And yet, since Solon and Plato, there has been no shortage of writings attesting to this reality, as well as to the Wisdom emanating from this people. But where could the knowledge of the people who lived on the banks of the Nile in the time of Menes have come from?

Even Plutarch, who was an eyewitness, was full of respect for the possessors of sciences that he considered inexplicable by human standards. The Egyptians measured the height of the pole, for example, with a tile-shaped tablet that formed a right angle with a level plane[2]. From this description, it is easy to recognise a type of

---

[2] "Des oracles qui ont cessé", chap. 3.

equinoctial sundial still in use in Thebaid in the second millennium BC.

What we have to admit is that such an instrument could not have come into being just like that. It only arose as a logical consequence of knowledge of the obliquity of the ecliptic, and had been around long enough to be able to control its curvature using specially designed measuring devices.

Who would dare to claim that a people capable of equipping themselves with such instruments for taming space, and of orienting their first religious buildings with rigorous precision, would not have been able to describe and accurately reproduce the state of the sky on a given day in their time?

But then, Anaximander? Anaximenes? Thales? Does this mean that these 'scholars' invented nothing? Clement of Alexandria, who knew exactly what he was talking about, and who was perfectly familiar with the contents of his city's archives, remarked wistfully in his *Stromata*: "If I had to cite here all the plagiarism and all the knowledge that the Greeks borrowed from the Egyptians, the entire contents of this book would not be enough to write the names of their authors!"

One thing is also certain, without going back to the Egyptian calendar, and that is that the famous sundial, whose invention is attributed to Anaximander by Diogenes Laërce, and to Anaximenes by Pliny the Younger, already existed well before the birth of these two so-called inventors. In fact, although sundials flourished in Millet during the 6th century BC, a text dating back one hundred and fifty years tells us that they existed much earlier.

In the Old Testament, in fact, we find (Isaiah, chapter XXXVIII, verse 8): "Here is a sign for you from Yahweh that Yahweh will carry out this word that he has spoken: I will turn back the shadow that the Sun casts on the steps of Ahaz by ten degrees. And on the sundial of Ahaz, the Sun moved back ten degrees on the steps he had lowered."

This significant passage mentions a king of Judah, Ahaz, who ruled from 736 to 716 BC, during which time he had a sundial built that had already been in use in Egypt. This dial indicated the passage of time by means of the variable length of the shadow cast by a rod on steps defined for this purpose by precise calculations. These were just some of the dials used two hundred years before their invention by Hellenic "scholars".

When we also remember that, in their respective philosophies, Anaximander taught his pupils that the Earth was flat and Anaximenes that the sky was made of stone, there is no comment to be made on the science of these "geniuses"! What can we say about their 'erudite' compatriots?

Their leaders were Eudoxes and Eratosthenes. Their position is just as uncomfortable. What's more, these unrepentant plagiarists knew very little about the subject they disclosed on their return to Greece. Their astronomical 'discoveries' will be explained at greater length in the chapter devoted to 'Combinations', which is why it is worth referring to it for those who want to see the obvious proof of them now.

On the other hand, let us ponder for a moment the words of a scholar who travelled to this grandiose country a little later than the Hellenic philosophers. His visit to the Temple of Sais, advocated centuries earlier by Plato, opened up an abyss of reflections on the intelligence of those who welcomed him. So, after contemplating the mass of archives accumulated in the building's underground passageways, Martianus Capella - for he is the one in question[3] - wrote:

> "You should have seen what books, how many volumes, and how many languages covered them, preserved the products of these learned Priests! Some appeared to have been written on papyrus strips rubbed with cedar; others were made of linen folded over itself. There were also many volumes in sheep skins,

---

[3] *De Nuptiis philologiae et Mercurii*, Liv. II, p. 35.

perfectly preserved. A small number of others were written on lime leaves, and still others were coloured a religious black, with letters representing the effigies of animals that seemed to capture your soul".

However little I know about the early hieroglyphics of Ahâ-MenPtah, the numerous texts compiled in several European libraries, as well as in certain monasteries in Egypt and the Sinai, have managed to weave together a solid framework of information that is extremely logical, and in which Logic has found its place with complete peace of mind. Particularly with regard to the understanding of "Divine-Mathematical-Combinations", which was hidden beneath the famous hieroglyphic anaglyphs already mentioned by Clement of Alexandria. Champollion only skimmed the surface of the rebus when he called this writing "Meditated Combinations".

Perhaps the library of the Centre Culturel des Fontaines[4], which welcomed me to finalise my notes and conclude my research, played a large part in achieving these results. Of the 650000 or so volumes housed in this den of learning, more than 2,000 are devoted solely to the study of Pharaonic history and its developments (books of this kind are rare today). Of these, 114 concern grammar and the hieroglyphic system.

From all these highly erudite interpretations, one conclusion emerges, even for the neophyte: there is no agreement on the basic data used for the translations, not the slightest thread to standardise a real understanding of the Sacred Language, hieroglyphics.

All the evidence shows that it has remained a dead letter, as Egyptologists have been violently at each other's throats on this subject ever since the Champollionesque attempts to read the famous trilingual Rosetta Stone. As we know, it was the discovery of this stone by soldiers in Bonaparte's army that triggered a

---

[4] This Centre, run by the Jesuits, is located near Chantilly, in the Oise region. All researchers are given a warm welcome.

translation 'mechanism' among French researchers. Champollion's grey matter resonated strongly in front of the hieroglyphs engraved in what are popularly called "cartouches", because he had understood that they were the patronymics of Roman emperors written *phonetically*, but in the language of Ramses. We will leave him with the credit for this idea, as our aim is not to reopen the controversy on this subject, as Dr Young, an Englishman, had reached the same conclusions twelve years earlier. Let's not be so perfidious, and let's admit that he was not aware of this preferential outcome, especially as many readings of signs turned out to be just as inadmissible.

Our learned Egyptologist had died a few months later, and the two "scholars" involved in the same controversy had been laughed at by many scholars who jointly denied any value to this aberrant system of understanding. In their defence, I would add that in 1830, the chronological horizon of the History of Peoples was singularly narrow. Sacred History, which could not be contradicted on pain of heresy-like excommunication, only dated the first man back to the fifth millennium BC!

This in no way prevented a number of scholars from very valuable discoveries that enabled them to adopt a certain approach to correct reading. In 1869, the Viscount de Rongé wrote in his *Étude sur l'écriture égyptienne (Study of Egyptian writing)*: "By a conception that no doubt has some mystical reason, some of the texts are written in a system that can be described as 'retrograde' group by group, because to read them, you have to take them in the reverse order of that which would be indicated by the arrangement of the characters".

This reading, which is the opposite of our own, is one of the fundamental notions of the Sacred Language. When sentences have a double meaning, certain parts are read from right to left, and others from left to right. Current phonetisation is too hazardous to rely on. It is, to say the least, adventurous to try to reconcile a phonetised *designation* of characters with a precisely defined meaning, with a *spelling*, even hieroglyphised, of words meaning only the proper names of emperors unknown in any form whatsoever to the Ancestors. It's as if we wanted to write "space rocket" in Latin, and today we would have to invent special words *to go with it*, the phonetics of which would have nothing in common with their primary meaning.

A typical example is the one I asked a distinguished Latinist to translate into French: pommes-frites", a term that did not exist in Christ's time because this "root" was not on any menu.

After careful consideration, this erudite researcher gave me the following interpretation: "*Solana Tuberosa ex oleo fricta*". In short, it's as if, a few millennia from now, a translator were asked to transcribe a text by Ovid, or Jules Verne, in the slang language so dear to San Antonio and which is unfortunately making its way everywhere.

In any case, it was a similar task that the Scribes undertook for the decree on the Rosetta Stone. Berenice and Ptolemy had no phonetic correspondence with the hieroglyphs in use under the first dynasties, or even with the understanding of signs as it existed from the reign of the Hyksos kings onwards.

It is undoubtedly not my place to set myself up as the last judge in this extremely interesting discipline, nor to engage in sterile battles in order to justify this or that statement made, by systematically criticising what more competent men have interpreted according to their conceptions of the Egyptian texts in relation to the all-powerful Christian theology of our time.

These scholars devoted their entire lives to research which, I confess without false shame, I am not very familiar with. On the other hand, I have carried out other mathematical and astronomical research, based on a logical analysis of all the data, chronologically classified and then methodically memorised. In this way, I was able to group together certain formulations that provided formal answers to the arithmetical construction in the progressions of the 'Divine-Mathematical Combinations' hidden within anaglyphic texts. Algebra, geometry and the use of fractional systems in astronomy completed the process itself. The strict rules that define it are beyond discussion, since they ultimately define the law hidden beneath the apparent complication.

As loyally and simply as possible, I ask all Egyptologists to consider the possibility of a complete translation of the Knowledge, which is obviously a long way from the abusive interpretation of the writings of the Sacred Language. It would be time to return to the original Creation of Tradition, transmitted by initiation in the "Houses of Life" following a strict teaching.

This would be the best way of escaping from this gully from which nothing has yet emerged but a Hellenised mythological affabulation, which pays little heed to the ancient intelligence passed on by God to his chosen offspring, and which was capable of building these prodigious monuments that defy time and our imagination, as much as our consciences.

We need to retrace the spiritual path that brought this hieroglyphic writing back into a known context, one that is more mathematical than grammatical, and more logical than literal. This is the only way to restore a complete understanding of the monotheism that was in use from the most remote antiquity among this original people of divine essence. The battle of the two clans that followed severed the very clear dissociation between good and evil as soon as the Great Cataclysm was over. The titanic struggle that continued among the survivors during the Exodus, over thousands of years and thousands of kilometres apart, was simply a continuation of this.

Generation after generation, century after century, the differences between the true and false divinities grew until the arrival of Ath-Ka-Ptah, where it ended by force of circumstance. In the meantime, the two populations followed parallel paths, scattering across the territories they crossed, meeting by chance and then fighting each other violently. The history of these fratricidal factions has undergone many changes. Among the "Rebels of Sit", there was little left of God, while under Menes, the successor of the "Followers of Hor", he still retained his predominance, preserving the fearful tradition of the rupture of the new Alliance between

Heaven and Earth, if the plates of the celestial scales weighing souls tilted the wrong way!

The greatest indulgence is therefore requested by the author who, with all his goodwill, is addressing his fellow men in this work which will include other volumes, and in which many points which are still obscure will only appear to specialists as the stammerings of a novice. However, it is sometimes a good idea not to take advantage of studies which are in line with the chosen discipline and traditionally in line with research. This can open up a new, unorthodox path, where criticism is obviously possible, even if it only leads to sterile disputes.

It is by no means a question of doing the work of a historian or writer by disowning or denying all significance to the work of eminent scholars, known for their brilliant hypotheses on Pharaonic antiquity, but of asking these same personalities to study in their turn this different conception of the Creator and the succession of the Pêr-Ahâ.

Having deciphered, or rather cleared, the secret understanding of ancestral texts through mathematical research into anaglyphs, I gladly leave open to them this only logical access to the traditional reading of hieroglyphic signs.

For this early language, which has been totally lost but can be reconstructed, is the one that has always put specialists off. Since the continent of Ahâ-Men-Ptah was swallowed up, traditional survival has only been possible through intensive oral memorization, which was constantly maintained until the arrival of Ath-Ka-Ptah, centuries and centuries later.

The rock engravings painted and carved into the rocks all along the route travelled, stretching from the West African coast to the banks of the Great River, the Nile, several thousand kilometres to the east, recalled with unique constancy the tragic times of the millennia since the Great Cataclysm, better known as the period of the Great Mourning. These drawings justified the hope of the survivors in a Land promised for so many generations by successive Elders, in the name of God.

During this long period, and right up to the I^{st} Dynasty, a script adapted to the new spiritual needs was reconstituted from scratch, based on the primitive language, ready to be restored when the time came to re-establish the calendar, and consequently the harmonic order uniting Heaven and Earth.

The Pharaonic civilisation thus survived the many ups and downs, its tradition being an incessant and sovereign reminder for failing human brains. Hieroglyphics thus became the protector of the Law of the Creator, as well as the preserver of the Sacred Texts, the only ones capable of ensuring the good ethics of humanity on its way to the eternity of the Beyond of terrestrial Life, accessible only to the chosen ones of the "Second Heart" who have committed no sin.

But then oblivion set in again, favoured by usurpers and forced by invaders! Decadence, brought about in successive stages, definitively wiped out this chosen people, "God's Beloved", when Cambyses, at the head of the armies of Persia, in 525 BC, carried out the first known genocide of a people. And AthKa-Ptah, the 'Second Heart of God', disappeared once again...

CHAPTER ONE

TA MANA!
(SUNSET-PLACE)

When Ifrikios saw this people of foreign race, and heard them speak a language whose varieties struck his ears, he gave way to astonishment, and exclaimed: "What Berbera is theirs!" This is why they were called "Berbers", because in Arabic, Berber means a mixture unintelligible cries!

IBN KHALDUN
(History of the Berbers)

These are the first days of the reborn Universe;
The centuries that have passed begin again;
Already Themis returns, and Saturn with her,
A new race descends from the heavens.

VIRGILE
(Eglogue IV)

The first book of this narrative, starting with the Origin of all things and all living beings, ended with the gigantic upheaval produced by the wrath of God, who was forced to demonstrate his omnipotence as Creator in order to restore the harmony that had disappeared on Earth, where humanity's forgetfulness of its duties was endangering the planet as a whole.

Despite numerous warnings from the Priests and celestial signs, the continent of Ahâ-MenPtah was destroyed on the appointed day in a series of earthquakes, before being completely swallowed up by an enormous tidal wave. Thus disappeared the famous Edenic territory that Plato immortalised, following in the footsteps of his ancestor Solon the Wise, under the legendary name of ATLANTIDE.

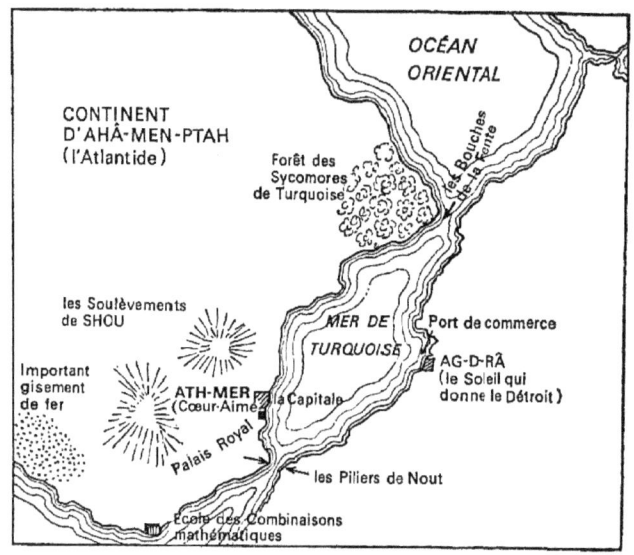

Continent of Ahâ-Men-Ptah (Atlantis).

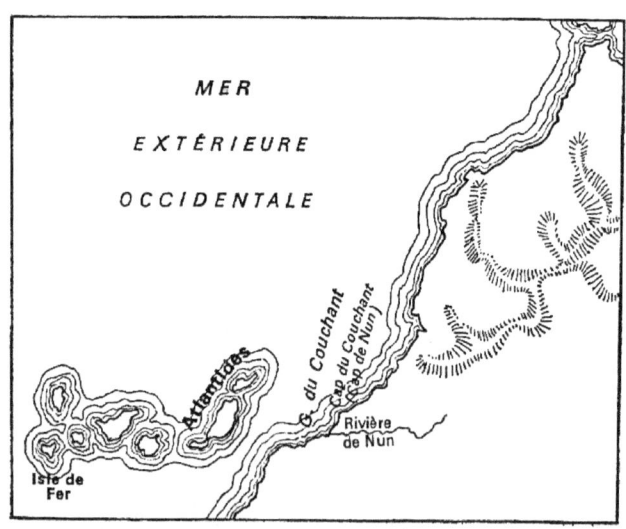

For research on the western coasts of Ptolemy's Africa, and on the islands known to the Ancients in the Atlantic Ocean.

The survivors of this Great Cataclysm and their descendants fearfully passed on the hallucinatory story, generation after generation. After many millennia, they still recounted the appalling catastrophe in meaningful texts, which were increasingly legendary and mythological.

This unparalleled fright, which broke out in cries of despair in the Annals, is recounted in all its details, so that no one can ignore it, on the walls of the first Egyptian temples. This Promised Land, which has become a place of welcome and peace for the descendants of those who survived, nevertheless suffered the jolts and aftershocks throughout the Pharaonic era. Its very name, that given to it by its first King, Menes, is significant: Ath-Ka-Ptah or "Second Heart of God", which is a kind of imploration to ward off bad luck.

Each convulsion of the earth's crust in a neighbouring country brought an extraordinary revival of faith among the people, who were inspired by fear at the time, and who bore at their head a new "Pêr-Ahâ", who became "Pharaoh", or "Divine Son", who brought together the distended links of the Covenant with God through grandiose constructions and offerings on the same scale dedicated to the Creator... and the earthquake passed far from the creatures of the Eternal One!

These upheavals coincided with the departure of a new dynasty towards its religious apogee. Berossus, a Chaldean priest three centuries before Christ, recounts *the* ancient tradition *of Idzubar-Gilgem*, which tells in terrifying detail of a flood that occurred in the time of Abraham, the original text of which was kept in the library of Erech, the famous Chaldean city that had had close relations with the learned Egyptian priests who frequented it at the time. The chosen people were therefore perfectly aware of this and other cataclysms, and the fear of an identical punishment, in the face of the polytheism that was implanted, led to the establishment of a new dynasty, that of Ramses, which rapidly assumed extraordinary power.

The chronicle of Ahâ-Men-Ptah, ending the first volume with the re-establishment of the real history of Platonic Atlantis, also completed the only era of integral monotheism. Time and oblivion distanced this civilised humanity from its origins and its duties.

Having become impious and selfish, unaware of its sacrileges, it profaned its Creator, until that fatal day of 27 July 9792 BC. The survivors of this collective shipwreck were scattered on both sides of the sunken continent. Those we are talking about here landed in relatively large numbers on the coast of Africa, whose land was close by, separated by a strait of around a hundred kilometres, the "Mouths of the Gap".

They had known all the contours *before, as* navigation was highly developed. But apparently, this territory seemed totally foreign to them, as if it were located in an indefinite distance, another c somewhere else... They had been thrown there by the fury of the waves and the barely calmed winds.

In their daze, these unfortunate castaways realised that they alone were responsible for this horror. All they had to do was get down on their knees and give thanks for being there. And they owed it only to the courageous indulgence of the last Pêr-Ahâ who, unconcerned by criticism and mockery, had imperturbably continued the programme to build 200,000 "Mandjit", unsinkable boats designed to float above the tidal waves and complete the evacuation.

All along the African coast, the cataclysm had much less strongly felt. But the natives and settlers had moved to higher ground as a precautionary measure. Trade, which had flourished before, and mining had encouraged the establishment of specialised personnel who, in time, would be able to help the survivors.

A few points of the shoreline had been submerged, but on the whole, there had been no major damage and the coastal configuration was identical. The same was not true everywhere, and far from it , since three upheavals had changed the rest of the African outline:

> - First of all, the collapse of Ahâ-Men-Ptah created a vast *eastern* ocean, which replaced the land that had disappeared, to become the *western* ocean and finally *the Atlantic*, from

which only a few volcanic islands emerged, aptly named the "Fortunate Isles", before becoming the Canary Islands.

- At the same time, the collapse of the Spanish-Atlantic chain led to the opening up of the present day Strait of Gibraltar.

- In this convulsive contraction of the earth's crust, the opening of the Bab el-Mandeb strait also separated Egypt from Arabia.

But that day, the survivors who disembarked were searching in vain for non-existent landmarks. The axial change in our planet's orbit had apparently "thrown the Sun into the sea, turning all geographical data upside down! Texts like those of Herodotus bear witness to this. But since everything was just an appearance, and the star of the day was 'fixed', it was the Earth's pivot that caused the solar navigation to retrograde at dawn on this new first day, *above the eastern horizon, and not the western one as on the previous day!*

This beginning of a new celestial era, in which the Sun ceased to follow its usual direct course, also changed the universal harmony and the rhythm of the "Mathematical Combinations" that make up the Law of Divine Creation. The solar star appeared to retreat into the constellation of Leo, where it had been in its normal advance before the Great Cataclysm.

The astronomical phenomenon can be explained scientifically today, as well as predicted mathematically with a very small margin of error, by calculating very precisely the difference angular precessional of the terrestrial equinoxes with various ratios of Force, Mass and Attraction.

The movement of the Earth shows us a Sun "na viguant" slowly across the sky, within a narrow equatorial belt, like a boat in a great milky river: the Milky Way, dotted along its banks with twelve geometrically defined astral configurations, shining differently and each with its own specificity. These are the twelve zodiacal constellations that encircle our globe at a distance of between 80 and 120 light years. From that day on, our Sun sailed inside this circumference, in the opposite direction, but still in 25,920 cycles; that's the BIG YEAR!

Leaving the west, where it used to rise, our star of the day now appeared in the east to end its journey in the west, where debris of all kinds was still stagnating on an immense sea, the only scattered and shapeless remains of a gigantic liquid tomb of millions and millions of Lives!

In this new retrograde era of Leo, the western horizon became, for the survivors, "the Kingdom of the Dead", immortalised in all the monumental engravings by the hieroglyphs reading A-MEN-TA and phonetising AHA-MEN-PTAH, the vanished Heart whose memory alone remained...

All kinds of buildings, such as the sarcophagus of Ramses II, also feature two lions leaning against each other, with a gleaming sun between them resting on an upside-down sky held up by a cross of Life. The symbolism is evident in this renewal of the sun's march, personifying a radical renewal of life on earth, and thereby marking the terrible fear and dread of a possible new cataclysm.

A Temple of Ptah with its imposing monolithic blocks rose on the Giza plateau well before the First Dynasty, and near it, carved into the rock, appeared at the same time the figure that the Arabs still call *Abu'l Hol*, the "Father of Fear". As for the Greeks, when they saw him for the first time, they were speechless in front of this enormous face with open eyes, which was the only thing sticking out of the sand at the time. That's why they called him "the Sphinx".

However, there was nothing enigmatic about his origin, for he personified a universal warning reminding all human souls that God was the Almighty in matters of Creation or Annihilation. With his eyes always open - like those of a lion that never close - staring towards the West and the Amenta of the Ancestors who died in the distance, the Father of Fear was a reminder of the Great Cataclysm and of Divine Power.

But for the pioneers, thrown onto a hostile shore, deprived of everything, and consequently experiencing the appalling drama that would later become literature, the Nile was still a long way off. A terrifying march of three millennia over more than three thousand kilometres awaited them. Their distant goal, Ta Merit, the "Beloved" land that would become their second homeland under the name Ath-KaPtah, was still only a faint light, if not a great hope. The surviving Pontiff would prepare the exodus, and his successors would lead it, generation after generation, to its conclusion.

Such a displacement of population remains unparalleled in human history, and leaves far behind that of the Jewish people. Numerous remains can be found all along this African journey, from west to east, engraved on the stones that mark out this arduous route braving eternity.

All the more so as this path was *split into two*. Sit is not dead, and neither is Hor, and a merciless struggle will develop throughout the long march, century after century and millennium after millennium. While the first volume ends with a sombre description, the new Sun reveals the first glimmer of light on Iset and Hor, who are very much alive, as well as on Ousir who, although dead and tied up in a bull's skin, will arrive on African soil. The Divine Triad thus reconstituted will be ready to guide the people, if they are willing to raise their eyes to the sky.

Clearly, having demonstrated to the rest of his descendants that he was indeed the Almighty, God could also let his anger sink and once again become the benevolent and magnanimous Father who must now be properly honoured to avoid the return of an even greater cataclysm.

For this reason, as soon as the ship crash-landed, after the first few moments of understandable daze, all the survivors prostrated themselves in collective thanksgiving to the Eternal One, asking him to restore Time to harmony with the Earth.

Every dawn that followed, in anticipation of being able to rebuild portable altars and then Temples, saw all beings kneel before the Sun in unanimous thanksgiving. From then on, a vibrant song of hope for a new life burst forth from every living breast, until the Golden Sun, dazzling and glorious, appeared in its entire circumference, thus approving the day that had begun with benevolence.

It became a very natural thing for those who gathered in this way, on the beaches where the remains of all kinds of broken ships still lay. With the same instinctive impulse, they thanked the Lord of the Sky and his avenging arm, the sun, for their survival. They finally understood that it was because they had forgotten the elementary Law instituted so that Life could reign in the Peace of each individual, that their "Heart" had been wiped off the face of the earth with all those who had not been able to escape. In their immense grief, they *realised* that this Universal Lawgiver was a tangible reality.

He was pure Force and Light before he gave birth to Creation, and everything was possible for him. The texts learned from the priests, entering through one ear and leaving through the other, were forgotten in the euphoria of AhâMen-Ptah's tranquillity. But they suddenly took on their true meaning in the new hope animating this reborn humanity.

It was this hope that still animated the builders of the Temples under the Pharaohs 4,000 years later. God had shown the limits of his Law, punishing as necessary those who had exceeded them.

The poor humans who had taken themselves for gods had not even had time to understand their misfortune and their defeat. But the survivors could see with their still bewildered eyes that the commandments resulting from Divine Law had not simply been formulated by the class of Priests for the use of the faithful who had become slaves to a false theology, but because this Law could not fail to exist. Life, and freedom, could only exist at this price by fitting into the Celestial Harmony.

And so, the fatal day of imbalance having arrived, nothing could stop it from being accomplished by the pivoting of the Earth on its axis. Thus were buried the foundations of the disorder caused by the inhabitants of Ahâ-Men-Ptah. This "Elder Heart", which seemed just as indestructible as the foundations of the religious morality instituted by the first Elder, sank at the same time as the collective egoism of the Cadets!

This primitive humanity, monotheistic by birth and by essence, had imposed on itself the most natural foundations of the first spiritual ethic. With no need to ask themselves pointless questions about their origin, knowing it perfectly well and not so far away that it could be challenged by others, they lived as normally as possible in constant communion with their Creator.

To overthrow this immortal conception of the soul, the idolatry suggested by successive unreasonable reasonings was enough. In the space of a few millennia, the tranquillity of a life free from war, the daily bread and wine that was guaranteed in all weathers, overcame Reason, destroying the Happiness of an entire people who considered themselves to be God's Chosen.

The instinct of the struggle between Good and Evil was an unknown concept, if not to the Priests, who read it in the Texts and preached it to their flock as it was, since they did not sin! This is why, over the centuries of prosperity, an unconscious blindness set in that sealed many an eyelid, implanting the seeds of selfishness, those painless seeds that were quickly activated, personalising themselves in different ways in each being lost in its own contemplation.

Places of worship were abandoned, for there was no longer anyone unconscious enough to come and thank God for an abundance that came naturally to them, or to implore him in anticipation of misfortunes that never came. Living blissfully had become the only watchword, contemplating one's own image in perfectly polished mirrors that could only reflect a *human* face.

This contemplation also led to the first quarrels, which were about clothes, showing a different way of passing the time. An unhealthy pleasure was born, generating quarrels where the reason of the strongest became the best, even if it wasn't the right one. Human strength thus supplanted divine commandments. Squabbles degenerated into pitched battles between clans, then into open rebellion against institutions. Men became like wolves, finally forgetting that, unlike wild beasts, they possessed a soul entrusted to them by God.

Thus began the struggle between Sit and Hor on the ancient continent[5]...

However much the priests tried to exhort the crowds to greater moderation for fear of heavenly reprisals, they openly mocked the sermons, going so far as to ransack places of worship!

So much so that the servants of God themselves came to doubt the validity of what they were saying, and some admired the need to revise the outdated Commandments.

The most reckless and carefree took advantage of the situation to wallow in indescribable orgies, while at the same time blasphemers invaded the temples and desecrated them in every possible way.

The Pontiff himself, although not doubting his Faith or the Law, no longer believed in the invincibility of the Eternal. He spent most of his time locked up in the Holy of Holies, searching for a new prayer formula that would be better adapted to the present, and that would once again serve the One God, an entity that was both im palpable and totally invisible. This ancient veneration of an original Father had been so disfigured by popular fickleness that the task seemed insurmountable before the Great Cataclysm. Faith wavered, died out completely and God was ignored... Ignorance is the mother of all misery. It wasn't long before these miseries descended on Ahâ-Men-Ptah without restriction. When the earth's

---

[5] *Le Grand Cataclysme*, by the same author, published by the same publisher.

crust convulsed, the immense crowd, most of whom had become unbelievers, was panic-stricken.

The temples, so long abandoned, were invaded. Fear filled the spans of stone benches with a terrible clamour, between which fell those who implored a forgiveness that it was no longer time to ask. Man had been denied by the One to whom he had denied all power over him. And his cries of distress were lost in the thunderous roar of titanic explosions, in which the elements of unchained nature shattered the ground and opened wide the bowels of the Earth. Religious buildings and their occupants were engulfed, as was the rest of the country, for there were no words of Faith among the cries. The ritual prayers had been forgotten...

As soon as they touched that other land, the survivors became aware, without any priest trying to convince them, of an absolute necessity: from that day on, no human feeling could or should *ever* be substituted for unconditional belief in the Divine power and its Commandments.

In order to better follow the extraordinary odyssey of the descendants of the "Heroes", the "Followers of Hor" and the "Rebels of Sit", it is important to understand that these people, left with only their arms to ensure a future that was still uncertain, had retained their intelligence, developed over millennia of civilising progress, as well as the memory of the Principles of all their sciences. Moreover, the totality of Knowledge was indelibly engraved in the minds of the surviving Priests.

From the very start of his new life, the Pontiff set out to find ways of preserving intact the literary expression of religious and mathematical culture, which he still possessed perfectly. So much so that, having succeeded in perfecting a method of oral instruction, the chapters of the various disciplines, repeated unceasingly after having been learnt by heart, and brought together generation after generation in immense colleges of learning, were finally engraved 4,000 years later on the walls of the main Temples of Egypt.

The dogmas of Creation can be found here, from An-Ra (Heliopolis) to Denderah, on a thousand kilometres of facades lining the Nile from one city to the next:

> "God is the God of the Universe. He created every star and every 'wanderer' before he created everything on it, and every living thing on Earth. For no life would have been possible if the Law of the Creator had not first ordered that the Sun should shine. Thus Light springs from Darkness!

Some of the monuments, it is true, are of only relative antiquity; the temple of Denderah, for example, dates back to Ptolemy II, but it was his *sixth reconstruction* based on the very ancient original plans. The numerous papyri, copied from ever older manuscripts, prove, if proof were needed, the unanimity of the various ancient accounts authenticating the history of this people and its Divine Ancestors.

This is how the origin of the Temple of Ptah at Giza, built near the Sphinx and mentioned a few pages ago, was re-established. This Temple, which can still be seen today in all its splendour, baffles the thousands of tourists who flock there year-round. Every visitor to is automatically filled with astonishment, as access is via a corridor where each of the base 'stones', admirably carved and embedded, weighs *several hundred tonnes!*

It was cleared for the third time by the Duc de Luynes, and it was well worth the effort. The immense alabaster monolithic pillars inside are superb in their austerity. There are no mouldings or engravings, no ornaments to detract from their polished appearance. What remains is the unconditional homage of a people finally reaching their "Second Heart" and thanking God for having made it possible.

This earlier date is proven by several documents. On an inscription preserved in the Boulac Museum (Egypt), the royal scribe of the Pharaoh with the Righteous Voice, "Khoufou", the Greek Khufu, notes the dedication that he himself noted on an *earlier* document, claiming that the Sun himself presided over the gigantic construction, whose origin was lost in the mists of time.

It is undeniable that, even in those days, mythology gradually replaced the ancient reality that had been erased by oblivion. But it is fairly easy to reconstruct the truth, as the monument was built to the glory of the sun.

Khufu's scribe went on to say that the Temple was buried in the desert sands when workers cleaning the Sphinx accidentally revealed it. "His Majesty, in a reign blessed by God a million times over, the Pêr-Ahâ Khoufou, then immediately ordered the monument to be cleared."

When we remember that this blessed reign took place around 4,000 years before our era, we are left stunned by the actual antiquity of this Temple, which we have to admit was built at least a millennium earlier!

Manuscripts and hieroglyphic inscriptions still buried in unexcavated monuments abound everywhere. Such is the case of a site bounded by Dendera and Nagadah, where the texts recovered in the course of research campaigns, year after year, tirelessly repeat the same phrases so that no one ignores them. They are those that recall the Original and Instrumental Cause of things and beings born of Chaos, born of the Supreme Voice, animated by a life of their own in minerals, plants and animals, before personalising themselves in Humanity.

Master of the Word, God is to be found par excellence in all the epistolary transcriptions of the earliest times. It was essentially thanks to his schools of Scribes, dedicated to safeguarding Knowledge and Wisdom, that the world, after the Great Cataclysm, relearned the Traditions handed down in Ahâ-Men-Ptah by the "First Elder".

The first 'written' stammerings were the rock engravings that dotted the long route of the African exodus along hundreds of sandstone walls and cave 'walls', which we will describe they were discovered in the chapters that follow.

At the same time, adults specially selected and educated for this purpose each memorised a part of the Knowledge, repeating it to themselves day after day until they reached an imperative age limit, in order to pass it on to their eldest son so that the unbroken torch of Knowledge would one day reach the territory that would become the "Second Heart".

Pharaonic civilisation was thus born in *one fell swoop, as* soon as the last generation reached the second homeland that would become Egypt. Although with limited means, it re-established its Science in its own right. This can still be seen today at Denderah, with the temple of the "Lady of Heaven", and at Nagadah, where "chambers of access to the Beyond of Terrestrial Life" are still being excavated, tombs *housing predynastic kings*, the famous "Followers of Hor" who reigned long before Menes.

These latest funerary constructions are a perfect illustration of the artists' mastery of all kinds of materials. The mud-brick mastabas were painted in three colours, black, ochre and white being easy to achieve with the resources available at. The pottery found in these tombs, the rustic but elegant furniture and, above all, the jewellery of all shapes and sizes, mounted in chased gold and set with the most precious stones, all bear witness to an unheard-of perfection in the way they were assembled, which seasoned jewellers of our time would find hard to achieve. Cut rock crystals alone require tools that experience alone would not be enough to perfect.

All these items were multiplied to delight in these funeral homes: ivory headpins, jade earrings, gold and lapis lazuli rings, jewellery made from all kinds of hard stones - agate, chalcedony, opal, carnelian, jasper and others - and porcelain imitating turquoise? Not to mention horn combs engraved with the first known hieroglyphics, and boxes of cooling, blushing and tinting ointments! And last but not least, a medicine chest - yes! - filled with various flasks and vases containing ammonia salts, ointments and turpentine, all wrapped in plaited rushes with a folding handle, in which the box was placed when being transported from one place to another to prevent breakage. Among the mirrors found in a tomb, one with a Queen's cartouche has its handle decorated in relief with a cross of Life, the Tau, thus resurfacing from an unforgettable past long before the first King of the first dynasty.

The Saharan journey is dotted with tombs, from the most primitive in Morocco four millennia ago, to those identical in Nagadah, with jewellery and pottery found in Libya. During this enormous span of time, the people lived as nomads, traversing the arid sands to the rhythm of heavier footsteps before reaching their goal. But they never forgot their task of transmitting Knowledge, nor their faith in the one God who would save them.

I know that there are still readers who bristle at the staggering number of millennia spread out in the first volume, taking monotheism back some thirty-six millennia! But before the Vatican's Biblical Commission gave the go-ahead for serious research into the chronology of the first chapters of Genesis, a work that no one can doubt wrote in the word GENESIS: "It can be said that there is no biblical chronology for the time before Abraham. The Bible therefore leaves scholars free to determine the antiquity of man.[6]

The following pages should not, therefore, be considered as an overture to polemical discussion, since they are not the starting point of any doctrine whatsoever. They are intended solely as a means of research, open to all, which should lead to a deeper and more accurate understanding of the theories put forward.

The misnamed *Book of the Dead is* simply a compilation of very ancient texts, which already announced exemplary punishments, or hopes for an eternal Afterlife, already in use on the 'First Earth' 10,000 years before.

The precessional cycle of the Great Year is the symbol of this eternal return, where each Cadet will continue along the same path

---

[6] *Dictionn. Apolog. d'Alès*, col. 290.

as his Elder, in the space destined for him, just as the new ear of barley grows in the place from which the previous one was cut. The great "Wheel" turns, very slowly, to the rhythm of the Sun replacing the little hand turning in an eternal circle.

This was understood by the successive Pontiffs responsible for putting the Divine Commandments into writing, who agreed beforehand, with the greatest humility, *that the reach of human intelligence does not exceed, and will never exceed at any time in the present or the future, the impassable limit where God wants Reason to stop so that Faith can begin.*

Hence this first fundamental axiom of the ancient priests, repeated over and over again and inspiring the most profound meditation: "GOD MUST NOT PROVE HIMSELF BY REASON, BUT HE MUST LIVE BY FAITH".

From the very beginning, the survivors of Ahâ-Men-Ptah lived by this lost ethic, which was rediscovered for the greater good of all. It was still in force 5,000 years later, at the inauguration of the Temple of Medinet-Habu, which bears the following formula engraved on its foundations:

> "The Breath is in your hands, O Ptah,
> for you are Life.
> The condition of the Earth is that which you have made
> and we will always obey it.
> You have struck down evil and vice
> and grant us goodness and peace.
> Let us remain attentive to your words.

What we need to bear in mind when reading these lines is, at the very least, that these men and women of the highest antiquity possessed a vision of God that is foreign to us! No human being of our time can boast of following so fully the Commandments instituted by God to enable them to live in harmony with the Earth, as with Heaven.

Few of today's Wise Men possess the spirituality essential to the tenuous maintenance of an agreement with Heaven limited to its simplest expression. And the cries of an active minority in the midst of an amorphous majority end up making them doubt the intangibility of dogma, even though it was expressly recommended by the sacrifice of Christ who redeemed the sins of the world.

But the subject is so vast that it goes well beyond the scope of this book. Let's just ask ourselves one more question: "God, why are we so blind?

These were the words spoken by the last great sage of Ath-Mer, the marvellous sunken capital, as everything collapsed around him, just as he had foreseen and predicted. This Pontiff of the College of High Priests, having prepared the collective departure of his subordinates and passed on full powers to his eldest son to replace him wherever he went, had preferred to go down with the 'Heart' that had been his whole life!

The answer to his ultimate question must have been given to him in this Beyond Life, where he had arrived in the company of millions and millions of his fellow citizens forced to do the same. As for those who survived, the horrible memory of this earth slowly sinking beneath the waters would remain with them forever.

Ovid, who had heard a few echoes of it, put this terrible phrase into the mouth of Pythagoras, a striking image of an unbearable reality: "I have seen with my own eyes what a solid earth was when it became the water of the Flood!

Once ashore, the survivors felt very much alive. Life soon returned to normal, and they called this place TA MANA, the "Setting Place", because they were not used to seeing the Sun set above the liquid horizon where it should have risen, and on *their* continent!

In 9792 B.C., when men, women and children were thrown into extreme destitution on the beaches of Africa, while still possessing their only priceless heritage, Knowledge, Europe was still living at the dawn of its humanity, in the most remote prehistory.

The "human bipeds" lived withdrawn in smoky corners, scattered in the heart of luxuriant forests in which the great beasts reigned in possessive clans, masters of precise territories, which were the object of bloody battles. And if the humans in their holes lived so miserably and nakedly, it was because they had never known anything else.

In that same year, Greece did not exist, and the site of what would become Athens, the capital of the learned world (sic), had not yet been defined. Even the first stone of what would later become the elegant Parthenon had not yet been quarried.

But from that day, 12,000 years ago, the survivors of the Great Cataclysm recovered their faith. With it, hope was born, along with the knowledge that they were still "Descendants of the Elder". All that remained was for them to reach this second land and rebuild their 'Second Hearts'.

If the former, which was as spiritual as it was scientific, was no longer there, the latter would not be left in the lurch, as the Knowledge acquired was well recorded in the brains of the priests. For the rest, the generous nature of the place would provide the necessities. Palm, coconut, mango, papaya and other fruit trees abounded, as did many varieties of wild vegetables.

The thousands of castaways still scattered around were thus safe from starvation, no matter where they were boarded. The temperature, mild below this 25(th) parallel, posed no problem for the open-air habitat, and the animals, easy to domesticate, immediately provided milk for the orphaned babies.

It was only the changing face of this land that posed problems of orientation. Africa, at least in the north, was not yet what it became after the Great Cataclysm. At that time, the Sahara was a very fertile region, covered with lush tropical vegetation that had followed an intense ice age. The waters flowed wildly in rivers carved out of deep gorges. It was along these paradisiacal shores, at least in the first moments of their exodus, that they carved out their history and recounted the adventures of their long march "towards the Light". It was during these millennia of exhausting advance that this people spread out into numerous families who later became the Tuaregs, the Kabyles, the Berbers, and who all spoke a similar idiom, barbaric to our ears, reminiscent of the roar of the lion, perfectly identical in its definitions to the language of the Guanches, the inhabitants of the Canary Islands.

Even today, in these various peoples who are very proud of their origins, women are capable of exercising political power. I saw for myself in 1974, in the Moroccan Atlas, a woman who was the chief of a Berber tribe and who, with remarkable serenity, ran an administration that everyone praised for its soundness.

Because, and this is the most important difference between Arabs and Berbers, the latter are monogamous. Their main law is the equality of men and women in all areas. Moreover, from a spiritual point of view, the cross is the symbol of recognition of these tribes; it is found everywhere: in the alphabet, on weapons, shields, and above all in the only tattoo they get. A simple cross with four equal points on the forehead for the men, so that their souls are eternally reminded of the First Law; and on the back of the left hand for the women, so that, with this hand over their heart, they swear to bring up their children in the Faith of one God.

So, from "Ta Mana" - the Sunset - to "Ta Meri" - the Beloved - we meet up with the ancient survivors of the original family of the "Descendants" throughout their exodus, which became more and more exhausting as they crossed, over the millennium, what ended up becoming a "sea without water" and which they called SA-AHA-RA, or "Terre-Brûlée par l'Ancien-Soleil", which is quite a programme! The contraction of the name eventually turned it into the Sahara...

Their wandering progress presented them with great valleys abandoned by the waters, but where plants and animals still abounded when the time came to leave. The valley of the Dra, in particular, which will be discussed in greater detail in the next chapter, began to guide the main group as it advanced through Morocco, the name given to it by Lyautey, but which in Arabic had the same meaning as "Land of the setting sun", *Moghreb el-Aqsa*.

Executed in red, black and white on one of the walls of a predynastic tomb near Nagadah, where the scene of the flight on the day of the Great Cataclysm is very well rendered. The tomb is from the time of a Scorpion king dating from before the 1st dynasty (around 5000 BC).

CHAPTER TWO

LIFE RESUMES

> *Praise be to you, O Ra, Master of Light, for your splendid appearances! You rose here during a Great Year. You have chosen this same retreat in the Western Horizon, which becomes your resting place. From now on: your setting will place you in Your Mana.*
>
> BOOK OF THE DEAD
> (Chapter XV)

> *My life would not suffice if I wanted to expose and prove in detail all the plagiarisms of the Greeks that vanity has led them to make, and who claim to have invented the best part of their dogmas, having taken it from the Egyptians.*
>
> CLEMENT OF ALEXANDRIA
> *(Stromata,* Book VI)

The western horizon, the one that should have cut across the coast visible against the light, no longer lit up Ahâ-Men-Ptah with the unreal, bloody crimson that a gigantic glow had macabrely made dance over the waves that night. The flames from the fire at Ath-Mer, the capital of the immense continent, had extinguished themselves as the rest of the country sank.

Everything had disappeared beneath the tumultuous waves at dawn on 28 July 9792 BC, when it seemed like an eternity had passed since the day before. None of the survivors would have dared to say, when he was thrown onto the seemingly solid ground, that he wasn't somewhere in the Kingdom of the Dead on the day after the cataclysm.

The day before, before the longest night in living memory began, the Sun had set as usual in the East. But as the catastrophe worsened, and the explosions of incandescent lava spewed and vomited their putrid excrement all over the "Mandjit", the inky blackness with its strong sulphurous odour had formed another sky, very low down, hiding the real thing with its stifling, apocalyptic cloak, and the night never seemed to end. It lasted so long that its mathematical counting would have been a delusion, but no one gave it a thought.

As soon as a few uncertain glimmers of light appeared, forcing the darkness to retreat elsewhere, cries of joy came from oppressed chests. But an astonished surprise tinted the eyes of the scholars, who wondered if they were really awake. In fact, a celestial phenomenon even more improbable than the previous ones was apparently producing this light.

Still faint, and poorly diffused by the unhealthy fog that still hung over the horizon, this light that heralded a dawn *came from the East!* It was rising from the land towards which the frail boats were now being pushed. As a result, *the Sun was appearing in the very place where it had disappeared the day before, at the start of the long, dramatic night!*

SO THE SUN HAD SUSPENDED ITS JOURNEY DURING THE CATACLYSM, AND RESUMED ITS COURSE IN THE OPPOSITE DIRECTION!

A tidal wave, undoubtedly caused by gigantic ground swells brought to the surface by the deepening of this new world of the underwater depths, had by this time attracted too much attention from the shipwrecked crew in total perdition for them to be overly concerned.

Horus takes the dead Sun into the Amenta after leading the Survivors of the Great Cataclysm to the terra firma of Ta Mana (the Sunset place), the starting point of the Exodus that will take them to Ta Merit (the Beloved place), i.e. from Morocco to Egypt or from Ahâ-Men-Ptah to Ath-Ka-Ptah the 'Second Heart of God'.

Trying only to stay alive by keeping a very precarious balance in their "Mandjit", which sagged heavily in waves of more than twelve metres, the unfortunate people could not think of worrying about an additional celestial strangeness. They would only fully realise the significance of this change in Divine Harmony when God granted them the possibility of returning to a more human existence. Only then would Time resume its meaning in a new, standardised solar year.

A few hours later on this unforgettable day, cyclical harmony truly took on its new meaning. As the elements calmed, the first survivors began to wash up on the sandy beaches; the Sun symbolised in everyone's minds the sign by which God demonstrated the action of his Power, while showing the Renewal he was offering.

In his holy wrath, the Creator had wiped out the unwholesome part of his creation and reached out to his surviving creatures. As eternal proof, he had changed the face of the Earth, reversing the face of the world. From that day onwards, the celestial movements of the "Great Celestial River" - the Milky Way - moved from east to west, ending above the horizon where the millions of "Blessed Ones" who had been swallowed up now rested!

For several days, hundreds of kilometres beyond the present-day seaside resort of Agadir, in southern Morocco[7], thousands of human beings, haggard and pale, came ashore in more or less a disaster. Fortunately, the beaches all along this stretch of coast were sandy. So the arrival did not add to the immense number of corpses that were constantly being washed up among the debris of all kinds that washed up along the coast.

---

[7] *Agadir* comes from the hieroglyph "Gad", which means narrow and, by extension, strait. It was the southern closing point of the "Bouches de la Fente", blocking access to the eastern sea. The earthquake that destroyed 98% of Agadir in 1964 is proof of the violence of this fault line.

Of all the dislocated and shredded bodies, whose eyes still bulged with the indescribable terror they had experienced before giving up the ghost, and whose limbs still twitching before stiffening testified to the effort they had put into trying to survive, the survivors kept an indelible memory that haunted their nights for a very long time.

In spite of their immense grief, not being able to ensure the burial of all their companions in misfortune, they watched in despair as they disappeared with the surf, which carried them to the shallows, where the fish of the sea would feast with delight on the human flesh so loved in that first 'Heart', gone forever! Hence the tenacious hatred, long nurtured and preserved over thousands of years against this progeny, and still very much alive in Egypt under the first dynasties.

As the waters calmed, everyone's eyes were drawn ever more painfully over the unfathomable western horizon. Men and women had to face the facts: *nothing*, absolutely nothing, was emerging from the liquid immensity!

Further south, but as yet unsuspected, peaks and volcanoes surrounded by islets had escaped total engulfment. When a few pioneers reached these places and found survivors, they were called the survivors of the "Fortunate Islands", a name that remained in use until the 16th century AD, after which they became the "Canary Islands".

Strangely enough, the maelstrom that spiralled out of control when the continent collapsed has become a warm, beneficial wind that still circles the same vast area: this is the Gulf Stream, which still perfectly encircles the immense area of the Atlantic that was Ahâ-Men-Ptah.

Buffon wrote in his *Histoire naturelle:* "The currents coming from the west and heading east are very violent. As a result, ships can get from Moura to Rio de Benin in two days

Even more precisely, Mr Dapprès reports in his *French Hydrography:* "As a result, ships thinking they were reaching Tenerife, in the Canaries, and not knowing the new current, have often ended up at Cape Noun, in southern Morocco!

Cape Noun, which still bears this name, that of the Lady of Heaven, mother of Usir and Iset and the last Queen of Ahâ-Men-Ptah, is precisely the promontory where Iset and her son Hor landed. So it was only natural that en should take the patronymic of the last direct descendant who paved the way for the new people.

The Annals record the tiny number of 144,000 living creatures who reached the extreme limits of their endurance, both physical and moral, in this place at sunset, Ta Mana, and were saved only thanks to the unsinkability of the frail but magnificently designed and built "Mandjit". The willpower and stamina of the poor souls thrown into this turmoil would not have been enough.

Fortunately, the boats ran aground on the sandy beaches, anchoring themselves deep in the sand through the tears in their hulls, thus avoiding becoming the plaything of the tides. This allowed the unfortunate passengers, who were on the verge of exhaustion, to regain some strength before attempting to get out into the open air. They then realised that they were safe, and in this haven of peace, they had time to meditate on their desperate adventure and their own smallness compared to the immensity that surrounded them...

Out of the total despondency of the first few days, with the deep sadness that filled everyone's eyes, and the obvious lack of any kind of organisation, a few initiatives sprang up here and there, bringing together scattered families and lonely people in various places, according to their affinities.

When, after the eighth morning apparition of the sun in the east, word spread like wildfire along the shore that the remains of Uzir had landed in the company of Nek-Bet, sighs of relief burst from many chests. Ousir remained God's 'Guide' and Elder beyond death, and he represented a certain hope, although no one could say why. Except perhaps Nek-Bet, who felt she had been entrusted with a divine mission. Iset's twin sister had therefore joined her husband the An-Nu, who had their four children with him, and was preparing her family's opinion to leave Ousir in peace, locked up in his bull's skin for a few more days.

When a messenger arrived the next day to tell them that Nut, the Queen Mother, had reached them, they received a thunderous ovation. There was a general stampede of all the souls in pain towards this favoured beach, where the "Descendants" became the magnet.

The location was particularly favourable for ethnic development. A wide bay bordered it, protected from the winds by a double curtain of tall coconut palms and dense palm trees. This bewildered humanity, which was arriving in great numbers, quickly placed itself under the traditional guardianship of the Elders, the only people who could give them the courage to face the many problems caused by this new blind departure towards a destination that only God could already know.

This rush of a multitude in distress was the lifeline that enabled Nut to overcome her own grief, for apart from the irreparable loss of Geb, her husband, an even more horrible tragedy had struck her in her own flesh with the fratricidal struggle between two children born from her womb, who were undoubtedly brothers.[8]

The souls in pain demanded all her attention, and she set about giving them courage and protecting them from their desperate feelings. As a start had to be made on providing more humane accommodation for all these people, she pointed out the primitive means that could ensure decent buildings.

---

[8] This imperative matriarchal law of the Atlanteans is still found today among the Berbers, who have a proverb that explains it succinctly: "The womb makes the child". If a noble woman has a child by a peasant, the child is noble; if it is born of a peasant woman and a nobleman, the child is a peasant.

Admittedly, the mechanical means used in the great royal constructions were lacking, were the stones, but that made it all the easier for her, whose solution was awaited. She herself in her younger days, kneading clay and drying it into bricks... when she was building a shelter to hide in.

And Nut began by having the palm leaves plaited into large clumps; she then had them assembled into panels and erected into huts that were precarious but constituted a first safe shelter. In a single day, a large town had sprung up, with everyone having taken part in these temporary constructions in a short space of time. The Queen Mother then had the village surrounded by a high wall of parched earth, very wide to ensure good resistance, since she assigned it eight cubits, or more than four metres thick.

There was nothing in its appearance to remind one of the majestic surrounding wall of his Palace of Ath-Mer, but Nut was not too melancholy about it; this wall was more reminiscent of the first defences encircling the ancient primitive villages of Ahâ-Men-Ptah. Thousands of years had passed... and the people were back where they started! Here, it wasn't a question of defending themselves, but of stemming the flow of animals that found food within their reach.

But it turned out that this enclosure had a more important and, in a way, unexpected use. Some of the many species of animal that proliferated in the area were peaceful, chewing on scattered plants, reminiscent of mammals that provided milk for certain peasants who caught them without much difficulty. There were moufflons, gazelles, fallow deer, four large oxen with hanging humps and several ewes whose milk was a delight to young and old alike.

In the midst of this period of adjustment, mixed with many movements, one fact went almost unnoticed. But it was of the utmost importance. Nek-Bet, with the help of a few women, had built a temporary "dwelling" on a mound to give Ousir a rest, which the surrounding wall barely encompassed. This was the "Iat-Ousir" or the Mound of Usir.

This construction emanated from a vision that the young woman had had, and which gave her, without her being able to say why, the order not to bury the body of the eldest son of Nut, nor to remove it from its bull skin. The Pontiff, her husband, had expressed some misgivings about this burial without a funeral ritual, but knowing the divine power of second sight that she possessed, he did not object.

As this mound also had a sycamore tree at its summit, the memory and similarity with the Sacred Nahi where Nut had taken refuge on the eve of her marriage to Geb prompted An-Nu to wait patiently for clarification to reach him one way or another.

The Pontiff had nonetheless decreed, for the reasons given above, that this "Iat-Ousir" place would be Sacred. A boundary separated it from the profane world by a small square enclosure that he designed himself. On this occasion, Nut made the first mud bricks, showing everyone the ancient technique of mixing reddish clay similar to that used to cover the roads to Ath-Mer and the Palace.

The first notion of divine unity resurfaced in full force with the devotion and veneration that were shown to the "Eldest-Descendant" from that moment onwards. But this did not calm Nut's irritation, for she still did not understand why the Pontiff had allowed her son to remain in this execrable skin with Nek-Bet's assent. The Queen Mother had told her daughter loud and clear what everyone was whispering. Iset's twin apologised with a half-lie, claiming that only her sister, the wife of Usir, had the power to decide what should be done with this bull skin, which had in turn become Sacred by its very content. When the time came, Iset alone would be able to make the decision "that would bring peace and a new reality to Usir".

These enigmatic words, while relieving Nut, intrigued her greatly, for she knew the power with which her daughter was invested. So she gave in, despite some reservations.

Let's stop the simple narration and take part directly in the dialogue, as it is almost entirely reported in the Archives des *Quatre Temps:*

- That's all very well, Net, but we've had no news from Iset...

- Have no fear about him, O beloved mother; she is looking after her son, who is very wounded but alive. But they are on their way here.

- What wonderful news! I've been so anxious! Tell me, couldn't we send some men to meet them? Where are they?

- They don't need anyone, O my mother, they'll meet the people they need along the way. Just provide plenty of extra huts to house all those who arrive with them.

Nout thought about how happy she would be to hold Iset and her grandson in her arms. She feverishly prepared a suitable home for the wounded Hor, who had always been her favourite, because "this son was his Father's protection". The Annals are quite clear on these terms.

Meanwhile, Iset, former Queen of a continent that no longer existed, former wife of an inert body awaiting her arrival, continued her ordeal. Stranded at the mouth of a river, exhausted by the interminable night, she had collapsed next to her son, still firmly attached to the broken mast of the "Mandjit "t, to which she had tied him. Hor, bloodied and eyelashed, with a broken right knee and a dislocated shoulder, remained in a second, fluid state, in which his soul struggled to stay afloat.

When the sun was high and her clothes had dried a little, she pulled her son out of the boat, half carrying him, half pushing him.

At the end of her strength, she dragged him as far as she could over the firmer fine sand, comforting him with her own warmth.

Barely rested, not knowing which way to go and wanting to find help as quickly as possible to care for her poor child who was unable to move about on his own, she clutched him to her shoulders. Thus heavily laden, she followed the course of the water upstream towards the interior of the country. It was very painful, and she soon realised that the panorama reminded her of nothing, and that God was their only Protector.

Hor, for his part, was clutching heavily and instinctively at his mother's frail shoulders, unable to hold back the groans that the pain was tearing from his swollen lips. The twinges rising from her leg, deformed by the knee-high wounds, became intolerable. His face, ravaged to eye level, prevented him from realising the pitiful state to which he and his mother had been reduced.

During this slow progression, Iset wondered what she had sinned to be reduced to this appalling nightmare. If her people had failed to preserve their traditional faith, how was she responsible for this impiety, to be punished so severely for it?

There was no answer to disturb the faint echoes coming from a surrounding world resistant to all pleas. Ready to let herself fall from exhaustion into a fading day already beyond the new western horizon, she suddenly believed herself to be the victim of an hallucination: she was hearing voices !

Frantic with fatigue, she stopped and looked up at the sky, but the shifting branches of the tall trees revealed nothing. She did not fully realise the situation until the words she had heard without understanding them were transformed into human appearances. Iset slid to the ground, haggard, but realising that the help she had been calling for was coming to her side.

They were a small group of survivors who had ventured inland and were stopped by high mountains. It was on the way back to their starting point that the meeting took place. As soon as she spoke, Iset was recognised, despite her extreme weakness. Men and women fell to their knees, while one of them quickly got up to support her, as she had just fainted for good.

Two thick layers of foliage were quickly prepared for the two bodies and juicy fruit placed next to them to wake them up, all camping there for the night. In the morning, after a brief explanation with Iset, the group resumed their march towards the mouth of the river, the advance having produced no results. Two men gently took Hor in their intertwined arms, providing him with a sitting position that took the weight off his legs.

The return to the starting point was uneventful, with Iset seeing this encounter as the favourable sign she had been hoping for. Her spirits began to rise again, and were finally lifted when their group reached the mouth of the river and spotted around twenty other survivors heading north along the shoreline. A messenger had told them the day before that An-Nu, his wife Nek-Bet, and above all Queen-Mother Nut, the Protector Beloved of God, were gathering around them all the survivors who wanted to find a Second Heart and a second homeland.

On realising that they had found Iset and her son Hor alive and well, a delirious joy swept over everyone. The ex-Queen, who for a moment had thought herself an orphan lost in a hostile world, was embraced by such gaiety that it turned into a nervous fit of tears, probably the first of her life, as far as she could remember.

She learned later, when the increased convoy had resumed its march in the new direction to join her mother, that the noise of this newly-established agglomeration ran at full speed through the tall trees, on all sides, because every time a group set off from any point, it delegated a solitary member to bring the good news to other lonely survivors.

After about ten days of less strenuous advance, with the men taking turns to carry Hor and ease his march, Iset estimated that they had covered half the road. That day, another messenger informed them that Nek-Bet had taken Ousir's body to a safe shelter while awaiting their arrival.

With the news not only that she was expected, but that she would soon be able to provide her husband with a decent burial,

Iset regained her zest for life. Her son was just as , relieved of all the useless effort. On the other hand, there were enough desperate pleas and inexhaustible sobs around her for her not to give in to her grief.

Faced with the unfathomable mystery that presided over the cataclysm, and with death posing the inescapable problem of human powerlessness in the face of a celestial phenomenon beyond man's control, the

Foi found himself tightening his ties with the 'Descendants' who had been so badly treated in the last days of Ahâ-Men-Ptah.

Hence the idea, which spread rapidly, of forming a second homeland, which would be a new heart linking the Creator and his creatures, where no one would think of fighting him any more.

But another problem, almost as distressing for her conscience, brought Iset face to face with her responsibilities when, the very next day, their troop was augmented four men who confessed to belonging to the rebel States, in other words to the ex-Provinces which had taken part in the annihilation of the 'Descendants'. Although these survivors had no doubt not been directly involved in her husband's murder and assured him of their complete devotion, they nevertheless posed a question that would become vital if answered: what should be said to the surviving 'Sons of the Sit Rebellion' who wanted to join them? And more specifically, what should be done with all those who would not say so, but who had been part of this band of brigands *before?*

Iset looked around, but didn't say out loud what she was thinking. Her brother Ousit, who had become Sit when he disowned his descendants, might even be dead. Confused, she ended up wishing for this with great fervour.

But this rebel brother was very much alive. He had endured the hallucinatory crossing very badly, after the dramatic battle that had pitted him against Usir, the "vile usurping bastard". This hatred, rehearsed in his solitude, was irreparably destroying Sit's weakened mind, as he found himself two days' walk further south, sitting on a stone at the mouth of a river that would become known *as the Iliouna*, meaning the "Survivors of Heaven[9] ".

But Sit, still retaining a few shreds of lucidity in the depths of his soul, took stock of the nameless slaughter that had precipitated the outbreak and annihilation of *his* country. The conclusion, of course, was that the 'abominable' Usir was indeed dead, and that he had been delivered, but that neither of them could rule over a country that no longer existed.

That's why the idea quickly germinated in his feverish brain of achieving another success in spite of everything, through posthumous revenge. He tried to round up the few human wrecks he came across. He easily succeeded with these wanderers, abandoned to their basest instincts, given over to whoever knew how to make the most of them. Sit, in his unconscious madness, had no trouble demonstrating to them that all the evils that had befallen their shoulders had been caused by the carelessness of the 'Descendants', now happily dead.

The leader of the former "Sons of the Rebellion" convinced himself that he was still a guide that no-one else could match. By dint of repetition, everyone became imbued with this truth. A few days later, the group, which was gradually growing, was informed of the creation of a large centre where Nout and Nek-Bet, with the help of her husband, were already organising a perfect life, and

---

[9] In Volume XVI of the *Revue archéologique*, M. de Rougé reiterates an untenable theory regarding this name. This name is engraved in many places, including the tomb of Sesostris. M. de Rongé cites a conquered country: Dardani, which became Dardanos l'Homérique (which is correct), as well as another: *Iliuna*, "that ancient city Ilios or Ilion, capital of the Dardanians" (*sic*). In fact, while Dardani is a Thracian name par excellence, Iliuna means nothing, not even in Greek. Hieroglyphic phonetics, on the other hand, give us E-Iou-Na, meaning "The Rescued of Heaven". It was they who initially enabled Sesostris, descendant of Sit, to become the "Great Victorious One".

some of them wanted to go there instead of living on the air of the times and fine words.

The next day, another messenger told them that the remains of Usir, from his sacred enclosure, provided effective protection for the new village, and that everyone was invited to gather there.

Foaming with rage and literally drooling, Sit strangled him with his own hands, before making a long speech to his 'troops'. To put an end to the dithering of the hesitant, he ordered them to set off for this city, which they would take over and place under their domination and control. This rather diplomatic announcement pleased most, who never realised that the first thing Sit wanted was to send Ousir back into the sea, believing that this hated brother had already been devoured by fish.

At the first stopover, he took aside those he thought might no longer have any faith or law, and proved to them that the reign of these two women had to be stopped in order to ensure their own, omitting to tell them that one was his mother and the other his sister, although everyone knew this.

But with their sights set on a lucrative new takeover of this community, the new rebels had a glint of greed in their eyes. Not a single voice was raised against this planned invasion, and Sit grinned with pleasure, blinking his eyelids in a nervous tic, so as not to show that his conception of despotism included his soldiers in the herd of slaves.

Around a thousand people, not counting the children, formed the first link in the chain of this clan that would much later become the bitter rival of the southern pharaonic dynasties. In the meantime, an incessant, titanic struggle would drive a wedge between the two giants that would soon become insurmountable.

Each evening brought them closer to the dazzling lighthouse that attracted them, and this gave them the opportunity to make preparations for the invasion, in a corner away from the camp fires. Sit having shown them how to make effective clubs and bows with lethal arrows, the "Rebels" set to work, more or less on the sly, so as not to frighten the women. However, it was becoming difficult to hide all the weapons, so to those who were astonished, they retorted that they were only devices to defend themselves against ferocious beasts.

Taking their time to travel, as they wanted to arrive at the end of the journey refreshed and ready to go, and in the company of their women and children, so as not to frighten the inhabitants and above all to give the impression that Nut would not fail to ask questions about Sit and organise a defence if all the reassurances were not provided immediately, they had all the time they needed to organise the "seizure of power"...

A few days before arriving, in a moment of terrible anger, the chief revealed his intentions, to the great horror of the most peaceful people. Sit had been seized with a sudden fury at the refusal of a young woman to follow him. He raged and threatened to kill her, just as "he would do with Nut, Nek-Bet and all those who opposed his desire when they arrived".

As the troop neared their goal, no one dared to run for fear of suffering an unenviable fate at the of the armed men with increasingly pudgy faces who flanked them.

Forty-eight hours before they arrived on the scene, Iset and her group, now numerous, entered the city walls. Comforted along the way by the friendly respect that had surrounded her so well, despite her exhaustion, she straightened up to respond to the ovations that greeted her arrival.

Hor, very weak, but having gradually regained awareness of his surroundings, tried as best he could to stand up on the layer of foliage where he was, carried by two men like a stretcher. His vision was impaired, his injured eye closed by the blood that had coagulated there, but his mother had kept him informed right to the end of the journey.

Cheered on and soon carried in triumph, Iset and Hor, stunned by the people's enthusiasm them, found themselves in front of the hut where Nut, Nek-Bet and An-Nu were waiting. There they were carefully deposited, surrounded by a thousand attentions from everyone.

While the Queen Mother finally held her children close and the twin watched this touching scene, her husband, the Pontiff, bowed respectfully, followed by all those present. In an instant, Tradition reappeared, bringing back civilisation, with the words pronounced by the An-Nu in a strong voice:

- O you, Iset, Divine Mistress of Heaven, by finding Hor alive, you have allowed the Great Cataclysm to cease! For he is the Son of the Son, and it is he who will henceforth lead the new reconstituted people of God. Welcome, Iset; welcome, Hor; this village is yours, eternally, for its name is Ta Mana today and for all eternity!

Everyone had regained their dignity during the brief speech, after which the outpourings and ovations resumed. Nek-Bet, however, simply said to Nut:

- It is urgent, O our beloved Mother, that Hor gets some rest in the hut you have prepared for him. I'll be back to help you look after him as soon as I've taken my sister Iset, my other self, to her husband. The "Iat", specially built to keep him in peaceful expectation of the one who alone has the delegation of celestial powers, is ready to receive her!

The groups went their separate ways, the Pontiff looked after the new arrivals who had gathered, dazed by this intense activity that had overtaken them.

On the way, Nek-Bet set about carrying out the first part of her mission by trying to clear her sister's mind completely, so that she would be highly receptive to certain influences when she arrived on the mound in the "Sacred Abode". To achieve this, she had to talk intensely about a subject likely to capture her sister's full attention.

So she chose to explain the meaning of the "Sunset" with which Ta Mana is adorned[10]:

- To show its omnipotence, divine anger chose invincible signs. It changed the course of the Sun by provoking the Great Cataclysm and all the upheavals it brought in its wake. No human could fight against it. The day before that horrible day, the sun rose in the west as it had done every day before. We've seen enough of the magnificent golden rays of this globe as it rose in the west, do you remember?

Iset nodded in the affirmative, proving that she had been following the monologue, despite her obvious tiredness and her desire to get to her husband. But she added nothing, and Nek-Bet quickly continued:

- The next day, after the catastrophe, the obvious became clear to all dazed eyes: God had manifested himself by making the Sun move back in the sky, forcing it set where the lights of the houses of Ath-Mer should have shone, and where all that remained was the sea that covered the millions of souls of our dear ancestors...

Shuddering at this bloody reminder, Iset was left speechless. She walked on without thinking about her own problems, trying to understand what had led to this series of catastrophic events. Her sister, who followed her twin's train of thought perfectly, was pleased with this development, which would undoubtedly facilitate the arrival of something extraordinary. She hastened to repeat, so that this state of mind would continue until they reached the Mound:

- The Divine Signs must serve as an experience for us, the survivors, because they are punishments that can be redeemed. The annihilation took place during the solar navigation under the

---

[10] Ta Mana is still the name of a village 60 km north of Agadir. And although it is now a few leagues from the coast, it is still built on sand, where non-fossilised shells abound, proof that they have only been there for around ten millennia.

domination of the "Fixes" of the Great Force: that which comes to us from Leo. The very Force that depended on our first Pêr-Ahâ, the Elder. So God wanted humanity to understand at last, "afterwards", that he was God and at the same time that the Sun was one of his own angry eyes, and that Leo served as his arm: God is everything, in himself.[11]

Subjected to the verbal pressure emanating from this evocation, Iset no longer noticed anything of her surroundings, in particular the crowd that was growing ever denser as they approached the Sacred Enclosure, or the embarrassed or pitying looks that were quickly turning away from the two women who would soon be standing in front of *the* skin containing Ousir.

The container and its precious contents were awaiting their arrival. Nek-Bet, who could only think of this moment, suddenly wondered anxiously if she had guessed correctly about the visions that had possessed her. But there was no turning back now, and Iset had to keep thinking about something other than her husband. So, in order not to concentrate too soon on the mound, she continued:

- Today, a Council met in Ta Mana. It was the first one and nobody knew you were coming, except me. But I didn't say anything, because the decisions taken were in line with the renewal that was needed. Harmonic links have been set up to reconnect the new Lion and his double, through a number of symbols that will only have their full meaning if a 'Descendant', and he alone, holds the firm link between his people and his Father, God. So as soon as your son, Hor, is cured and fit to take over the reins of Pêr-Ahâ, a ceremony will crown him by the immolation of a lion. The lion's tail will be used as a belt, as a sign of the Celestial Alliance 'girdling' *the Twelve*. This link, uniting Earth and Heaven, will be his protection, as well as that of his people, for eternity. For the day it is otherwise, an even more horrible cataclysm will destroy our

---

[11] "I am Ra! And I am also the Lion" ( ) *Book of the Dead*, chapter 62, VIII.

civilisation forever, and all that will be left of it will be stones, symbols of a past glory.

Predynastic pottery in which the great cataclysm is also well depicted.

These last words echoed mournfully in Iset's head, and without realising it, she climbed the mound that led them under the sycamore tree, in front of Ousir's Iat. Only then did Nek-Bet's sister feel a blow to the heart. On the other side of the weak wall, the body of her husband was waiting for her... She felt herself being pushed by the firm hand of her twin, who watched her enter the "Abode"...

The first part of her plan had succeeded, and NekBet thought it was time to join Nout, who was busy looking after Hor.

Chapter Three

OUSIR THE RISEN

He is the eldest, the head of four children, and it is he who will make peace reign on the second earth for ever. On the Throne, he will place his son Horus, who was the praise of Geb and the love of Nut. This will be imposed on the very man who hates him for having cowardly killed him: his brother Sit.

HYMN TO OSIRIS
(I - 17/24)

Away with you: "Celestial Bull, enemy of the Sun", for you have no body, no arms and no legs, and you can no longer live because you have no head! O dead soul, turn away from the sun, for you have become an abomination to all! My soul will never replace yours in this skin, and you will no longer rise up against me!

PAPYRUS OF NESI-AMSOU
(The Wrath of Sit)

The knee seemed to be back in place, and the pieces of bone consolidated by a thick plaster made from a kind of clay that we would describe today as 'radioactive'. Nout had discovered it on the very day of her arrival, smoking next to a hot spring where she came to wash. She felt a new vigour come over her and quickly realised its purpose. Before applying it to the broken kneecap, she soaked the mud in seawater.

As soon as she entered the room, Iset had nodded in approval. It was obvious that Hor was in experienced hands, and that he would make a speedy recovery, as far as his legs were concerned at least. She leaned over his face to examine the bloodshot eyes that had just been washed out. One eye socket was empty, but the other, whose closed lid was swollen, did not look too bad. Nek-Bet deduced that the retina must still be healthy.

Whilst murmuring soothing words of comfort to her nephew, the young woman placed her left hand over both eyes. She allowed some of her vital fluid to flow into the weakened body, allowing the partially destroyed tissues to regenerate more quickly.

Hor instantly felt a general calming take hold of the inside of his body. An essential force was immediately returning to him, calming him, while relaxing a number of his cells, forcing them to reform and reproduce all the interrupted functions once again.

Suddenly overcome by sleep under his closed eyelids, he fell asleep so peacefully for the first time in a long time that the two women, moved and touched, let their feelings for each other show as they wept in each other's arms.

This did not last long, as Nek-Bet sensed that the big moment for Ousir had arrived. She had to get back to her sister very quickly, who was in danger of missing *the Event* in her haste. Leaving her mother at the bedside of the recovering patient, she set off again for the "Abode", where this bull skin would no longer pose the very particular enigma that was making her so feverish.

As she entered the room, surrounded by a truly extraordinary peace, she was relieved to see that her twin was still collapsed on the skin containing her husband's body and that she hadn't touched anything yet. As she drew closer, she realised with a smile that her sister, understandably tired, had fallen asleep after encircling the neck, as if the skin were non-existent, and was simply clutching her husband by the neck.

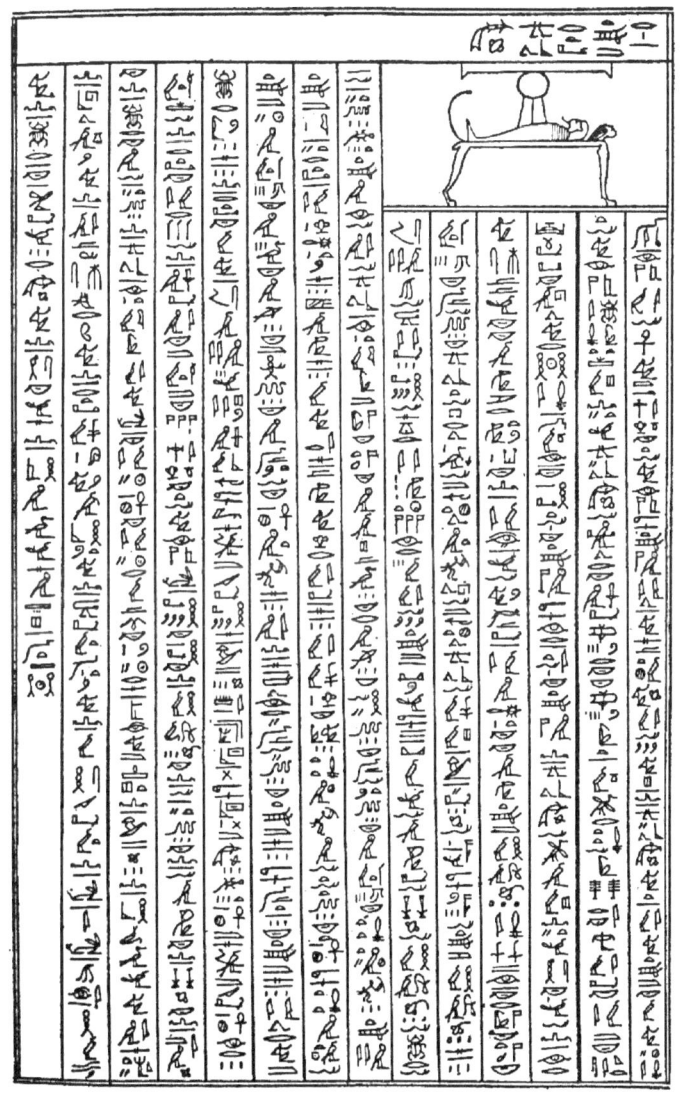

Here is an extract from the "Book of the Afterlife" explaining the epic of the "Rescapae" and the resurrection of Osiris.

The sound of her sister leaning towards her was enough to wake Iset, who jumped up, as if caught off guard. She frowned before asking in a hesitant voice:

- Tell me, Nek, you who know everything... Why am I not crushed with grief, I who loved him so much? It should drive me mad and I shouldn't be able to talk to you, and yet I'm shamefully calm!

At the sight of Iset, so distraught at her lack of sadness, her sister replied in a slightly mocking voice:

- Perhaps you are in this state of mind because your soul is in perfect communion with that of Ou sir, your adored husband and my beloved brother.

- Don't make fun of your sister who's in desolation! It's too horrible to be like that! Her spirit is certainly still with me, all the time, but it's dead!

- Perhaps, yes; and perhaps... no.

- What are you trying to say?

Suddenly very frightened, Iset stepped back, pointing her finger at the bouncing skin of the body there:

- Is... Is he there?... Or are you trying to make me understand that he's not the one in that awful skin?

- As far as I know, it is Usir, your husband, who lies there, with his soul linked to yours. This skin has been tightened tightly, preventing his spirit from joining those of the Blessed.

- That must be why I didn't dare cut the shackles: I was afraid his soul would be gone forever.

A small, mischievous smile crept across Nek-Bet's lips. She moved closer to her sister, and offered in a soft, persuasive voice

- Do you want to leave it like that and build it your own?

Final residence?

- What are you suggesting? Would you like me to leave him in that skin?...

Horrified by this image, she covered her eyes with her hands, but only for a short time. In a fierce voice, she continued:

- Oh no! This animal envelope won' serve him as a ceremonial robe when he enters the Eternal Beyond... never!

- You're going beyond my thoughts by lending me such an idea, O you who are my other self! I just wanted to know if your desire was to see Usir in another 'elsewhere', or for him to stay close to you.

- By my side? It would be so wonderful if life had not been taken from him by his Father. He'd still be alive... And to think that I can't even feel any despair, or even the slightest feeling of loneliness!

It was hard to see her expression as she drew closer to her sister and asked, eye to eye:

- Tell me, Nek, would I become a body without a soul, to feel no sorrow at the death of my husband, whom I adored so much?

Nek-Bet laughed mockingly, the better to hide her tenderness and emotion, for the pathetic moment was fast approaching with the arrival of her mother and her own husband. She stroked her sister's hair as she "saw" Nut, the Pontiff and two other priests make the short climb up the mound to them. Indeed, it wasn't long before they entered the room.

When everyone was assembled, Nek-Bet knew that the moment God had willed had arrived. It was up to her to carry out what had been written by Him so that Faith would be reborn in this "Second Heart". So she left Iset lost in her reflections and turned towards her husband, whose noble appearance she had finally rediscovered, despite the simple air that had won her over so many years before.

She raised her forehead to rest it respectfully in turn on the two strong shoulders, so comforting when she felt the need, as at this moment when she had to ask for his spiritual as well as moral help. What she said, however, did not fit in with her innermost thoughts, least on the surface, so she was not surprised to see the Pontiff frown slightly in incomprehension. But he tried to understand the hidden meaning of the words in order to help his wife, who needed him.

- Our beloved Iset, finally reunited with her family, our revered sister, finally welcomed into our family circle of "Elders", is experiencing a dilemma in her conscience. O you, my husband favoured by God and his counsels, now is the time to help her regain perfect balance. This should be easy enough, since her son Hor is going to get better and our sister confesses to feeling no sadness at the body of the noble Usir locked inert at our feet. She doesn't despair at this animal notion of the end of a husband, and...

Outraged by this persecutory tone, Iset rose on tiptoe to cut him off:

- Nek! How can you talk like that?

The incomprehensible irony of Nek-Bet's diatribe took them all by surprise, and even more so his sister, who in turn ran to the Pontiff, his brother-in-law, who had just pushed his wife slightly aside to look at her and try to unravel the mystery he sensed was brewing without yet understanding what was going to happen.

Interspersed with restrained sobs, Iset's anguished voice continued:

- Have you forgotten, my sister, the horrible end to Usir's life?

Nek-Bet's enigmatic smile persisted, without her even pretending to justify herself. Iset continued, more vehemently:

- This bull skin contains the body of my husband! Have you forgotten him? It's him you mock by mocking me!

Taking one of the Pontiff's hands and clasping it tightly, she implored him:

- O you, who are the venerable guide of our souls on the fragile path of rebirth, you, who are the Pontiff introducing the new hope into all hearts, you, who are the justifier of human actions before God, give the order to build near here, the "Abode of Usir". May it be as simple as possible, but as pleasant as possible, so that his soul may remain eternally in the Peace he has always asked for us!

All present remained silent in the face of these just words. Nut kept a reproachful gaze on NekBet while An-Nu, suddenly very worried, cast furtive and embarrassed glances at him, for he had to appease Iset. But it was his wife who had almost demanded that the skin be left like that and not opened. This went against Sacred Tradition, even though he was working to re-establish the ancestral ritual in its entirety.

Nek-Bet, who was obviously reading him, didn't let him venture any further into harmful expectation. Before he could utter any regrettable words, she intervened, beating him to the punch:

- If such is your wish, O my sister, to build a simple dwelling for Usir to rest his body, whose praises will be eternally glorified, there is nothing easier. And the Annals of the grandchildren of our great-grandchildren will sing of a Soul flying out of a bull's skin, and carried on a golden boat to the Kingdom of the Happy Ones, propelled by the Twelve...

Iset burst into convulsive sobs, at a loss for what to say or do, as her twin sister read the future and seemed to taunt her. The An-Nu held her close, making his disapproval clear to his wife. As for

Nut, she turned into a statue like the other two priests, no longer understanding anything about a situation that was beyond her comprehension.

However, perfectly calm, Nek-Bet did not hurry the events, which were to take place shortly after sunset. As only she knew, she knew that Time was present, the last rays of sunlight casting their changing glow on the mound and the sycamore tree.

Moving towards the opening of the "Abode", she asked those waiting silently outside to join them in the "ceremony willed by God". Retracing her steps, she crossed the room in silence and stopped in front of the air vent at the back to remove from under a flat stone one of the metal knives she had saved from the debacle and salvaged from the debris strewn across the beaches, which she had placed there in anticipation of the exceptional task that would be hers.

She returned to her husband, who in turn sensed something extraordinary without being able to define its quality. She raised the blade in both hands, looking at the crowd that had gathered and turned into a mute immensity, and this time spoke in a solemn tone:

- Let our venerated Pontiff pronounce the words of purification on this knife so that it can cut through the fetid bond and all its impurities, to free the body of Usir from its long sleep in this skin. Let the ancient ritual for the "Protection of the Living" take place before us. May the "Eldest Son" be returned to his wife and all the "Cadets"!

Very puzzled by the content of this imploring speech, for it was rather the phrases of the rite dedicated to the "Protection of the Blessed" that the Pontiff intended to utter, he nonetheless came to his wife to delicately take the outstretched blade, "to which would henceforth be attached the power to open all mouths, with the help of the most just and good Father". This, at least, was Nek-Bet's thought, as she carefully followed her husband's movements and turned to the two officiants who had accompanied him there.

With a quick glance, he asked for their help, so that he could be effectively assisted during the ceremony that was about to take place. In the same way, they nodded respectfully, before taking their places on either side of the Pontiff. The three servants of God then slowly approached the plump skin, taking the same slow, solemn step.

Having arrived in front of the Sacred Form, the An-Nu raised the knife high above it, suspending all movement for a few seconds. There was a hushed silence until the officiant took a deep breath and implored the Creator with poignant fervour. At his first words, all present fell to their knees.

Let us glorify God at this exceptional moment, so that he may assist us with his immense benevolence, and guide us as we open this mouth. Glory to you, Father of us all, for the benefits you have made available to us since we landed on this second earth.

The two officiants then raised their arms equally in supplication before the Pontiff continued in a voice vibrating with passion:

- Come to us, O Almighty Father, and support us throughout this ceremony that will bring Usir, your son and Hor's father, back to us. He came from You, the Creator unlimited in his creations, and has returned to You, the Father of all the Blessed.

But we beg you to give him back to us in human form, so that his soul does not become a "wanderer". May this sharp blade, which we present to you for purification, be washed of all its impurities and may the severed bond, the gaping lips of this skin, of this mouth, reveal Usir to our eyes, as you desire[12]...

Nek-Bet approached carrying a kind of small jug carved from the woody bark of a large coconut. She had purified it herself the

---

[12] The liturgical implorations reproduced throughout these pages come from the various texts relating to the "Hymn to Osiris" and the "Lamentations of Isis", as well as from the chapters of the *Book of the Dead*.

day before, meticulously preserving the ancient ritual. One of the two priests bowed and took the precious amphora, handing it to the Pontiff, who dipped the knife into it, before raising it and saying in a loud voice:

- Look kindly upon this living water, O God of Eternity! May the purifying offering of this liquid renew the scope of our actions and the Faith that animates them! May this purified metal, blessed by You, become your liberating instrument and present Ousir to us as we have always known him!

Lowering the jug, the Pontiff was about to formulate the beneficial incantation preceding the long-awaited act, when he felt the pressure of the fingers of his wife's hand tugging lightly at his linen robe. Surprised, he paused his words for a moment. As if on cue, she took advantage of the moment to utter words that made up sentences that could scarcely be believed. The An-Nu trembled inwardly from the start, for prophecy was manifesting itself in the unreal and unbelievable. But he made no protest and did nothing to stem the flow of sounds that penetrated all the initially dumbfounded souls:

- O You who are our splendour, resplendent in the gold of your millions of years, You whose face no one has yet contemplated without being blinded by it, You the Master of Justice and Truth, You our Lord, adored by the two sisters here present who implore you, You, the Beloved of all your Cadets gathered here who implore you, You, the revered by Nut, the Mother of your son, who implores you... May your blessing extend over this Abode where Usir lies, in this skin still sewn! May your powerful Breath purify the opening of this mouth, and restore his sleeping human appearance to the one who is still alive in our hearts, for he will live there eternally! Give us back the Elder, O Almighty One, to whom *nothing* is impossible.

After a short silence that oppressed all those kneeling there, Nek-Bet seemed to regain consciousness and gently pulled her husband up so that they were exactly above the imprisoned body. She stiffened again and raised her arms until she could feel her husband's hands holding the jug. She helped him lower the jug, all the while saying in a fierce voice heavy with extreme inner emotion:

- May this purified blade bring about the rebirth of our people! May he whose body lies here inert be reborn! May he whose limbs are imprisoned here be reborn! May he who is your son, Usir, be reborn and reappear among us! Let Usir no longer be inert; let his limbs come back to life, for he is your son, to You who created the multitude! Make him ALIVE!

The astonishment at these words reached a climax, and the entire assembly froze in amazement at the fantastic way in which the ceremony had unfolded. Everyone unconsciously sensed, without yet fully realising the precise meaning of what was about to happen, that something unusual was about to happen.

In the growing darkness of the room, everyone held their breath, trying to understand the incomprehensible. The impossible would happen before their very eyes, to prove that Divine Power was no illusion and could achieve anything.

Nek-Bet waved one hand at her husband, clearly up and down. The Pontiff understood what he had to do, but he could barely control the trembling in his fingers as he took the action of a lifetime. Taking a deep breath of air from his lungs to give himself the confidence he needed, he leaned towards the withered leather strap that had tightened, enclosing Usir's remains even more tightly.

He, in turn, uttered a fervent prayer aloud, while looking for a crack in the edges of the skin to insert the blade:

- May your faithful and submissive servant, who celebrates your power, use this arrow to sever this bond according to your will! May your son be preserved from all impurities and all past and future curses. May your will be done, O Mighty Lord of the Universe...

This last phrase was repeated once by the two officiants, then three more times by the other attendants. This time allowed the Pontiff to strengthen the grip he had just found under the blade. In the silence that followed, everyone heard the crunch of the knife, which, like a scalpel wielded with the consummate skill of a modern surgeon, found its way without difficulty to the posterior base of the skin, at the junction of the leather binding the bull's two thighs together.

Following the sort of dotted line left by the lacing, the point moved upwards, guided by a steady hand. It wasn't easy, however. But the Pontiff had acted with such speed, as if in a second state, that he only realised his success when he saw the skin suddenly relax. The lips parted widely, opening this enormous mouth which gave back its contents.

All the chests exhaled a breath held too long, while the kneeling bodies, in a single reflex, dragged themselves backwards, as much to avoid smelling the effluvia that must have come from this rotting flesh, as to avoid seeing the dreadful sight it must have presented.

After a brief, understandable hesitation, Nek-Bet leaned forward, however, because the darkness was almost total. Had she made a mistake? It didn't take her long to realise: she had correctly guessed the meaning of the premonitions that had assailed her so many times. Usir had not been reduced to dust; he seemed to have been asleep for only a few hours.

Only the beard had grown, darkening the face and disproving the simple sleep; but the general attitude of the body denoted a languor and somnolence that were far from mortal stiffness.

Gradually, in the face of Nek-Bet's joyful immobility, his sister in turn approached and let out an exclamation. The sobs that shook her again, seemingly in no way horrified her, gradually drew all those present back behind Nut. Shouts erupted, most of them surprised and joyful at this miracle of preservation of a body whose facial features were even serene.

Then nothing seemed impossible to Iset, from a God who allowed her to see her husband restored in this way, after having been "devoured" by a bull. This miracle of contemplating a cherished image, always the same as the one she had kept in her heart, made her foresee an upheaval even greater, spiritually, than that caused by the Great Cataclysm. At this vision, she burst into hysterical screams and collapsed on the body of her rediscovered husband, with all his *living* elasticity intact!

She flooded the bearded face with her tears, thus beginning the process of triggering the Event, the echoes of which the Annals would echo forever. Iset undertook to make heard the litanies of her c Lamentations, which have become the very embodiment of Love in its purest state. They are transcribed on the walls of dozens of royal tombs in Thebes, Saqqarah and many other places, so that a person loved by another may live again as a result of these incantations. They can only be the oral replicas that have been transmitted, generation after generation, since the time when Usir's wife addressed them to God.

An engraving that comes close to the truth, despite being 12,000 years old, is followed by this invocation[13]:

> "O you, Supreme Master of flesh and spirit, this dwelling is also yours! O you, Lord without enemies, it is your children who implore you! Answer the prayer of your daughter, whom you cannot abandon with the hope you have given birth to in her heart. My soul flies to you, to whom I will give my eyes, begging you to return to this Home that is also yours. Come and see the woman who loves your son with all her heart and soul, just as she loves you in the same way. O Lord, come to the call of your daughter! Come! COME!"

Overwhelmed by her pleas, and the sheer intensity of her spirit, Usir's wife fell back onto her body, which she flooded again with

---

[13] Quotation from the "Berlin Papyrus", recorded in the Egyptian collection under no. 3008, and better known as the "Lamentations of Isis": "Lamentations of Isis".

tears. She gently caressed the rediscovered face, so warm and *alive!* Clearly, the body seemed to be resting. But was it possible?

Night had fallen in the room, where all the heads piled up just above hers reinforced the impression of phantasmagoria. Luminaries bathed in smoky oil appeared at that moment, creating dancing lights that created a most hallucinatory environment. An unreal halo was created on the skin spread out around Ousir, surrounded by an extraordinary mystical ensemble, from which rose incredulous and astonished cries.

But Iset was not living this moment for those around her: she was concentrating on her husband. With a voice vibrating with emotion, she spoke to him, whispering in his ear:

- My beloved, whom I love so deeply! O you, Usir, come back and stretch out your arms over her who has your blood in her, who is of the same mother as yours, who is also the one who gave life to your son Hor!...

She paused for a moment, to convince herself that her words were penetrating to the very depths of her husband's still-drowsy but receptive soul. Unmindful of those panting above them, she pressed her cheek against his thick beard several times, as if to remind him of some past shared joys. When nothing happened, she continued in an even more imploring tone:

- I am your wife, O my beloved! She needs you, and so do all your people. Come back to us all, no longer lie motionless, so near and yet so far. Bring your soul back to earthly life, to keep company with mine that bathes you with its tears! I beg you, WAKE UP!...

Ready to collapse under the prodigious mental effort she had just made in trying in vain to bring her husband back to life, Iset lifted herself up to admire this face where there was nothing to suggest any understanding of the message she had so ardently launched. Nek-Bet knelt closer to her to try and help her in this attempt at resurrection, which she was certain was God's will. It would only be a question of Faith and Prayer for the result to happen.

She stretched out her two hands above the inert body, closing her eyes to perfect the vision she had of what would happen next. Certain from then on that only total communion of all in a single fervent prayer would allow the return to the Light, she prophesied in a low voice:

- All of us here, let us unite our requests in a single, *tangible* prayer. May all our words take root in Usir's soul and bring him back to us... Lord our Father, wake up your Son, we all beg you! Awaken him before the Sun touches the Western Horizon and caresses the Blessed. May Usir be reborn among us to guide us according to your commandments!

At this point, the Pontiff let himself fall to the ground, realising that the Lord could no longer remain insensitive to the strength emanating from the two sisters. With his face crushed to the ground, he cried out his prayer as loud as he could, because he suddenly felt so weak and helpless before the greatness of Divine Love; the two sisters had to obtain this "Renaissance"[14]:

- God Almighty! Yes !... Let Usir awake! Ousir awake!

The two priests in turn prostrated themselves, their foreheads touching the widely-spread skin, repeating the same words in the form of an incantation, which in turn were taken up by the almost trance-like audience:

- Awaken Ousir! Awaken Usir! O You Almighty!

AND SHE FELT THE REVERED BODY TREMBLING IN HER ARMS!

---

[14] Text of "The Vigil of the Two Sisters" at the Little Temple of Isis in Dendera.

Numerous grandiloquent narratives attempt to describe the Event accurately, but without quite succeeding. Engraved on the Temples dedicated to Isis, Osiris or Horus - the majority of religious buildings - the texts highlight the veneration that followed the Resurrection of the Son of God, the Eldest of the Cadets.

The summary, which we quote here, of the scene that followed, while not the oldest, underlines the intense Faith that achieved the result[15]:

> "Then the dead God, the one who would become the Celestial Bull, awoke. Usir took his soul back from his Father, who gladly gave it back to him, faith having regained its place among the people. Iset's husband first stretched out one arm to lie more comfortably on his side, as if he were simply waking from a long sleep. He rested his head on the two trembling hands of his wife, who was ready to faint from the strong emotion that was gripping her. He smiled at her to calm her nervousness. After so much time spent in the darkness of this skin, where he had been protected from everything and everyone, his wife's immense love, accompanied by fervent pleas, had awoken him from his long sleep. The triumph of the Faith burst forth in all its splendour with the Resurrection of Usir!

A moment of collective delirium around the couple tenderly embracing on the bull's skin, which had immediately become a sacred object of veneration, seemed to suspend time. A spiritual intensity beyond description gripped the entire audience.

The two young priests shouted as loud as the others, their arms raised, dancing their song of joy on the spot. The pale An-Nu felt the Divine Breath brush past him. He hugged his wife and Nut to calm them down, for they were both crying their eyes out, but he

---

[15] Taken from the "Ritual of the Resurrection" at the Great Temple of Medinet Habu.

could not have spoken, as his astonishment had rendered him speechless!

Usir finally stood up, without too much effort, gallantly helping his wife to do the same. The crowd returned to their knees and prostrated themselves at their feet, before kissing the bull's skin and tearing it open so that everyone would have a shred of this animal skin, this conservative mouth that had already become Sacred.

C.G. Jung, the famous philosopher who took a great interest in symbolism, quoted in one of his books the meaning of this skin "the container of the soul[16] ", which he would certainly have developed much further in a subsequent book if death had not taken him at that moment, for if the container contains the soul, the latter itself contains "the Divine Force which, through its Breath, gives and restores Life".

The fact remains that this skin very quickly became the object of very special veneration, symbolising, a few millennia later, through a privileged cult, the alliance of the people of the "Descendants of Hor" with the "Celestial Bull". Hieroglyphic subtlety led to a series of misunderstandings on the part of the "translators" *(sic)*, who transformed the understandable religious rites into a series of "abominable tales".

Texts referring to the "bull" mention Apophis, "the serpent"! Now, just as Ptah became Phtah in Greek (the P being read as "fe"), Apophis is, in hieroglyphic, "Ap'Pis", or *Api-Apis*, i.e. "Bull of the Milky Way", which is the sacred name of Usir. So there's nothing abominable about it - quite the contrary

Returning to Ta Mana's "Iat-Ousir", an extraordinary effervescence reigned throughout the night. Not wanting to wake Hor, who was sleeping peacefully for the first time in a long time,

---

[16] In his remarkable study *Wandlungen und Symbole der Libido*, C.G. Jung cites a bas-relief from the temple of Denderah, where the body of Osiris, wrapped like a mummy, is held in place by a sycamore branch.

Iset and her husband withdrew far from the joyous cries that continued to resound in their honour. It is likely that God's name was not often glorified and thanked as fervently as it was that night.

But in the midst of this popular enthusiasm, Iset's outpouring of love for her Risen Usir, which soon became her husband's name, was even more proof of her return to Life. However, he had only returned to carry out a very specific task: to educate his son Hor so that he could reign, while teaching his people about his destiny as "God's chosen one". This new covenant should never be broken again, for this second time would mean an even more appalling destruction than that which had engulfed Ahâ-Men-Ptah.[17]

Although he knew what was coming next for his younger siblings, the Elder knew that God alone would always have the power to direct the future by combining the movements of the stars in a way that he alone could judge. It was in this way, and so that he could inform Hor, that Life had been given back to him.

For seven millennia, Usir's Resurrection was glorified throughout the Second Heart. Thanks to his return and the teaching that his son subsequently provided, God's work, his law and his Commandments were very well understood and respected. The same was true of the arts, letters and sciences, which were passed on to posterity for the greater good of the Creator's work. But then oblivion set in...

By the time of the Caesars, hundreds of stelae glorified nothing but a carnivalesque pantheon. Greco-Roman elucidations took the place of theogonic decadence, and mixed hieroglyphs that were already partly incomprehensible with a new, wild iconography, devoid of any monotheistic spirituality.

---

[17] This text, "Nahi of the Bull's Skin", is engraved on the walls of the staircase leading to the famous Hall of Records in the Temple of Denderah, behind which the successive Pontiffs, and they alone, came to meditate in the "Holy Place".

And if, before tackling the story of this "long march" and of the "Struggle of the Two Giants", a preliminary is introduced in the next chapter with the Life of Hor, it is because he did indeed become the Guide who directed the first moment of the immense Exodus towards the "Second Heart" while beginning the battle against his uncle Sit, and succeeding in neutralising him most of the time thanks to the Knowledge he acquired by listening to his Father. And so he became "Horus the Pure"...

The best existing hieroglyphic reference to this important episode is the so-called "Metternich" stele, which was the most important discovery of the Russian Egyptologist Vladimir Golenitschef. Its translation is highly questionable, as the "abominable tales" are to be found beneath the eulogistic and emphatic epithets, and the French retranslation did nothing to improve them.

It is therefore through a personal understanding of the anaglyphs inserted in this stele that the history of Hor-le-Pur has been rewritten for your instruction. This stone was certainly not engraved until the reign of Nectanebo Ier, of the XXXth dynasty in 365 BC.

This is what we learn from its scribe, who copied this text at the request of the High Priest Nestum, of the temple of the necropolis of the sacred bulls of Am, or Heliopolis, so that the ancestral spiritual ritual would survive. A very old manuscript in the process of being lost, itself reproduced from a very ancient document, attested to its origin and veracity.

The general title, according to the first translation by V. Golenitschef, is *Horus the Saviour*. However, we prefer its true hieroglyphic name *Hor-Ro*, i.e. "Horus the Pure". The extract below (col. 126/130) is a perfectly logical conclusion to this chapter:

> "He approaches his wounded child:
> He is Sirius, who sails like the Sun,
> He is also the Celestial Bull!

He has left his temporary home
HE IS OUSIR THE RESURRECTED!"

Chapter Four

HORUS-LE-PUR

Of all Egyptian theology, the system of emanation dominated, which consists not only in distinguishing but in separating the various attributes of the Great Being, so that each of them becomes a separate person and one God passes through a multitude of gods.
G. F. CREUZER
(Ancient religions)

I am Horus, the Descendant of millions of years! The throne has passed to me and I shall rule it, for the mouth spoke but fell silent! Osiris has left for the Western Horizon; I become, through his Breath, the one who possesses within himself what he needs, and who, cycle after cycle, once again becomes the Guide.
HORUS THE PURE
(Temple of Edfu 3, IV)

The different interpretations of the Horus stele, discovered by the Russian Golenitschef, stem essentially from the adaptation carried out to bring the text into line with the Plutarchian elucidations of the *De Iside et Osiride*, which was an authority on the subject, albeit at the extreme limit of indecency, or perhaps because of it. Only a Greek of 2,000 years ago could 'translate' a very high spirituality with 'abominable tales' that were within the reach of his feeble understanding, but which greatly satisfied his compatriots in need of superiority.

Let us therefore re-establish, with the help of other, much earlier documents, the original wording of a story still engraved on stone, barely distorted by a hieratic anaglyph from ancient times. The affabulations perceptible in the last centuries before Christianity were essentially made by the High Priests themselves, who wanted the Greco-Roman Barbarians to believe that they were not the savages.

Hor-Pa-Ro remains the title of this ritual, symbolising this transition from the ancestral ritual. The hieroglyphic article "Pa", placed between "Hor" and "Ro", has an importance that goes far beyond a simple linguistic and philological study. Like each of the signs engraved in the 249 vertical and horizontal columns relating to Hor's heroic life, it has a *precise* meaning.

Although the ancient language does not usually use articles in its usual context, either definite or indefinite, leaving it to the general meaning of a sentence to determine the type of article (for example, in a Latin sentence, the word *frater* means "brother" or "a brother", or "*the* brother") In some cases, such as on this stele and on the walls of the Temple of Edfu, ideographic characters provide essential precision.

The article "Pa", in particular, which is masculine singular, elevates the noun attached to it to celestial precision. "Pa" is represented by a flying duck: It gives all its symbolic value to the name, in this case "Ro": "Pure". Hor-Pa-Ro is therefore the certainty of the purity of Hor's soul, because it is linked to God through this part engendered by the Divinity.

This purity is totally lacking in the interpretations concerning Horus, whether they come from texts preserved in the museums of Turin, Leiden, Berlin or the Louvre in Paris. On the other hand, scenes of magic and sorcery abound, even though they do not exist in the real story.

One of the many copies that have been constantly copied over the millennia, recounting the life of Horus, son of Isis and Osiris.

But now it's time to follow Usir, who in the morning, well rested, entered the thick, cool foliage of the hut where Hor was sleeping. Spotting him lying on a thick litter of feathers and fur, he remarked:

- You hoped for God's mercy, my son, and you were right: as long as your soul remains pure, your body will not rot.

Seeing that his Elder did not wake up, he went over to him and ran a soothing hand over his crippled but de-suffused eye, murmuring:

- Hor ! Hor !... Your soul has not yielded to the fire of the Great Cataclysm. The march of Time was suspended pending your decision. That's why your heart continued to beat that night. Then the day came again; since then, fear no more!

At the sound of the "Voice", as much as under the gentle caress, the convincing words made the able-bodied eye open. Hor smiled beatifically.

- Father! I am saved!

- You already were, my son, for you must succeed me. You will heal very quickly, and those who do not despair of Heavenly Goodness will heal in the same way. Your strength will be reborn and those who rebel against your orders will have to flee. No one will ever seize this land, our "Second Heart", which God has placed within our reach *and where only those who bear the title of "Descendant of the Eldest" will reign!*

This pious vow was always fulfilled throughout the millennia that followed in the land of Ath-KaPtah, for even the usurpers, all the invaders and the Romans themselves adorned themselves with the title of *Pêr-Ahâ* (Pharaoh), which in hieroglyphic means "Descendant of the Elder".

Usir already knew this, but he thought that, since God allowed free will to work in humans, the Elders could prevent this degeneration which would bring about the end of the chosen people: the Cadets of the Second Heart. It was therefore necessary to educate his own son without further delay. To do this, he had to get back on his feet. Nut and Nek-Bet had prepared the healing of the broken knee by compressing the mor ceaux of the kneecap with dried mud; also straightened up to say, raising his eyes to Heaven, in the monologue of a father addressing the Father:

- O You who are my Creator, You who are the First, the Only, the Only, You are Hor's protection because he is pure. You stopped the disc from sailing for millions of years so that it might survive. You protect Hor because he is the hope of the Cadets. You placed yourself on "Meskit" so that the Lion would be overthrown and push the "Mandjit" onto Ta Mana. You protect Hor because you heard his mother's cries and his sister's screams. You protect Hor because you allowed the darkness to disperse. You protect Hor because you are his name and his soul. O You, my Father, make our Elder rise, so that he can carry out the task assigned to him. May he regain the use of his leg and recover his sight!

Bending down without waiting for an answer, Usir began to carefully remove the thick layer of mud consolidating the knee. Seeing that everything was perfect, he applied his hands to the broken kneecap, compressing it. He looked fixedly at his son, who was still staring at him, speechless with astonishment and even wincing at the pain he must be feeling, and he said to him:

- Your head is yours, Hor, as strong as the Lord's: it will support your steps and guide them as best you can on the road to the second land. Your right eye is always yours, Hor, as perceptive to all visions as that of the Lord; it will support the realities that will guide you towards the eastern horizon. Your right knee is yours, Hor, as valiant as the Lord's: it will withstand all the hazards sown on the path to the "Second Heart". All forces are already reborn in your body, as powerful as those of the Lord, for you are now the Protector of the wounded and the Defender of the weak: they will valiantly bear the heavy burden of all human hesitations in this march towards the Light, to meet the Beloved, to meet God.

At this last word, Usir took a firm hold of one of his son's hands and helped him to rise from his bed. He held him upright for as long as it took for *both* legs to regain their confidence on the ground. The knee regained its natural pink tinge, very quickly. Before long, this epic struggle before the Great Cataclysm would leave no visible trace, apart from the irretrievable loss of his right eye. Only posterity would likely seize upon the event to create a legend.

Ousir, thinking of this popular reflex, and wanting to avoid it, remarked:

- May your eyes become a living symbol that will preside over the renewal of history. The people will learn from tomorrow that as long as they respect God's Commandments, you will remain their defender thanks to this total vision of *your two eyes*. The new cyclical time will only continue its harmonious course if this condition is in no way disavowed by you.

Your left eye will symbolise the day, because it will be the protection of the day, watching over the solar navigation during its journey of millions of years in the Great Celestial River. Your other eye, closed, will be the Justifier of the night, when time is as if suspended. You will be the appearance of Light and the separation of Darkness, until the end of time. You will be the "Guide"...

Hor stepped back a little and stood alone, his eyebrows furrowed:

- But you are still with us, Father! It's up to you to guide the people. I have time to learn everything by watching you. Usir shook his head slowly.

- My days are numbered, my son: from now on I must teach you the initial symbols and their meaning. Let's both go down to the seaside and talk in peace. But be prepared to face the liveliness of the good people when they see you on your two feet!

-But you're more of a miracle worker than I am, Father! If there is a symbol to perpetuate in the future, it is the bull's skin that has preserved you so well.

If the first steps were rather uncertain and stumbling, the following ones were more assured. The enthusiasm aroused by their appearance side by side helped to control the last nervous spasms in the knee, which was now back in place. The ovations continued all the way to the beach. The waters were calm and limpid blue, reminiscent of an outlawed era. With a weary sigh, Usir waved his arm broadly before talking to his son, who leaned on him to rest.

- You see, Hor, the sea is the same as before, but it's different because the sun rises on the opposite side. A new cycle begins...

- I remember the prophecies of your Father, the venerated Geb. They have all come true... Why did such a great misfortune have to happen, Father?

- So that people can understand, Hor. This raises the whole problem of intelligence, with its essential link to God, the Soul. But it is very fragile, because it is made up of both strength and fragility!

- What do you mean, Father?

Usir did not reply immediately, scanning the area to find a suitable place for them to talk. He spotted a small rise not far away led his son to it, while answering:

- The Soul is invisible and impalpable, like our Creator. To forge a "Second Heart of God", the multitude of spiritual consciousnesses must have *only one*, *in* the very image of the new "Mathematical Combinations", which will build harmony with celestial movements day after day.

- But we've lost all the writings, Father! We no longer have any...

- Like a few survivors, I know the keys Knowledge, my son. I will open doors for you that no one else knows about, and then the Pontiff and Nek-Bet will help you to shape that Knowledge. What you must never forget, Hor, is that our souls must be in perfect balance between the designs of Earth and Heaven. For it was they who created the fatal imbalance in AhâMen-Ptah!

- Did it have to be this destructive anger, Father? Everything could have been wonderful in the best of all possible worlds. Why did you destroy it? Why did you do it?

Usir paused for a moment, as if to think about his answer. Then the two men slowly made their way back up the hill. Then he said:

- Perhaps, in fact, he was no longer the best, despite appearances. For he was no longer Ahâ-Men-Ptah the "Beloved of God". Are you forgetting that Geb, my Father, died because this country had ceased to be one long before he disappeared?

- Isn't God the only one responsible for this, Father? Man lacked reflection...

- In the beginning, perhaps; but then came sacrilegious impiety. In the beginning, this great tranquillity established by the reign of God, generation after generation, over hundreds of centuries, became so accentuated Time went on, that it seemed quite natural, in the order of things established once and for all. And so Man's duties towards the One who had fashioned him were forgotten, by giving him a soul capable of far more magnificent things than what it was accomplishing. This led him to deny any form of prayer or thanks to this God who could no longer provide them with the material well-being they already possessed. Thus began this unholy and sterile happiness, in which spirituality had no place.

- I certainly understand that, O my venerated Father, but since Man is what he is ultimately by the Divine Will, he is not completely at fault: he is only the depositary of the constituent part of the Soul...

- No, Hor! Because the humans made a solemn pact with God, and their Cadets broke that covenant. It was this perjury that unleashed the wrath of Heaven. Long before Geb, selfishness, envy and hatred began the work of destruction. If the people had continued to go to the places of worship to pray, God would certainly have relented, for he is the Father of all. But the temples were abandoned or became places of abomination. It was this impiety that triggered the horror of the Great Cataclysm.

- Yet this impiety cannot justify the tens of millions of deaths, Father! It's so monstrous...

- Apparently so, my son, but the few thousand survivors who have landed on these shores are proof of Divine clemency. If they understand, thanks to you and the "Descendants" who will follow you, that they must follow the Commandments instituted by Universal Harmony, they will rebuild a second country, which will be their "Second Heart". And this new humanity will form a powerful nation of millions and millions of beings living in accord with God, and will begin Life anew within a new reconstituted Alliance, where happiness will once again reign over the whole Earth.

As they talked, they reached the small hill. Father and son climbed it slowly. Hor felt his knee crack, but the bones held. He made a quick grimace to show how little faith he had, before remarking in response to Ousir's last sentence:

- Given the weakness of the human soul, isn't there a risk that such forgetfulness will recur?

- As long as the Priests keep reminding everyone of the story of the swallowing up of the "First Heart of God", Peace, Prosperity and Happiness will progress in the Second Homeland.

- You are right, Father: as long as the priests themselves do not forget the meaning of the teachings they give, they will be the guarantors of the Resurrection that you personify today. But what if they forget, or allow their dogmas to be led astray by the new generations?

- Then it will be the definitive denial of any right supremacy of Man on Earth. God will remove him from the ranks of living beings or have him enslaved by another category made of flesh and bone, to whom He will transfer our Souls.

- So we need to find ways to establish eternal veneration for the Creator who made us what we are.

- Veneration is not exactly what is needed; nor is adoration. He is the Father, and must be honoured as such, always. It is this worship that must be eternalized and put back into everyday use. It is a duty of filial piety as much as of gratitude for having endowed us with this Divine particle that allows us to emerge above the mass of animals of all kinds, to be *men*.

- I learned about the formation of this Soul, Father, when I was still studying with the Great Master of Measure and Number, at Ath-Mer, and how all these convolutions received the weft of the emanations of the Great Celestial Breath. And I am well aware of the faults that men have to fight against, in spite of themselves!

- Not all of them, my son! This is a long-term study, which you will then have to teach again and again to all the young boys and girls, with the help of the Pontiff and Nek-Bet. They themselves will then have to pass on their knowledge to their children in subsequent generations, and so on until the written texts reappear in the new Homeland.

- And the "Sacred Words"?

- Each An-Nu and each Elder will hold a part of it in their spirit, which must never be lost, until the solemn reopening of the "Houses of Life".

As they reached the top of the mound, they were pleasantly surprised by a slight warmth in the air, as well as by the silence that seemed to have covered everything here.

Usir pointed to a soft spot, carpeted with tender grass.

- Let's sit down here and continue our conversation. The Life Force that makes up the Soul is the very symbol of the Faith that will always blaze. It is You. It is each one of us, like a living flame, as bright as the Sun itself. It is this Force alone that dispenses in hearts the multitude that will form bodies around the multiplicity of immortal souls. This is what the mind forgets most quickly...

- O Father!

Have you forgotten that just eight days ago you were considered enlightened and the godless man wise? The hypocrite became brave and the soul was no more than an outdated concept, useless to say the least. Hence the denial of God and His works, and the preference of Darkness over Light.

- But the Soul remains present in us, Father!

- This is why we must no longer rely solely on popular understanding to be certain that the "Sacred Words" reach Souls. And if certain symbolic figures in the written texts perfectly expressed the ideas represented, they will have to be explained as soon as they are used again, because they were not enough to prevent the destruction of the carnal envelopes that believed themselves to be intelligent. The Soul is the only Divine personification in man. It is the "Ka" symbol, with its two arms raised and hands open in a call for unity towards heaven, to link the human soul to its creator.

- And that's what we'll have to explain from now on, because the image alone has not created this bond of union.

- I see you understand, my son. May your descendants be like you, and may there be no more divorce between God, the "Ka" Creator, and his images of flesh, the "Ka" begotten. The "Second Heart" will then be called *Ath-Ka-Ptah*, as much to perpetuate the motherland as to thank Divine Harmony for having led the survivors to a new habitable land, similar to the first, so that there can be a new beginning.

- This memory will be eternal, Father! Ath-Ka-Ptah will remind everyone of the beautiful land of Ahâ-Men-Ptah, the "Elder Land", the "Beloved Land". She will be its physical double for Eternity.

- The "Ka" symbol shows that you can't grasp God with both hands, but you have to implore his help with both arms. And that help will come. Never forget the comforting words of our departed writings: "Life and prosperity are given to you more than to all other living beings. I have destined you for excellence and abundance, and for all the good things I have placed on earth, by giving you this Life Force that will make you like me; you will be my image, my double, my "Ka"!

- This is how the soul was born in a quadruped that rose above the others by walking on only two feet. But it can be lost forever, and the Great Cataclysm is the warning.

- You're beginning to understand, my son! You have a tough job ahead of you if you are to avoid an even more catastrophic renewal of the human race.

A short silence followed, during which both speakers allowed their thoughts to wander back to that atrocious past, so near and yet so far away for those who had escaped it. This prompted Ousir to murmur:

- Of the streams of blood that still stain the bottom of this sea, all that remains for our eyes is this celestial blue. Everything is already beginning again; the past has been forgotten while the people have not yet woken up to the future that awaits them. It will be up to you to do everything you can to constantly remind them that they must live in constant fear of a worse and definitive abomination if they do not forge indissoluble ties with God. For truly I say to you solemnly, Hor, if the survivors do create a new bridgehead to Heaven by signing a new Covenant with their

Creator, this time they will perish in the throes of eternal punishment.

- They will sign this pact, Father, because they will never forget the shock they suffered.

- Not them! Perhaps not their children either...

But what about their grandchildren? And what about the new-born babies of the hundredth generation?

- The very strict Commandments of the High Priests will help them to remember.

- If the people remained united, perhaps! But there are already two enemy stocks. Many other branches will populate not only our second homeland, this land promised to all, but many other regions, forming other clans...

- Why would this cause further dissension?

To justify a desire for independence, new fictitious gods were invented and invoked, provoking original impiety, as in Ahâ-Men-Ptah!

- So what can we do?

- Looking back over dozens of centuries to predict what will happen when our people reach the 'Second Heart'? What will happen then? Total oblivion of the past, which is our present. It's obvious... Your only aim will be to make sure that it doesn't happen again. That every man feels watched over by God and a multitude of facets, throughout his life, every second of the day, for every act he does every day. Let every man know that the slightest deviation will bring the worst calamity upon the whole human race, and that his own entry into the Beyond of Life will only be granted after a rigorous weighing of his soul, where the smallest bad deed committed will be deducted from the weight required by the regulation of the Commandments. Let everyone be educated in this priority understanding, and let it be perpetuated deep into the mists of time, whatever governments may be in power.

- Won't the people wonder what all this fear is about? Especially if they live in a new comfort, similar to the one that prevailed when Ahâ-Men-Ptah was swallowed up.

- The history of the Great Cataclysm, with its precise date and its consequences, must be engraved in imperishable stone for these forgetful generations. The two lions opposed by a central Sun could be the symbolisation, understandable by all the young future minds of the coming millennia, whatever their degree of intelligence. Fear will live on...

- Do you think, then, Father, that it would be preferable for the Covenant with God to be based on an absolute and unconditional belief in the Almighty Power of the Lord?

- It can only be effective and efficient if it is automated by certain daily acts that ensure its omnipotence as well as its omnipresence. Divine Goodness and Divine Wrath must never again be doubted. From now on, the Sun will set at the opposite end of each day's navigation, in the same place where it meets the millions of souls of our Blessed Ancestors on the horizon every evening. What better proof could there be to inspire fear in that distant future when the sun will do the same?

- You're right, Father, and I still have a lot to learn. But as far as we are concerned, we will have to redo all the "Mathematical Combinations", in order find ourselves in harmony with the movements of the sky. This will take a long time, since the Sun's course has totally changed.

- I don't think there are so many complications. If I'm not mistaken, you'll soon realise that, in his great mercy, the Creator has kept the movements of the Universe intact. Only the Earth tilted, and the offending living beings disappeared from the very place where they had sinned. So there was no change in the spatial swirling order. So nothing has changed in the pre-established order!

- So the Sun is always in the same place?

- Yes, but because the Earth has changed its course, the solar star is "moving backwards" for us alone in the constellation "Akher", Leo.

- So we could easily get back into harmony with the sky?

- I told you that Divine Goodness is immense. If the Sun has stopped its advance on the Great Milky River on its golden boat, in this configuration of Leo, it is precisely as a sign of anger and opposition to this fratricidal slaughter unleashed by my brother Usit. But that won't do much to change the meaning of the 'Mathematical Combinations'.

- What can you tell me about these calculations that I don't already know, Father?

- There are so many important problems to tackle that I won't have the time to help you solve them all. But this Mathematical Knowledge will come to you as and when Knowledge forces you to tackle them. And the elements of understanding that I am going to instil in you will enable you to complete your education alone, in meditative contemplation. You have learned that God originally created through the Word. He was the fire from which the Light gushed forth, giving rise to the material, physical world, from which the earthly human image was then born. This is why the Word-Light is now within you. You, in turn, must transmit it to living beings, through your "Ka" to other "Ka", so that the elevation continues gradually, of disappearing. It is this soul that will enable you to hear the Commandments of God, to act in this Knowledge, to create and procreate, in complementarity with the Word, through the Word!

- I knew about this Divine Force that generates from nothing, Father: "God said, and it was..." So it was God, but He destroyed everything! So it was God, but He destroyed everything!

- Not everything, Hor, because we're here, alive and well, to see how we can teach the thousands survivors the best way to live again in Universal Harmony.

- Do you think I'm capable of carrying out such a missionFather? I feel so diminished...

- You are all the less so, because your mind, surely intact, is developed towards an understanding that no human will ever possess! You will know how to make yourself worthy of this superiority by teaching Knowledge. The Word is based on twenty-two phonetic articulations, which reflect the Soul that moves it; this is why it is the mirror of each individuality within the multitude. Thanks to your name, and the name that identifies each personality, everyone becomes himself and no one else. It is the foundation of the edifice that will soon emerge from the gathering under your protective wing, if it is to survive thereafter as a "Second Heart". From now on, therefore, you must lay such a deep foundation for it that it will become unshakeable.

- Will human reason accept this new effort, when the soul has just suffered such a shock, O my Father? The dead have not even been given the burial they deserve!

- God gave them the most beautiful of all: AhâMen-Ptah! That's why, for the survivors, the Spirit will once again take precedence over Reason, as a sign of rebirth. The new Sacred Word will give rise to impulses and intuitions in everyone, opening the way to the future. The Soul, finally emerging from the sterile lethargy that kept it from God, will at last perceive the meaning of words. This will be the illumination that forges ideas and shapes all the awakening faculties.

- The Word will truly be a Divine gift, if that's what happens!

- That's how it will be, my son, but this gift is outside human nature, and therefore very fragile and dangerous.

- It would therefore be necessary to surround the Sacred Words with all the predictable oratory precautions, with an intangible rite, planned for Eternity.

- Yes. There should be no room left for any intervention of personal intuition, whether popular or emanating from an elite who would like to demonstrate intelligence, where this would be of no use.

- So the catastrophe we have just experienced will remain the historical event willed by the Creator. It will remain engraved in everyone's minds, always occupying pride of place in daily concerns as a symbol of Divine fear. The Annals that will emerge from it will trace its true origins.

- Once again, you forget that the survivors will have children, who will have children of their own, and so on for each new generation. The Truth will change and weaken over the centuries. In 10,000 years' time, what will be left of it, Hor?

- It's so far away, Father!...

- The cycle of the Sons of God will only be perpetuated by foreseeing what will happen a hundred centuries from now. And if strict Laws are not enacted now for the rigorous observance of the Commandments, the foundations will crumble and chaos will be reborn, before the final disappearance of all.

- You will not be able to avoid the revival of Scripture, which will allow thought to flourish, aided by reasoning. There will then be this development of all the faculties which will bring with it constant progress forming a new civilisation, but also a retreat from the spirituality necessary to any harmonious life.

- That's why we have to set faith against religion, my son. The revelation that has been ours will undergo many changes over the coming millennia, which will be the price of this progress. Faith in God must therefore be involved from the very first words you speak. Faith will have to remain unshakeable, so that despite the future blows dealt by unreasonable reasoning, it remains intact in its eternal inviolability. Faith will continue to be the flagrant and tangible proof of the Divine Origin of Humanity, and it cannot be undermined in any way, anywhere.

- What will become of the reasoner, Father?

- Simply human Reason, Hor, will never possess any reasonable reasoning to reach an understanding of God. Its perception and conception of the Divinity being null, this Reason is doomed to annihilation by its very formation. This is why Faith must take the place of Reason, because it has no need of reasoned justification. The certainty of a single original Law and the Commandments that flow from it to avoid a cataclysmic renewal should be enough to occupy reasoning. For who, if not God, could be the Lawgiver regulating Celestial Harmony, since Man did not yet exist?

- This logic is very well reasoned, O Father! This Law of Creation needs to be clearly stated, in a humanised form, so that the whole population becomes imbued with it and follows its rules.

- It is one of God's intended difficulties to allow this doubt to persist. It is precisely Faith that should enable human beings to rise on their own, recognising all that they owe to the Eternal One, even above their own doubts. The ancestral parabolic form of the calculations of the "Masters of Measurement and Number" remains the only valid one, and it is not up to us to make it perceptible to the masses. From now on, we will even have to make the teaching of "Mathematical Combinations" a little more complicated, because the example of those who have gone before us has hardly been conclusive, at least in the sense of Faith.

- What a shame for the College of High Priests, Father! They gave in everywhere and humiliated themselves in vain. The mockery and sarcasm of countless sceptics still ring deafeningly in my ears. Poor Geb, who tried everything to save all the sons of the Light, born on Earth, and whom he considered to be his own children!

- That's why Master Geb will be remembered as the Father of the Earth, and for two reasons, because it was thanks to his tenacity that the "Mandjit" enabled us to escape this horror. You are his grandson, Hor, and you too will have an Elder who, by perpetuating you, will link us all with the next 'Descendants'. The path you must follow from now on to strengthen the new stock that is already developing is blind obedience to the Commandments of the Law, and the fear of not following them.

- Pending the formation of a new College High Priests to teach novices this skill, this is clearly the best method of instilling the unshakeable Faith that will ensure a smooth journey towards the Light that is the second home.

- It is the promise of the Covenant, and it will have to be called Ath-Ka-Ptah when the propitious moment defined by the celestial configurations arrives. In this way, future generations, when they set foot on it, will know that they have indeed reached their second "Soul". Until then, you and your successors will have to act as if you were talking to the blind and pointing out a road to the deaf.

- I understand, Father; the people must be allowed see without seeing, and hear without understanding. That way they will obey more easily and above all without any restrictions.

- In this way, this "Second Heart" will welcome the multitude who will live there eternally, under the enlightened guidance of "Pêr-Ahâ" from the first Elder of God, begotten in Ahâ-Men-Ptah, who disappeared through the blindness of its inhabitants.

- To preserve its memory intact, we should call this vanished kingdom, which made us happy, by a name that will be venerated forever.

- The "Kingdom of the Blessed" would be a perfect image of the welcome God has given it. It would be called *Amenta*, recalling the original land where souls that had not sinned would join those of the Ancestors...

- In this way, our lost continent, so dear to our memory, while remaining a warning of a terrible cataclysm, can also be a refuge for all those who have earned eternal life.

- You have understood this lesson very well, my son. All our Cadets have truly become Blessed, in remission for the collective faults of which some were not guilty. And it is for this reason that I shall not be long in joining them...

- O Father!

- Someone has to be present at the Weighing of the first Souls who will soon present themselves to God! And remember, Hor: beware of those who have transgressed too much of the Law and its Commandments!

- I'll be sure to keep reminding everyone of this, O my venerated Father!

- Now we're going to look again at the mechanism of "Mathematical Combinations", so that you know the Celestial Harmonic Whole and can carry out the work for which you were born.

- Including that of being "my Father's avenger[18]"!

---

[18] This phrase begins all the papyri dedicated to Horus, i.e. Hor. This hieroglyphic grouping means: "Horus, avenger of Osiris, Son of God and of the Sun, Twice Living and Risen".

CHAPTER FIVE

THE COVENANT WITH GOD

Understanding God is difficult, talking about him is impossible, because the body cannot express the incorporeal, because the imperfect cannot embrace the Perfect. How can we associate God with something that lasts such a short time?

STOBÉE
(Florilegium, LXXVIII)

May he live the Elder who comes from the Lion! May he henceforth live under the sceptre of the Protector of the Opposite Lands. Let him follow the path of the Fixed Stars to be led with his people into the second Soul of God. And the East, thus united with the West, will sanctify the arrival of the "Elders of the Sun".

REGISTRATION OF OUNAS
(Northeast Saqqara Tomb)

After the crazy night that followed Usir's resurrection, which had kept the An-Nu awake to preside over the thanksgivings that the crowd, suddenly aware of its origin, had not ceased to address to heaven, a much more active life had spiritually renewed the Souls. The desire to re-form a second nation suddenly materialised, anchored on the cornerstone represented by the 'Son' who had reappeared alive among them.

At dawn, at last, the Pontiff came to contemplate his wife peacefully asleep. He then caressed the foreheads of their four children, before returning to the temporary altar that served as a springboard for the celebration of the rising of the sun and the thanksgiving to the Eternal. As he made his way towards the consecrated area, pursued by the shouts of joy from the living, he thought with anguished dismay about what would have become of Ousir if Nek-Bet had not had this vision of his resurrected brother.

He would have gone to his last 'Home' on this earth! But on reaching the place of prayer, the Pontiff agreed with his conscience that God would have provided him with another sign to demonstrate His Power by returning His Son to him.

Ath-Ka-Ptah, the "Second Heart of God" is the meaning of this flame, which is that of the second heart reborn from its ashes thanks to Osiris, the Elder, and his descendants.

This sacred festival also includes the transport of the "Mandjit", or holy bark that carried the body of Osiris during the Great Cataclysm, without decomposing it, to Ta Mana.

The first beneficial rays of the Sun appeared in the east. As they penetrated people's minds, they still aroused the astonishment of those contemplating this unusual prodigy. This 'natural' habit was not easily accepted. Even the An-Nu was astonished, despite himself, while thanking the Creator for the daily miracle of this solar apparition. At the end of the ceremony, the faithful dispersed, leaving him to meditate on the incredible destiny that had become his, bringing him to the head of those who would restore God to his Throne until the end of Time. His soul was revitalised by the Divine Breath, which gave him the extra strength he needed to carry out the mission he knew he had been entrusted with.

The resplendent day stretched out and enveloped him. Before going to his teaching, he could not resist the temptation to contemplate the "priceless treasure" that one of the settlers of this land had entrusted to him that night. The sight of Usir alive had transformed all minds, restoring values to their proper proportions. The An-Nu carefully removed from under the table a kind of tub, hollowed out of a large tree trunk...

The man explained that he had owned the 'machine' for a very long , after bartering it with a nautonier[19] who had exchanged it for *Kesbet*[20]. It was a very old *Gô-men*, dating from well before the cataclysm, and now had an exceptional value that nothing else in Ta Mana could match.

For this bowl, roughly hollowed out, contained the most precious instrument in the world at that moment! It swam with the movements of the liquid inside. The An-Nu gazed with tenderised delight at the full, floating wheel; it reminded him of the old writings of his youth, when he learned that this object remained horizontal, whatever the movement of the tub. The liquid mass was in no way influenced by the inclination of the container. The light wheel always hovered on the same horizontal line.

The most important feature of this old work was the rod that stood perpendicular to it, whose large shadow made it possible to pinpoint the exact location required, with the calculations being carried out daily at zero zenith.

A series of concentric circles carved into the wood at different widths, precisely defined in advance, enabled its owner to go anywhere. The development of navigation, due to the foreign trade of Ahâ-Men-Ptah, had necessitated the development of such a

---

[19] He was the experienced pilot of coastal ships trading to the ends of the earth.

[20] *Kesbet* was a metallic derivative with highly valuable properties. It was probably orichalcum, as mentioned by Herodotus. In hieroglyphic texts, this name came immediately after gold in the list of precious metals.

device many millennia before. It was only much later that it was abandoned in favour of more sophisticated dials.

The Pontiff sighed deeply at the memory of his Father compiling the Combinations on the 'Golden Circle' of Ath-Mer. What a long time ago! But it shouldn't be too difficult to create a more 'modern' dial with the resources at hand. Twelve mutually inclined planes in a terrain well modelled for this purpose will always cut from 15 to 15 degrees the 24 equal spindles of a terrestrial representation whose first plane would be the meridian of Ta Mana. Starting from this point and heading towards the western horizon, and no longer towards the east, they will mark from 1 to 12 below this imaginary line, and from 1 to 12 above it. In this way, the Sun, uniformly describing its new celestial navigation, will intersect the hour circles on the western side at night, and on the eastern side during the day...

Another sigh rose from the An-Nu's chest at the thought of the ignorance that risked covering this land if he didn't find fifty or so young people to learn the Sciences in depth. But perhaps this machine, docile before his eyes, sent by Heaven, would make it much easier for him to teach the neophytes all the ancient data that had gone before. The Sacred Words, those ancient texts that each Pontiff revealed to his Elder, had led him not only to know perfectly well all the workings of the "Divine-Mathematical Combinations", and to understand the accomplishment of the terrible cataclysm, but also to foresee the mechanism that would make it possible to renew the New Alliance between God and his Second Heart.

This pact, if kept, would ensure Peace, until the occupation of this other Land that was promised to them. This would be the tangible, human reality of God's forgiveness, whatever the suffering endured beforehand to achieve it. Fortunately, the survivors were not yet aware of this clause.

How many tragedies Hor would have to thwart before giving the go-ahead. This long march "towards the Light" would be so perilous! Usir already had to teach his son what this ordeal would be like. Fortunately, the presence of a Pontiff was not required for such a teaching, which allowed him to reflect on the best ways to organise the journey spiritually. The machine, bathed in a myriad of solar reflections, gave him the opportunity to do just that, as *it ensured that its owner would know exactly what route to take to reach the 'Second Heart', Ath-Ka-Ptah!*

Certain basic annotations differed, delimiting the known lands; but as the Sun was starting from an opposite horizon, he would necessarily have to calculate new landmarks. All the more so as the aim here was not to steer a ship on the high seas, but to guide an innumerable caravan overland. The unknown point was a long way off, of course, but the appropriate 'Combinations' would perhaps be easier to study than it seemed, as it *was located on the same parallel as Ath-Mer*. The manuscripts were quite definite, and it was for this reason that this land had been designated by God.

In his studious youth, An-Nu had learnt that, although each dial was calculated in relation to a single location, it could be reproduced in the same way for any other place on the Earth situated under the same meridian, *provided that it was placed there in a situation parallel to the one it had previously been in.*

Now, the "House of Life" of the "Divine-Mathematical Combinations" in the Temple of Ath-Mer had the same coordinates as the current location, as shown by the path of the fixed stars, which had changed course, and also had the same configuration as the place chosen as the rallying point in the Second Homeland to establish the new place for calculating celestial data. THE DESCENDANTS WOULD LIVE UNDER THE SAME SKY AGAIN, THANKS TO THEIR ANCESTRAL ALLIANCE WITH GOD.

Knowing the coordinates of the sunken capital, still engraved on the gently floating wheel at a point almost invisible to the uninitiated, and which lay at the edge of the eighth circle, it would be easy to determine the route to follow to reach the distant land promised by God, and towards which successive Pontiffs would lead the faithful 'Descendants' without any weakness, as long as they kept the Eternal in their hearts and souls.

As Ta Mana's point of departure is perfectly well known thanks to the Ath-Mer exhibition, all it would take is a little daily calculation based on the shadow itself: would it be too long? The long caravan would have to curve southwards to reach. Would it be too short? On the contrary, the entire population would have to head northwards.

Since the route taken by the Fixed Stars is always identical to the opposite route taken by the Sun in major configurations such as Leo, night-time observation of Orion and Sirius would give the position that would lead without fail to the Second Homeland.

So, as the texts would later affirm:

"The East united with the West by the *Heart of the Lion* will guide the arrival in Ath-Ka-Ptah, the Second Heart of God[21]."

It should be possible to teach all young boys and girls without exception. But there was a glaring lack of initiates with the necessary skills. Tradition and Knowledge were not chess games to be put into every hand without prior explanation. And yet, the revelation had to be made in its entirety and repeated over and over again to young souls until it took root without error, and could then be repeated from father to eldest son, generation after generation, until the Word was transformed into a Scripture that would re-establish civilisation.

The ultimate 'Descendants' who, in several centuries, or perhaps even several millennia, will reach God's chosen destination, should be prepared to re-establish immediately the sciences they have learned, including the mathematics of 'Combinations', but in a specialised school from the outset.

---

[21] The *Coeur-du-Lion* is the star Régulus du Lion, whose very bright but highly variable brilliance makes it resemble the palpitations of a heart.

At the time of the first settlement in the 'Second Heart', the people blessed by the Creator in his Covenant would assert their supremacy over the indigenous peoples who were still in the same state in which they themselves, by a deliberate irony of fate, found themselves: carving stone tools! But the 'Descendants' would have recovered very quickly, while the others would still be in that state in two or three thousand years' time.

Teams had already set off for the high mountains to obtain copper and lead from mines that had already been opened ten or so days' walk from Ta Mana. The difficulty would be in smelting the ores to extract the metal.

The Pontiff began to smile: God wanted the survivors that they were to start again from nothing, like their distant ancestors, but also like the men they would meet up with there, at the end of the world, so that they would better understand the difficulties of these people and come to their aid. Instead of annihilating them or simply ignoring them, the 'Descendants' would make it their duty to show them the means to adapt and rise to the same civilised structures.

But until then, time would progress slowly in its desperate retrograde march through the Great Celestial River, approaching the zodiacal constellations, the *Twelve*, one after the other. The solar cycle would take an appreciable time before leaving this Avenging Lion, the personification of Hor. At an average of one degree backwards for every two generations, the education of these rising youngsters would be no small matter.[22]

Time never catches up, so the forecasts should cover the following eras as well. After Leo, the star of the day entered the

---

[22] In the precessional cycle, in which the Sun appears to be retrograde, this recession *is one degree in 72 years*. A generation is therefore counted as 36 years.

Squilla, whose dangerous claws almost closed off access to the next configuration, that of the irreducible 'Two Enemies'.[23]

As the journey would be very, very long and strewn with terrible pitfalls, it had to be harmonised with the celestial probabilities. Nek-Bet had told him that Sit had not died in the cataclysm, and that he had landed not far from Ta Mana, thanks to one of those 'Mandjit' he had so decried. He would arrive in the vicinity of the new city shortly after Iset.

If nothing happened here, according to his wife, it would not be the same in the merciless battle that would continually pit the "Two Brothers", or rather their descendants, against each other throughout the Exodus. This stellar coincidence could not be a coincidence, especially as the arrival in the "Second Heart" would occur when the Sun also entered the constellation of Taurus, which was the victorious emblem of Uzir, the "Heart of God".

This 'Battle of the Giants' would pit the *Followers of Hor*, all born of the descendants of the 'Celestial Bull', against the *Brothers of the Rebellion*, those 'Sons of Sit' who nevertheless come from the same original mother. Perhaps then there could be reconciliation in a single community where Wisdom and Knowledge would reign, and not Ruin and Desolation.

Already today, the advantage would go to the clan of Usir, who knew that Sit was coming, thus avoiding any disastrous surprises. But his wife would still have to tell him why victory would go to them without a fight...

- If you were to take care of bringing together the members of the College you are planning to form, O my dreamy husband, you

---

[23] The constellation of the Crayfish has since become that of Scorpio, but the claws retain the same mortal significance. As for the constellation of the *Two Brothers*, it has of course become that of *Gemini*.

would make it easier to return to teaching our people. Only you can solve this problem.

The Pontiff smiled at this affectionate reminder of his wife, who had come to him unheard. Nevertheless, he remained worried.

- But for Sit?

- I'll let Ousir and Hor know when the time comes. Do you really think he won't invade our peaceful village?

- I'm sure of it. With the help of our Elder, I have prepared the welcome that will stop his progress towards us. Go to work in peace, O you who are my life!

- Thank you, you're my pride and joy!

- Thank Anepou personally as soon as you see him. Our Elder helped me like a mature man, you know[24] ?

The An-Nu shook his head in satisfaction; at thirteen, Anepou promised to make an outstanding Pontiff in the future. Couldn't he already entrust him with the organisation of a course, and let him choose around thirty young people of his own age to teach them, in particular, how to develop their memory?

A three-year course would teach them one of the essential chapters of "Mathematical Combinations", for example. Thanks to Anepou, this first link would be put to work, the first episode of the fight against Sit over. With the adult class he planned to open that same day, learn the elements of Knowledge that could be assimilated by the uninitiated. The greatest difficulty would

---

[24] In Hellenic phonetics, Anepou became 'Anubis'. It was this son of Nek-Bet (or Nephthys in Greek) who taught the secrets of embalming and Eternal Life after the Weighing of the Souls, which he carried out personally.

undoubtedly lie in recruiting those who would be destined to learn the teaching that only first-class High Priests should know! As...

- Don't forget, my dreamy husband, to put away your precious "Gô-men". It's the only one to have been saved from the debacle. God used a roundabout way to give it to you, so don't lose it. If one Sit's friends were to see it tomorrow and understand its value, a war without mercy would break out for its possession.

With a jolt of retrospect, the Pontiff agreed with his wife's wise recommendation. Caught off guard, he stopped meditating, for it was high time to get back to work. He lifted the precious tub, smiling contritely at his wife, and led her back to her hiding place, which he camouflaged with large pebbles stacked on top of each other as an extra precaution.

Calm and serene as usual, Nek-Bet left slowly after making sure that the tub was invisible from the outside. She set off in search of Ousir and his son, her large black braids swaying harmoniously to the rhythm of her steps.

Shortly afterwards, she stopped; voices were calling out to her respectfully, as she was considered to be somewhat of a magician, at God's command, and therefore inspired considerable fear. The calls came from a group of crouching women who were pointing out something they were doing. Their cheerful tone already indicated that it deserved her attention and compliments.

The young woman walked towards them, smiling. At the centre of their circle, she recognised a primitive mill used to crush grain. The women had quickly spotted a type of wild barley growing in abundance not far from the village. They immediately looked for the best way to extract the flour, which was so good when cooked. They looked for and found oblong-shaped stones that acted as rollers, flattening and crushing the grains on large, more or less elliptical stones, whose slightly convex upper surface kept the creamy flour in its hollow.

This method, so dear to the great-grandmothers of forgotten times, was regaining all its splendour. Admittedly, it required a lot more effort, but these women put all their strength into it to prove that they were fully participating in the revival as best they could.

Nek-Bet's sincere congratulations went straight to their hearts and made them coo with delight. The young woman made her way more happily towards the hut where the Father and Son were standing. She knew that the important part of their conversation had already taken place with the announcement, made to Hor, of Usir's definitive departure, allowing the people to set off towards their new destiny.

As soon as she arrived, the young woman appeared to the two men as the referee who, knowing all things, would judiciously decide between opposing opinions. As she knew what made them feel this way, she smiled, addressing Hor instead:

- What's wrong, O you impetuous son of my sister?

- My venerable Father advocates a Covenant with God, sealed by unconditional Faith in our Creator.

- Don't you agree with that?

- With the Alliance, of course it is! But since Faith is not eternal, it will only be by appealing to Reason that the agreement will be lasting.

- That would apply to any signature other than a Covenant with God, Hor. I imagine that's what your father wants you to understand. Because in this Covenant, there *is only one* human signatory, who is imperfect because of this, and who lasts for such a short time compared to this Perfect Partner who is the Father of Eternity.

- I understand that very well, O revered Nek-Bet, but reason might more readily admit that...

- That your dispute is nonsense. It proves that Faith is still the only possible foundation. One after another, the rising generations will reason more and more falsely about the Power of God and His Wrath.

- Would it be wrong for God to remain God?

- Not for you, since you yourself experienced the terrible plague. But when the Cadets of the two hundredth 'Elders' begin the ultimate polytheistic revisionism of the one original truth, there will be nothing but Nothingness.

- Are you saying that another cataclysm will sweep away our new homeland?

- After all, wasn't it total atheism that caused our country to be wiped off the face of earth? Have you forgotten already? If appealing to Reason to justify Faith seems inevitable to you, it is because Faith is useless in advance, just like the Soul which depends on it, and just like the carnal envelope which encloses the Soul.

- In other words, Man would no longer have a reason to exist!...

The young woman did not reply. Her silence obviously reinforced the observation that had naturally come to Hor's lips. Ousir, who had nodded his head in agreement, also knew that his son would never be a prophet, despite his miraculous return. Nek-Bet had the incomparable gift of always having the right words to touch the heart. So he waited for her to speak again, which she soon did in the same inspired tone:

- God presides over the government of the Universe because he is God. How can you persuade human reason of this incontestable fact? By an axiom that a whole life would not suffice to demonstrate? Don't complicate Divine Law, when Faith is enough to explain what is immutable in the permanence of the incessant movements of "Mathematical Combinations". The Priests and their Head, as well as the "Masters" who will follow, of whom you are the first, must unite to maintain, in the depths of the ages to come, the intangibility of the dogma of the Power of God, and of His Power over all things and all beings, on all occasions.

- Isn't that too heavy a load for me to carry just starting out?

- Absolutely not, Hor; for you are the image of the Creator: his representative through the flesh. As such, you will limit the free will of souls, so that they do not reason about the Law and its Commandments. Only this notion will preserve the people. You must only inculcate in the children this fundamental Principle of Divine Law, which they themselves will teach in due course, without omitting or changing anything, to their descendants. In this way, they will all remain imbued with God's permanent work on the whole of nature, whether it is mineral or vegetable in essence, or animal flesh or human, *because the Creator is God, and no other can carry out this Great Work in perpetual evolution.* Faced with his son's frown indicating intense reflection, Usir added:

- Since the Origin of all things, it is a fact that physical changes, biological transformations and organic migrations have multiplied under the empire of this non-human Law, which is the only possibility since it takes place over millions and millions of years. What does Man represent in the midst of this immensity, he who does not even live the time of a celestial second? His reason, however developed it may be, even on a par with yours, is in no way parallel to that of God.

- Your father has the Right Voice, Hor. Faith must become an integral part of everyone's daily life.

As the "Descendant of the Eldest", you must be the Guide whom no one must question under any circumstances. Everything will be linked to this process of continuity in the divine lineage and in Faith in God.

The agreement will thus appear very natural to the living of each new generation. It will be this reasonable rhythm in their hearts that will unceasingly link them to the events decreed in the celestial combinations. None of the survivors living in Ta Mana is aware of the importance of the links that bind each event to the next. This is the case for Sit, who will be arriving in the vicinity of our village very early tomorrow, with a thousand people. This is only the minor effect of an ancient cause, but one that will last for a long time, which only God can predetermine.

Nek-Bet's tone of voice had not changed during this unexpected conclusion, so it took several seconds for the two of them to react. Hor turned pale and sat up slowly. As for Ousir, with a small smile, he held back his son with one arm, confirming what he already knew:

- Yes, Sit escaped the burning forest. Yes, Sit managed to escape from the earth that he helped to engulf! Yes, he has reached thanks to one of the "Mandjit" that he had previously failed to destroy. Yes, he will persevere in Evil so that he can triumph phe... That's why, Hor, it's up to you to ensure that it's Good that triumphs. Evil is already being called upon to prevent Good from returning to our people; this is your test, Hor. A signed Covenant that no one asks to be disavowed is no longer a Covenant. The people must ratify it in its entirety.

- But, Father, is blood going to flow again between the members of our family?

- If we let Bet do the talking, she'll come up with the solution. Her calmness shows that she has prepared a trick of her own to defeat Sit...

- You know everything too, my revered brother! Our brother's fighting spirit is... delirious, to say the least.

So I thought it wiser to act on his mind rather than provoke him on the spot.

- Tell us what you imagined.

- The bull's skin, which struck all the souls here by the way it preserved your body, remains the weak point that will disarm Sit's soul and arms. This is why, with the help of Anepou and some his little friends, we forced three oxen to race, killed them and butchered them. Then, like a wise little man, my eldest, in the company of two of his companions, went to place them in full view in two precise places, through which the whole troop of rebels will inevitably pass. The first spot is four hours' walk away and the skin will hang from the lowest branch of a tamarisk tree; the other is a vast clearing less than two hours away. They are due to hold their final gathering there, and the other two hides will be spread out in full view.

Ousir frowned in turn.

- Your idea is very appealing, Bet, but why are you so sure he won't come here to fight?

- Because the skins are just the prelude his mind running wild. After two hours on the road, and three dazzling reminders of his crime, he will say to himself that after all, with neither you nor your son among the humans to effectively block his path, Ta Mana, barely an hour's walk away, is under his control. So he'll keep moving in our direction for a while longer, until the moment comes when, prematurely savouring his victory, he gives in...

Hor couldn't resist the curiosity that was piquing him. And it was maliciously that Nek-Bet had stopped to allow him to ask:

- If you say that Sitan will flinch, then you already know why...

- Because it's you who will ensure this victory. A smile lit up Usir's face as he understood, while his son, stunned, could only repeat:

- Me? Well... But how do you expect me to...

- When Sit reaches the last hill protecting Ta Mana from the inland winds, he will have to go round it to continue his journey. At the first bend, on a mound halfway up, stands a huge sycamore tree. You will then appear from behind the trunk, which will have hidden you completely. Our Sacred Emblem will also camouflage Ousir, who will only come to light later, and protect you both. But I doubt that Sit, or any of his followers, will want to stay in your company. They will take the opposite route if they can.

- I realise that I have a lot to learn from both of you.

- This is the beginning of Wisdom. God will inspire you better than us for the rest of your life, Hor. You can always learn from us the science of the stars and their influence on beings; the nature of animals and their instincts; the thoughts of men and their faults; the virtues of plants and their venoms. But all that is hidden and makes up the Power of God, you will learn only from the Lord himself. The Wisdom that will be yours will support you in finally acquiring Knowledge of all things and all beings.

From that moment on, you will be the first Pêr-Ahâ of the generations that will follow for all eternity.[25]

An emotional silence followed, which Usir broke, as time was running out:

- And the souls of men will be your support. May their desire for independence not separate them again, willingly, from this new Covenant that you will forge, link by link!

Nek-Bet decided it was time to let Hor meditate at his leisure with himself the following night.

---

[25] Pêr-Ahâ, literally "Descendant of the Elder", hence "the Elder", is spelt Pharaoh.

So she proposed:

- If you'd like to see my husband: he's in the new house where he'll be giving his first 'Divine Mathematics' class tomorrow. That's where he's waiting for you to come.

Usir held back a smile at his sister's manner. He bowed his head gravely before replying:

- As our very special mission gives us a moment of free time just in time, let's pay a visit to the venerated Pontiff. In fact, I'd like him to put a time indicator back into use as soon as possible...

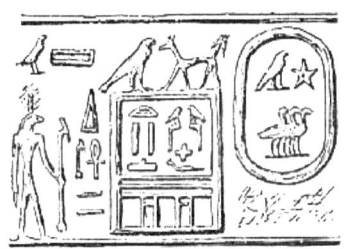

Chapter Six

THE PARABOLIC OF NUMBERS

> *As the most sacred land of our Ancestors, which is situated in the middle of the earth, the middle of the human body is the sanctuary of the heart, the advanced fortress of the soul. For this reason, my son Hor, the people of this country are as well endowed with qualities as the rest of mankind, but incomparably more intelligent and wiser, because they were born and brought up at the birthplace of the Second Heart.*
>
> STOBÉE
(Exc., XXIV - 11)

> *There was nothing veiled in the Knowledge of this Sage. But he covered it all his life with a veil that thickened everything he taught his pupils!*
> (Inscription at the bottom of the statue of Ptah-Mer, Pontiff of Ath-Ka-Ptah - Memphis, on display at the Musée du Louvre in Paris).

Stobaeus, who has Isis speak to her son Horus in the extract above, cites a Queen of the second dynasty who had adopted this sacred patronymic, and did the same for her son, a worthy "Descendant" of the first Elder. When the latter reached the age of sixteen, he learned of his Divine original lineage, and his attention was drawn to the difference to be made between the natives 'integrated' on the spot into their civilisation, and those coming in a straight line from Ahâ-Men-Ptah, the 'First Heart', who alone possessed Wisdom and Knowledge.

Those who had preceded them, throughout the I[st] Dynasty, had worked to restore the integrity of writing, the calendar, medicine, mathematics and the arts, with absolute priority given to a rigorous monotheistic theology, which had to be followed in every detail, on pain of the worst punishments. Thus, the second dynasty was already at the height of its civilisation.

Thereafter, the main concern of the An-Nu was to preserve intact the hereditary Dogma beyond all time. As soon as the first manuscripts saw the light of day, each Pontiff laid bare his memory, compiling, annotating and commenting on the texts of his predecessors in fine handwriting in the narrow margins, using signs and abbreviations that only he could understand. These markers made it easier to re-use mathematical formulations and instructions, as well as the numerical interpretations to be drawn from them.

By the 2nd Dynasty, schools of scribes were flourishing, and young people were proud to enter them. It was they who first recounted the origin of the History of the distant Ancestors, long before hieroglyphics reappeared engraved on the walls of the Temples. Papyrus manufacture had become a veritable industry, and the Sacred *Written* Word was born!

It is obviously very difficult to say who was the scribe who first had the idea of transforming his obscure annotations into *anaglyphs* that could be understood in the main text itself, but only by the initiates who would possess the key. It was at this time, so long ago, that the Pontiff of Ath-Ka-Ptah was already covering his teaching with a veil, specifying that from now on it had to be this way so that Faith remained Faith, the symbol of Light in everyday life.

When, as at Saqqarah, tourists still see this inscription at the entrance to a tomb: "God created man in his own image", they are bound to be troubled. On the other hand, it is tempting to associate this phrase with the idea behind these animal representations with human bodies, *images of the Divine "Ka"*, that of a similar animal in the anaglyphic idea, which serves as a "double".

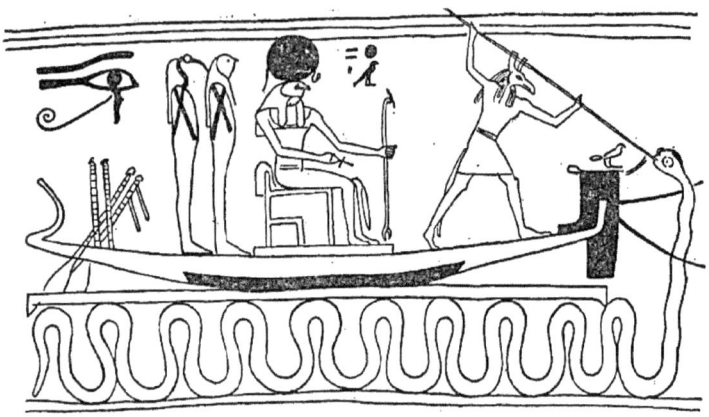

The symbolism of the Numbers begins with the study of the sky and its "Combinations" in order to understand the process that put an end to life on Ahâ-Men-Ptah. This is why there are so many representations of Horus mastering the new solar navigation.

This is perhaps a slight excuse for *the* ancient Greeks to have so readily accepted the theme of "barbaric tales" of "abominable savages". They had an easy opportunity to place themselves above a spiritual level a hundred cubits above their own. Without mentioning the "mathematicians" and other "philosophers", who will be discussed later, let's just mention the case of the famous *(sic)* Plutarch who, with his "Isis and Osiris", published a "bible" that served all the exegetes-egyptologists for 2,000 years to establish the incomprehension of the religions of ancient Egypt. All the absurdities accumulated at will by a man overwhelmed by the grandeur of the ruins he contemplated on the banks of the Nile were taken as gospel by generations of scholars.

In an identical vein, the myths of Amun, Aten and Ra were born, treated as the specific figures of distinct divinities, whereas they are, by virtue of the name that differentiates them, separate manifestations emanating from a single origin of the Word that distinguishes the various aspects of God's principal earthly instrument, the Sun.

This essential cosmic element is formally explained in the oldest texts as being the conditioner of all life. This is why, from the earliest times, the sun has been considered the most powerful numerical symbol in all iconography, and the instrumental parable of Divine Justice. This was easy to understand, since the memory of the Great Cataclysm was kept alive in the souls of that era by the image of the Sun not reappearing one morning above the horizon, which had become oriental, in which case nothing living would survive on the surface of the earth.

The primordial chapter of *Memphite theology*, the earliest of those that have come down to us, unequivocally regulates the respect due to the Sun as *an instrument* of Divine Harmony:

> "After the chaos[26] of summer and the death that followed, Ra brought forth from the liquid a second living universe; a Creation repeated by Ptah for a second cycle in which his cosmic power, opposed to that of men, will only end in the Creator's victory!

Throughout the enthronements of the "Descendants of the Elder", and for more than forty consecutive centuries, the Pontiffs welcomed the Pêr-Ahâ as "Sun and God", thus preserving the apparent unity of the two branches. The ritual formula remained identical: "O Mighty Amon! Behold your Second Heart, where from now on Your order and Your power will reign".

Five millennia of incessant repetition, incomparable patience and total self-sacrifice led to the immediate realisation of Ath-Ka-Ptah, which still astonishes our contemporary researchers. To understand this, we need to retrograde like the Sun, to find ourselves once again "in Leo", on the eve of Sit's presumed arrival in Ta Mana, where Ousir and his son, the Pontiff and his wife, were preparing for their second march, which would defy Time. It was the Risen One who said, resting his two hands on the shoulders of the first An-Nu of this new cycle:

---

[26] The word *chaos* should be taken here in its true sense: "fissure in the bowels of the Earth".

- You are the Pontiff of the Two Lands. This will be the title of every new Great Sage, head of the College High Priests, and therefore yours, O you who teach the survivors so masterfully! You are already preparing the future of all our "Ka" so that they can join their Ancestors in peace.

- I'm trying to do it in the most positive way that God allows on this occasion, O venerated Usir!

The Lion, who watches over the Sun and your Mana, becomes the new symbol of divine supremacy, which you will symbolise for all eternity. From now on, the Lion will tread on the water of the sky beneath his feet to make a rock-solid foundation.[27]

- That's all very well, but people's memories will become shorter and shorter as civilisation advances in comfort and peace.

- And therein lies the greatest difficulty. The evolution of minds will reproduce all the errors that have just cost our people so dearly. And impiety, thoughtlessness and recklessness will renew the eternal curse, if we do not find a way to put an effective end to them before the evil develops.

- Humans can only think in a very short space of time, at most their lifetime. This is why our future descendants' appreciation of ancient texts must be rigorous down to the smallest detail and not open to interpretation.

- However, these must be established using celestial mathematical emblems, to the exclusion of all others.

- Why is that, Venerable Pontiff?

---

[27] The Lion in his boat, trampling underfoot the sign of the Flood ( ) guiding the eleven other celestial constellations in his wake, backwards, leaves no doubt as to his significance on the "Planisphere of Denderah".

- Because the Word and the Scripture such as our Ancestors of Aha-Men-Ptah knew them will undergo appreciable variations, but mathematics and its combinations will always be founded on the same principles. Thus, at any time in the future, the restitution of the astronomical state of a sky will be a simple matter. And the solemn warnings that we will add to it, as to the Power of God and the fear to be observed in his regard, will not remain a dead letter.

- It's a good thing the new calculations have been made easier!

- God has been good to us, O Usir! These new 'Combinations', which are in fact the same but following a completely opposite course, will be the main subject of my first lesson, tomorrow. And as we are on the same parallel as AthMer and that of the second homeland, we will begin to draw up the celestial map which will serve to control the march towards the Light, this second Heart. The new movement of the Sun will determine the rises of the marker stars that its light obliterates when it appears on the eastern horizon. It will enable the measurement of time to be re-established and the calendar to be restarted at the exact moment when Harmony is perfectly achieved.[28]

- You will therefore keep, as your cyclical time, the rising of Sep'ti, which has always been the perfect year from this point of view. It will remain *the Year of God,* while the Year of Man will be maintained at 365 days, so that the mathematics of 1,460 is not disturbed by 72 human years of life.

- And the Great Cosmic Year?

- It is unlikely to change, at least in terms of its duration, because its rhythm is already evolving in a retrograde way, but still in 25,920 years.

---

[28] This rising of a star is its *heliacal rising*. It is the particular day of the year when the star, hitherto obliterated by the sun's brilliance, becomes visible when it rises on the western horizon, above the Amenta for the ancients.

- Around the same celestial pivot?

- Thank God, yes. The slow march of the 'Fixes' across the sky remains unchanged, which will make it much easier to find the route to the 'Second Heart'. Being situated on the same parallel as our "Ancient One", and therefore as Ta Mana, Harmony is intact. The Law that governs the "Divine-Mathematical Combinations" does not undergo any variation in its entirety, except as regards solar navigation, which follows an opposite route.

- This sign is destined to be an eternal reminder that we must never again break the New Covenant with God.

- That's right! And that's the main reason why we're reinstating the Sep'ti year.

- But this year of God is a long one!...

- But it is the only valid one for ratifying our agreement. Weak human time is of little importance in relation to the overall harmonic rhythm of the Universe. The Sun, while remaining fully and entirely the Divine instrument for providing the bread of each day, is non-existent in the eternal round of the 'Fixed'. It sails only according to the will of the Creator, and of him alone...

- So the new calendar will continue round of 365s, which will change the rhythms of the seasons the years?

- The 365 year is only approximate and requires meticulous calculations that will never be exact. But the year of God, the year of Sep'ti, with its cycle of 1460 true years, will have a sunrise every 1461 years, rigorously in harmony with the whole sky. And the Sun will be the sign of the start of the march of the "Descendants" towards the Light...

- When will the new timetable start?

-- The observations, which have been repeated over the last ten days or so using on-board resources, are very interesting. The Sun's new retreat in the constellation Leo shows that it has returned to the mid-point of its precessional path, and that it will therefore have to retrograde for almost a full Sep'ti cycle.[29]

- What good news!" exclaimed Hor. The Pontiff nodded, adding:

- This will allow us survivors to regain our strength, and those of us who are old enough to start a family to do so!

At this, Usir smiled, while Hor burst out laughing:

- I'm thinking about it, O Pontiff. You'll be the first to give me your blessing. But don't you think it will be very tempting for large families living peacefully here not to want to leave?

- No, because the land promised to us as our second "Heart" is the very sign of our Covenant to rediscover happiness. This second homeland will contain all the elements of prosperity that we will always lack here. Water, which will be God's gift to fertilise the land; minerals to forge our civilisation, that of the Cadets.

- In any case, our Cadets here will have plenty of time to learn at their leisure and retain all the chapters of Knowledge. How long do you think it will take to get each of your pupils to recite the bit of Knowledge you have taught them?

- A tour of 4 solar navigations, or one of Sep'ti. We'll need these four times 365 + 1 to perfect our memory.

---

[29] The cycle of Sep'ti, or Sirius, is 1461 years; we saw in the chronology at the end of the first volume that the new cycle gave Sep'ti 1440 years to 'navigate' in Leo.

Usir straightened up, for it was time to prepare for the hard day ahead, so he concluded:

- So nothing in our history can be distorted! Our Knowledge, combined with the Wisdom that God has instilled in his "Descendants", will enable our Alliance to survive all misfortunes, until the end of Time.

An-Nu nodded his approval:

- May you tell the truth, O you who, by your resurrection, have become the "Lord of the Two Lands"...

- This name will describe me perfectly before long, O Pontiff! May your progeny have sons to advise Hor's sons until the end of time!

- God will certainly see to that.

They embraced, as if they would never see each other again. Then hugging Hor, the An-Nu added:

- The year of God will be perpetuated by your name O you worthy son of Usir! Its first month will symbolise, through your heart, communion with your mother Iset, and with that of the future homeland: we'll call it *Ath-Hor*...

- The 'Horus-heart' is very welcome; its triple meaning will undoubtedly bring good luck to our descendants.[30]

This verbal tradition, which began in the aftermath of the Great Cataclysm in order to preserve the story of Ahâ-Men-Ptah intact while serving as a warning to those of Ath-Ka-Ptah, eventually became a barbaric tale. The simplest things had become

---

[30] *Athor* became Athyr in Greek, the month of Taurus. This was the beginning of the Sothian year. The precessional shift placed it in April in our time.

complicated despite all the precautions taken. The very people of the "Descendants of the Eldest" disappeared as such, leading to the oblivion and destruction of what had once been the Kingdom of God. Multiple invasions erased the last vestiges by burying them under the sands: the Persians, the Romans and the Greeks, the Christians and the Arabs left nothing but barbarism behind them.

Only the "Zodiac of Denderah", the last warning to emerge intact from the distant past, was preserved until its message was retransmitted to us following an odyssey that goes far beyond what fiction could have imagined[31]. The various Pontiffs religiously preserved the original engraving, even when they no longer understood it, such as during *the sixth reconstruction of* the Temple of Denderah under Ptolemy, "so that the Cadets could understand the history of the Two Lands and know the exact moment when the cyclical period coming to an end could degenerate into the end of the world if unbelief continued".

The Masters of Measurement seemed as sure of themselves as they were of the intelligence of future peoples. The intermediate calculations of dates between two periods of Sirius did not allow for any error of interpretation, since there was no fraction of a day more or less. There was no need for verification or rectification in this simplified arithmetic. The primitive "Mathematical Combinations" remained eternal, unaltered, with very specific characteristics for each state of the sky that would retain their same meaning century after century, since they only evolved in their relationship to each other in Space, and not in their Time, which remained cosmic and not solar.

It is for this reason that the precessional planisphere at Denderah, as well as those found elsewhere in Egypt, such as at Esneh, always began with the constellation Leo, which the "CombinaisonsMathématiques" and modern astronomical

---

[31] The adventure of the Denderah planisphere, brought back to France by two Parisians after a remarkable journey, will be featured in the next volume: *Et Dieu ressuscita à Dendérah!*

backtracking, calculated by computer, all place at the same date: July 9792 before the beginning of the Christian era.

The Lion advancing, then retreating after the Great Cataclysm, was symbolised by the two lions back to back, above which rose a new Sun. He admirably shows the true meaning of this famous iconography: Death on the western horizon, where he looks as the Sphinx does; and Resurrection at Ta Mana.

Manetho, the famous Egyptian priest whom Ptolemy II commissioned to research the dynastic chronology of the Pêr-Ahâ in the original texts, explains that the first recorded dating of this Lion goes back to the summer solstice in conjunction with Sothis, or Sirius, which marked Year I of the calendar put back into use by Menes' son Athothis Ier, the Atota of the hieroglyphs, who legend has it that he became the famous Thoth.... in the year 4241 BC.

So 5, years passed before the "Descendants" re-established in Ath-Ka-Ptah the chronology interrupted in Ahâ-Men Ptah.

The Tradition, even if it had become incomprehensible, was retransmitted as is, in all its parabolic Numbers. Various details in the form of a key leave no doubt as to the power of Sep'ti, to which he would later return to confirm, with the discovery of Sirius B, the black star that seriously disrupts the orb of the first star, everything that the Ancients affirmed.

And when Plutarch asserts that at the great summer solstice, when Sothis rose at the same time as the Sun, "all the goats of Egypt were obliged to look at the Fixed One to thank her for being alive precisely on that day", we mustn't sneer unthinkingly for once, because there is a great deal of truth in it. In a ceremony dating back to the beginning of the New Era, the shepherds who survived the cataclysm, having captured their first goats on the spot, prayed at sunrise to thank God for this new day, which brought them a life so similar to the one they had before[32]. It would be easy to laugh if so many aberrant examples were not provided by the Greek "philosophers". They taught monumental nonsense!

The stars are but muffled cloves of air, full of fire (Anaximander).

The stars are incandescent clouds that are never the same, but always new, every day, every night (Xenophanes).

The sky is a solid vault to which the stars are very firmly attached (Anaximenes).

To paraphrase Clement of Alexandria, I could add after these three transcendental meditations that a thousand pages would not be enough to write the names of all the Greek 'geniuses' who learned their knowledge on the banks of the Nile, and who were ashamed to admit it.

It's even so funny to demonstrate this today that you wonder how humans fell for it. Erathostene, for example, was "the inventor *(sic)* of the Sphere. The one he presented to the people of his dazzled world... was a false manifesto. The sky he represented as being that of Alexandria in 255 BC could in no way correspond to it, but he was too ignorant of stellar combinations to know that.

Any modern astronomer with the same sphere would reply, after a few simple calculations, that the sky represented was not that of Alexandria, but that of the latitude of Denderah, certain stars only being visible from this point eight hundred kilometres further south. And that the precessional phenomenon dated this sky to the year 2864 BC...

Poor Erathostene! How could such a mistake be made? Simply because in his time, the Theban era was coming back into fashion

---

[32] Plut, "Esseque, id firmissimum documentum maxime Tabulis Astronomicis consentiens".

thanks to a number of Greek poets who had visited Thebes. Homer, in particular, praised this capital city in the words of Achilles in his famous *Iliad* (in Canto IX): "What a fabulous city , full of treasures, and each of its hundred golden gates allowing the passage of two hundred warriors with their horses and chariots!

This most prestigious of periods brought back to life the dissident High Priests of the College of Pontiffs in the "House of Life" at Denderah, seventy kilometres away. Erathostenes therefore rushed to Thebes, where he was able to look at papyri and copy the one that inspired him - clumsily - to establish his sphere. This indicated the state of the beneficial sky during the fourth reconstruction of the Temple of the Lady of Heaven at Dendera, 2,600 years earlier.

Other 'Great Ones', such as Eudoxus, suffered many setbacks. In the case of Methon, the Priests clearly mocked him, since only half of his sphere was of his time, the other half being 586 years older. Eudoxus' sphere, with its solstice in the middle of Cancer, was a thousand years older than he claimed.[33]

Poets, on the other hand, intuitively rediscovered much of the lost information. Virgil and the aforementioned Homer are striking examples. There was also another Greek, Nonnus, who described the Great Cataclysm through ancient celestial disturbances and the annals of Necepsus, right up to the moment when the Earth was renewed by "the whitening foam of the great waters".

> "The last day ended and the last night began at the time of the Great Fear, rising above the horizon through the sign opposite the sun then in Leo, and which was Aquarius!"

---

[33] At a rate of 1°39' per century of retrogradation, the arc bringing the Dragon, the Polar of Eudoxus' time, shows a difference between the two longitudes of 45°96'39", a difference of 3321 years. As Eudoxus lived 2346 years ago, the exact difference *is 975 years*.

This constellation is symbolised in the "Zodiac of Denderah" by an urn pouring out two rivers of living water, held by Ptah.

Clearly, God is hesitating about who should bring forth the Light or the Darkness: the one who will sweep away everything in his path and bring about the final destruction; or the one who will nourish the world by dispensing fertile silt to all.

We must not lose sight of the fact that behind the engraved symbolism lies only the reality, reserved for the pure of heart. The constellations are the most powerful instruments that unite heaven and earth. To put it more clearly, each of these twelve astral configurations has a "Heart", a star of the first magnitude similar to our Sun, but whose Radiance, *its Vital Force*, is so fantastic that it is barely imaginable to our minds.

Regulus Leo, for example, which is about a hundred light years from our system, *is 12,000 times bigger than our star of the day*. This means that if it were in the place of our Sun, we would not exist, because the Earth would be nothing but impalpable ash itself. The same applies to the other eleven 'Hearts', whether Aldebaran in Taurus, Antares in Scorpio, or any other star.

So if, instead of allowing Reason to postpone meditation, we thought about the incredible but real Forces of these 12 Hearts, we would understand that the distance of an average of one hundred light years which separates us from them, is nothing compared to this radiation, which has been travelling for billions of years at a speed of 300,000 kilometres per second in space, and which strikes the Earth with such power that it passes right through its greatest circumference in $1/40^e$ of a second, a figure provided by a laboratory which studies this phenomenon assiduously near Moscow. Which explains the instrumental power God has made of it.

From the of birth, every newborn baby who emerges from nothingness, whose umbilical cord is cut, *finds itself isolated in terrestrial space as a living human being*. For the first time, right from that moment , the baby is literally bombarded by this fabulous radiation, imprinting in the cervical cortex *a pattern* that is therefore different for everyone, and to which he or she will react personally, according to the configurations of the "Mathematical Combinations".

> "The human Soul participates in the creative activity of the Earth, being united to it by its carnal, animated envelope, which enables it to call upon God in case of need. If Heaven and Earth are at odds, the influence the Soul is subjected to by the Twelve "Fixes" and the Sun could subject it to extremely harmful passions, which would be opposed to its true Divine destiny."

A stele from the Fourth Dynasty recalls these fundamental facts. Perhaps Manilius, that 'astrologer' of ancient Greece, was already aware of them when he wrote in his *Astronomica*, in verse: "In my songs, I undertake to bring down truly divine knowledge from the heavens. And the stars themselves, confidants of destiny with power directed by the supreme power, produce so many vicissitudes in the course of human life!

But this Marcus Manilius remains nothing more than a joker, for he prefaces the whole thing with this beginning that distorts everything: "I was the first to penetrate the mysteries of heaven *by the favour of the gods.*"

Not having been to Egypt, he contented himself with the explanations of Porphyry and Plutarch, thus praising the gods and not Ptah the One. He re-established what were called the decans, which are part of the "Combinations". These signs within the signs were called "Khent" in hieroglyphic. The Denderah inscriptions explaining the march of cosmic time are formal about the very principle of their mathematical value: "*The 36 Khent form the half-crown of the celestial equator.*"

Mathematically, this logically demonstrates that the entire corona, which forms the complete equatorial belt, comprises $36 \times 2 = 72$.

Faced with the "Combinations" he advocates, Manilius himself feels a sudden respect. The reciprocal actions and reactions that he sets in motion from nothing, like a wicked sorcerer's apprentice, because he knows very little about what he thinks will shape the figures to come, only lead to a dangerous alteration in the purpose of the "Divine-Mathematical Combinations".

In fact, this "poet astrologer" was followed by a host of charlatans. Time has not even done its work, since some of them, certain of not being understood, are still lauding him.

On the other hand, when it comes to the symbolism of Numbers, it is interesting to reread various papyri that describe "astrological themes". Dating from the beginning of the Christian era, they are inspired solely by Chaldean and Babylonian configurations, derived from "those of the Egyptians". To what extent? That is difficult to establish.

One of the most remarkable is the "theme of Titus", drawn up in the third year of his reign (i.e. 81 AD). sance that we know. It is preceded by an unambiguous introduction, urging fidelity to the immutable rules of the "Divine Heavenly Compositions" that were in use in Antiquity.

There is also papyrus N-98 in the British Museum, which traces the "theme" of an unknown person, but which was drawn up in the year 102 "according to Egyptian mathematical laws"; another document, number 110, is the theme of the sky of Anubion, drawn up in the first year of the reign of Antoninus (i.e. 138 AD) according to instructions "contained in a very old Egyptian scroll". There therefore absolute certainty that the mathematical coordinates for the study of the stars date from Egyptian antiquity.

There even exists a little-known but authentic work, *a Manual of Mathematical Celestial Observations for Studying the Plot of a Soul*. The manuscript indicates that it was compiled from Egyptian hieroglyphics by the Greek astrologer Paklos at the end of the 5th century.

This remarkable study, which provides the parabolic key to certain Numbers, solves several riddles throughout its original 149 paragraphs. Here too, it seems that the general lack of understanding of the apparent mathematical complications has relegated it to the back of a vaulted cellar for another 'Great Year' of 25,920 years, with successive archivists, faced with this unfathomable length of time, having mistaken it for sheer delirium.

The stellar movement, infinitely slow though it was, beat out the rhythm of the c Great Year, at Denderah, for the whole of Ath-Ka-Ptah. The crossing of one degree on the equatorial belt meant that 72 years of life had been consumed in the ether, and that the corresponding human being was reunited with his Creator. As we have seen, there are 72 Khent or decans bringing 72 primordial influences, so this Number seems to be endowed with remarkable properties.

Each of the 36 Khents is beneficial, while the 36 opposite Khents, the "N'Khents", are malefic! They are each only 5° wide, and cannot be called decans. The hieroglyphic symbol for this asterism is a 5-pointed star. It also qualifies the Number 5 in anaglyph, the whole forming the configurations of the complete fabric of the human mental psyche.

These 72 Khent, fixed on the zodiacal circle, necessarily have their Laws predefined by their geometric relationships with the "Fixed" and the "Wandering". These laws are based on the celestial harmonic affinities willed by Heaven, and which mathematics can make *predictable by drawing the configurations and their arithmetical results* in relation to the original framework drawn in each cervical cortex.

Ever since it arrived in France, the Denderah planisphere has continued to be opposed by both sides. A very lively [34] polemic involved all the renowned scholars of France and its various

---

[34] The term 'polemic' is a charming euphemism for the storms of insults that, for a hundred years, upset learned scientists such as Ampère, Arago, Baron Cuvier, the astronomer Dupuis, and so many academics!

academies in highly learned discussions. Three theses were vehemently defended or contested with equal vigour.

1) The Denderah planisphere was a meaningless ceiling ornament;

2) The planisphere was a rural calendar that made it possible to harvest in good time;

3) The planisphere had a completely different sky to Hipparchus, so no harvest was possible.

Then there was one more troublemaker, and not the least of all, who raised a possibility that the defenders of the other three points of view found absurd: by performing a celestial half-conversion of the planisphere, everything became clear thanks to the grace of precessional recoil, which the Egyptians knew all about. In this way, the ancient primitive zodiacal configurations were back where they belonged, in the Space of that time, *some 12,000 years ago*.

At the Académie des Sciences, an uproar broke out against an eminent scholar called Charles Dupuis, who had already published an enormous work, *L'Origine de tous les Cultes*. For a good twenty years, the polemic grew among the members of this learned Academy, where Dupuis's simple logical truth was described as heretical. At the time, there could be no question of endorsing a thesis that asserted such human anteriority, when biblical truth only dated the Flood to five millennia before our era.

When, in 1822, the "Zodiac of Denderah" reached the Royal Library in Paris, the discussion resumed. The Memoirs accumulated, in which the tone of the signatories was not only acerbic, but also highly polemical. The next volume, devoted to the history of Denderah, will give an account of this. The following extract from a major Parisian newspaper of the time, *La Quotidienne*, of 27 October 1822, shows how far scholars had come:

"Narrow minds, people who are frightened by the slightest objection, seemed to want to prevent the acquisition of the Denderah monument! Seeing with difficulty the books by M. de Volney and M. Dupuis, which are monstrous assemblages of false science and apparent erudition, being peddled not only in the smallest French hamlets, but also throughout Europe, and even to the very ends of Russia, these men seemed to fear that the exhibition of this monument would serve to spread with even greater activity these ideas of an indefinite antiquity of the world, which tend to do nothing less than destroy the authority of the Holy Books, in order *to* destroy any idea of religion!

Unfortunately, in 1822, that was still the case. The relatively recent Hebrew texts of the Old Testament took precedence over the rigorously chronological texts engraved on stone, which recounted the entire history of the first monotheism.

The idea of re-establishing the primitive Annals with the help of calculations based on these famous "Mathematical Combinations", derived from the eternal and har monic movement of the "Fixes" which brings about the equinoctial retrogradation, is therefore not new. But the starting point of this temporal and spatial spiral remained lost in the increasingly shrouded mists of the distant past. Researchers came up against the insurmountable wall of heroic suppositions, hearing nothing of anaglyphs and starting from a very primitive axiom about the intelligence of barbarians. Newton was the most famous...

The calculations of this great Englishman were the most resounding falsehoods imaginable. By way of conclusion, he convinced himself, in an attempt to drag the scholarly world along with him, that the famous biblical diluvian time was even closer to us, instead of putting this antiquity back some ten thousand years. So much so, in fact, that his shattering assertion, *a* major part of his book *Chronology of the Ancient Kingdoms,* made us forget for a time the lofty mathematical speculations that his genius delivered to mankind, and which, fortunately, have come down to us.

Perhaps he was referring to Pliny, who attributed the first description of the sky to Atlas, and to Anaximander for the constellations. He couldn't have known then that the mythical giant personified Hor in his crossing of Africa, carrying on his shoulders the heavy burden of repopulating the decimated Land of God, by saving the Cadets from the pitfalls sown on their way to the Second Heart of God, Egypt.

And while Bossuet and Leibniz's hopes that Louis the Fourteenth would take an interest in excavations in the land of the Pyramids were only disappointed, Bonaparte made up for lost time during his famous campaign, during which he was accompanied by a top-notch scientific team.

The "Zodiacs" of Esneh, Oumbos and Denderah were undoubtedly the most magnificent trio of discoveries. Fourier, after Denon, who drew the Denderah planisphere on the spot before it was transported to France, wrote to Berthollet:

> "The discussion of the astronomical monuments that have just been discovered serves to fix ideas on the many polemics. It justifies the chronology of Herodotus and that of Manetho. It remains constant that the present division of the zodiac, which dates back some fifteen thousand years, has been preserved without any alteration, and thus transmitted to other peoples."

So let's go back and follow the survivors, to experience with them the first shock of this battle of the ancient Giants, a historic event that took place shortly after the Cataclysm, near Ta Mana, between Ousir, Hor and Sit. In this way, the reality of the situation will be better conveyed, with the focus on the symbols carrying more weight than the actual description.

CHAPTER SEVEN

THE RA-SIT-OU
(THE SIT-SOLEIL REBELS)

He filled Sit's heart with fear! You are the Eldest because you were born before him. You are the Eldest whom Geb has put in his rightful place with Iset and Nek-Bet at your side.
O Usir! Hor has avenged you, and your soul may dwell in peace among the Blessed in the Amenta! Your name will remain engraved in the Second Heart so that it may be Eternal!
PYRAMID TEXTS
(7 d - 575/583)

It would be a ridiculous and unjust presumption to claim that we have more energy or intelligence than the ancients: while the substance of our knowledge has increased, our intelligence has not.
C.G. JUNG
(Metamorphoses of the Soul and its symbols)

In the clearing still partially flooded by the recent torrential rains, the horde of "Rebels" surrounding a rough leader jealous of his prerogatives, arrived completely exhausted from their exhausting march through the forest. It had been hard to make headway between the giant trees, among the luxuriant vegetation that proliferated higher and higher, bushy to the extreme and dripping with water that always seemed ominous.

The area they had suddenly discovered seemed like a haven of peace. The energy displayed by Sit during the advance that had brought them here had made the troop forget about the acrimony and sudden mood swings of their guide, who acted as if he believed himself to be invested with celestial authority. But perhaps, during the last few days, a relative calm had settled over this angry front. But perhaps, during the last few days, a relative calm had settled under this angry front, for he had found himself a solitary young companion, who instantly became very devoted to him, and on whom he subsequently spent most of his madness. The approach of the village, just a few hours away by walk, even made him rather amiable, as he savoured in advance a total victory over the "Descendants" still alive, knowing that he would show them no mercy.

The sigh of relief and cries of joy that greeted their arrival in the full light gradually turned to astonishment, murmurs of fear and then to a thick silence barely disturbed by the hoarse cries of birds of prey flying over the clearing. A crowd had formed around something enigmatic lying on the ground.

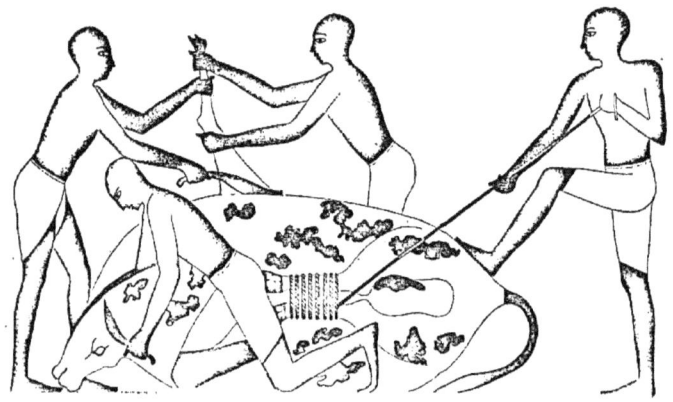

The Ra-Sit-Ou or Rebels of the Sun, the "Descendants of Set", practised the festival of Set (or Sed) during which a bull was ritually sacrificed so that its skin, according to tradition, would imprison the body of Osiris and cause it to perish and rot.

Suddenly breaking through the widening circle, Sit came to a halt in front of two *skins*, spread out wide, flattening the tall grass and bloody from the shoulder down. His bewilderment grew at this intriguing sight, for the previous night, his troop had stopped in front of a similar skin, hanging from a low tree branch, similarly stained scarlet, like a warning from heaven. Some of his rebels had whispered that this sign warned them not to go any further with their project, on pain of being reduced to the state of this emaciated skin...

The chief's anger had been terrible, because in his madness, he couldn't see who could have sent him such a message. These skins could only be laid out to dry, and the isolated man who was doing it was doing it like a beginner. But they were *bulls'* skins! It remained a bad memory. But there was no need to show any fear in front of those around him, who were watching him intently, trying to get to the bottom of his thoughts. As there was no one left alive on this earth to taunt him or send him a warning, it was better to laugh about it. He stood up, roughly gripping the shoulders of his close companion, and raising his voice fiercely, he said:

- Rest assured! You're in absolutely no danger. These skins are not a sign of weakness or a bad omen: they don't have the smell of death. On the contrary, they represent the signal sent by Heaven, which has sent us these bullskins, so that our hearts remain energetic in their legitimate resolutions and that weariness does not penetrate them. On the contrary, let us rejoice at the imminent arrival of our clan at its planned destination. This place will be ours, it will ensure our well-being and prosperity. Our great family will become the most powerful on this Earth, prospering under the new Sun, our only Master.

The murmurs started up again, the incomprehensible appearance of the skins remaining unresolved in the tired minds of the travellers, despite Sit's grandiloquent phrases. What appeared to be supernatural took precedence over what was not quite reality. The chief understood this so well that he hastened to order the last break before the investment of Ta Mana:

- The food carriers should stand by their group and distribute the food to the families! It's time to regain your strength. When the sun's rays cover the skins, the stopover will be over. We will then complete our journey and arrive at our destination together. Let my Ra-Sit-Ou join me to take their final orders. We'll all eat together, working out our final plan.

Sit was proving that he knew the souls of those who accompanied him. He knew that full bellies soothed consciences by putting recalcitrant wills to sleep. This would allow him to infuse his rebels with the ultimate energy needed to successfully carry out Ta Mana's general attack. As for the rest, there would always be time, afterwards, to think about the promises made.

The various groups had already dispersed, gathering by affinity and happily sharing the meat quarters. The young people were bringing back plenty of fruit; they had only to lift their hands to pick it from the shrubs growing on the edge of the jungle; papayas, mangoes and bananas were proliferating. There was also a curious green fruit, round and covered in prickles, which had to be sought on the high branches of a tree that was often centuries old, a good opportunity to play a little. It was prized for its soft, floury white flesh, which was reminiscent of the consistency and sour taste of the cereal cakes so popular in Ahâ-Men-Ptah.

At ease among his soldiers, Sit regained his feverish, distant eyes. As he tore his gazelle leg to shreds, he waxed lyrical for the circle of his people:

- From now on, we are all bound by our desire to re-establish the Creator Sun everywhere as the universal power. He created us, and it is up to us to re-establish his kingship on earth, if we do not want him to make us all disappear through his displeasure at seeing us worship a god other than Him, who dazzles us and allows us to live. The only solution for those who refuse to join in our worship of Ra is death!

The approvals that poured in here and there were not deliriously enthusiastic, but Sit felt he could continue his speech:

- To make sure of that, you will always be the Ra-Sit-Ou, the 'Soldiers of the Sun'. My *Rebels*... Our stockpile of bows and arrows is sufficient to ensure our supremacy; I think all we'll have to do to get the job done is scare people. We'll use our clubs to kill anyone who runs away...

One of the leaders, with his powerful musculature, was surprised:

- Why kill those who could work for us? We'll have the power, the supplies... and their wives! Why not keep at least the strongest?

Forcing himself not to let his annoyance and anger show, Sit frowned at the man asking such a stupid question. However, he managed to answer in a monotone voice:

- Ra demands the blood of those who have dared to raise prayers to someone else. If we do not annihilate them, they will resume their impious worship of something inconsistent and non-existent, which will unleash the new wrath of the Sun, who this time will take revenge in a more terrible way against us by annihilating us all. Is this what you want? Then go back to worshipping that sacrilegious god, the same one who caused our downfall and threw us onto this earth. We are alive thanks to the Sun. It is he who shows us the way, today more than ever, by illuminating these two skins. Either we will re-establish its authority everywhere, or we will all die a death far more terrible than that suffered by our parents. Which would you prefer? To disappear with the godless, or to help me eliminate them, just them?

Horrified whispers left him in no doubt as to the choice made by his fellow fighters, so he went on to address himself more specifically to the one who had so clumsily questioned him:

- Would you be among the godless, you whose strength has become weakness for daring to doubt my orders? The man realised that he had gone too far, so he hastened to answer humbly, without looking up at Sit, whose icy gaze pierced him:

- Far be it from me, O Lord of the Sun! You alone are capable of putting enemies out of action.

- Very well answered! And if we need slaves, there are enough primitive peoples in the mountains, the same ones who used to work in the mines, to replace the manpower we need...

Satisfied with the conclusion of this misunderstanding, he served himself another leg of gazelle. There would be no shortage of bodies devoted to him, willingly or unwillingly, just as there was no shortage of game. He had nothing to do with insidious questioners. And this lump of fat with a human face that had challenged him would soon become like the meat he was tearing apart with his sharp teeth. He would club it to death himself, and enjoy the mash he would make from that empty head. This allowed everyone to finish their meal in silence, in their own thoughts.

Moreover, after a furtive glance at the hides spread out, Sit saw that the moment was approaching when he would order the departure. He took the opportunity to give his final advice, as if suddenly inspired:

- Our salvation comes from Ra, who is the greatest and most beautiful of all the stars, and therefore of all the gods. He appears to us in all his glory to order us to set out and conquer what belongs to him. We will act very quickly, and in agreement with him, so that the conquest is complete before sunset. You are divided into groups of eight men; each of your leaders knows my orders and you will obey them without question. We will enter Ta Mana by all the exits at once, shouting as loud as we can to frighten these worshippers of a false divinity. We will prove to them the power of ours, by the vigour with which we will exterminate them. Glory be to Ra, who will shine at every sunrise as long as we prove his glory through our actions!

Some of the warriors rose to their feet, screaming hysterically, as if to express the savagery that would be theirs in a few hours' time. Sit was reassured by this and smiled, apparently satisfied with his exhortation. The other men remained seated but vigorously approved. These wild cries, more or less hoarse and similar to those of angry lions, would undoubtedly impress the villagers. To put heaven on his side once and for all, Sit held out his staff towards the sun as he rose to his feet. Clutching it tightly, he invoked Ra:

- Flood me with your beneficent rays, O Mighty Creator! May my sceptre command by your grace the annihilation of your enemies!

All the rebels hastened to repeat:

- May the Ra-Sit-Ou destroy all your enemies, Ra!

On all sides, the groups quickly finished their meals when they saw that the time had come to leave. Sit finished his peroration:

- All my soldiers will stand in front of the assembled women and children, except for the eight who will close the ranks at the rear. It's time: the rays are flooding the skins with light. Let's finish this march; let's attack and KILL!...

As soon as the whole horde had gone into the thick undergrowth, the dampness clung to everyone. As no one had turned towards the clearing, no one saw that the leather of the hides was taking on a pretty pink hue under the Sun, forming a kind of very bright halo, within which played myriads of joyful luminosities. Fear would certainly have taken possession of all simple minds.

But their feet were sinking into the marshes, making their steps heavier and heavier, and that alone was worrying them. Nevertheless, the advance continued at a satisfactory pace, with the presumed imminent arrival captivating the spirits. Galvanised by the approach, these men no longer doubted the validity of the arguments put forward by Sit to justify the appalling slaughter they were about to commit.

Yet the nervousness in the hearts of the animals was increasing, and was being expressed more loudly by the voices that were rising from all sides in high-pitched tones. The animals were fleeing their usual haunts long before this vociferous pack reached them. Even the indifferent elephants were turning away from their usual route, not out of fear but because the din was deafening them.

The noisy echoes, however, did not yet reach the spot where Ousir and Hor were standing. The rebels crossed a marshy hollow before reaching the dunes before the sand of the beaches. The rising ground slowed the progress of the men at the front, who were laden down with shock weapons. When they reached the top of the highest mound, they let out their wildest cries at the sight of the calm blue sea, which seemed so close. These powerful sounds, carried by a favourable warm wind , inevitably reached the ears of the Father and the Son, who were patiently waiting on their mound for the events foreseen by Nek-Bet to unfold.

The movements of the soil, aided by the run-off from the torrential rains of recent weeks, had formed terraces all along the slope of the highest mound. Trees had grown there long before the cataclysm, intertwining their roots in the stabilised soil. Halfway up, amidst some lush vegetation, stood a centuries-old sycamore tree. Behind this venerable trunk, out of sight of those who were advancing, the two calm and attentive Giants waited, in accordance with Nek-Bet's instructions. It was here, in this very spot, that the fate of the current community of survivors saved from the waters by the Almighty God would be decided.

Sensing the first burst of voices, Hor straightened up. Ousir, lost in thought, did not move; he preferred to leave the initiative to his son, who would have to get used to acting alone. The latter, as if reading his father's soul, felt all the tension in him disappear; his muscles unclenched and even the pulsations that painfully agitated his empty eyelid ceased. His valid eye regained perfect acuity, allowing him to scan carefully where the cohort led by his father's brother[35] would appear.

---

[35] During the Pharaonic millennia, the hieroglyphic expressions of all consanguineous kinship were based exclusively on monogamy. *Atefen-Atef* is the "father of the father"; *Sonen-Atef in Mau* is the "brother of the mother's father", hence the great-uncle; *Haï* is the husband and *Shime* is the wife; *Atefeh-Haï* is the father-in-law, literally the "father of the husband".

He who no longer believed in the God he was profaning would no longer gloat as soon as he reached them. Uzir, who was watching his son from the side, understood the meaning of the vengeful gleam in his able-bodied eye. Hor would be his father's avenger, elevated to the status of a god by future generations. This made him smile in the midst of his sadness. Why couldn't he simply have been a man like any other human being? He would have loved so much to live far from the complications to which God had subjected him in order to justify a renewal of Goodness and Faith in those who had been begotten in the Divine image... He sighed for a long time, in spite of himself, and this complaint from the depths of his heart was heard by Hor, who, mistaking the cause, set about reassuring him:

- Have no fear, O my venerated Father! Everything will happen as planned. I feel invested with a strength far greater than that which was mine in that forest destroyed by the divine wrath of Ahâ-MenPtah. I'm a different me, even if I don't know how to explain this transformation.

Usir rejoiced inwardly; he understood very well this feeling which had often been his. He nonetheless approved gravely:

- You are flesh of my flesh, another me, and my name and my heart are yours. You are protected in this way by the Lord, as will all those who sincerely call on you for help until the end of time.

You will be the Eldest, O my son, the most illustrious Elder, the First whose victory over Evil will be celebrated! That is why all the "Descendants" to be born through you will resemble you and have the same powers, as long as they personify the image of their Creator in the smallest acts of their lives. And only God, who makes water fall evenly and equally on all things, will always notice this. What can tell the difference between two similar drops of water, one falling on a rose and the other on a foxglove? Divine power alone, for it transforms the first plant into the crumb of the earth and the second into deadly venom.

As the shouting intensified, Ousir rose to his feet and concluded:

- You will receive offerings from all over the world, Hor, and give glory to God in the name of all three of us: Iset, me and you.

Hor's hair swayed in energetic denial:

- I do not desire this, O my Father! This privilege is yours, the harmony obtained at Your Mana is your work I would so much like to live simply as a man...

Both of Usir's arms stiffened helplessly against what he himself had wanted without getting:

It's impossible, my son. I would have liked it to be that way for your mother and for me, but God decided otherwise... By the way, protect Iset and keep her safe until she joins me in the other world.

Hor groaned at the end of this sentence. The dialogue was interrupted on this sad note, however, because the horde of Ra-Sit-Ou had just appeared at the top of a dune, about a hundred metres away. Sit, recognisable by his tall stature, joined this vanguard. He cast a piercing gaze over the horizon, before holding out his hand to show them the mound of sycamore trees from which Ousir and Hor watched invisibly as the men descended the slope and marched straight towards them.

When they reached the bottom of the mound that Sit was about to climb, Hor suddenly sprang up from the large trunk, shouting from his overhang of a good dozen metres:

- Get back, you enraged venom, despair of your mother All Creation hates you and you are vomited out by Humanity of divine essence! Back, Sit, back!

Lightning falling at the feet of the walkers could not have created a more intense stupor. They looked up at this inexplicable apparition, instinctively retreating a few steps, before remaining as they were, paralysed by the panic that gripped them. Only Sit, realising at once the cause of his troops' sudden halt, tried to understand how his nephew could be *alive* in this place!

Curiously, at the same time, there was silence - the women and children were still a long way behind - as if in anticipation of the confrontation that would soon pit the two Giants against each other.

Taking advantage of his undeniable advantage, Hor spoke again. His loud voice reverberated in a sort of cavernous echo along the surrounding slopes:

- Stand back, all of you! I, Hor, command you. God has allowed you to escape total engulfment, and in gratitude you accuse him of your blasphemy and sacrilegious conduct; shame on you! And I tell you: your souls will perish without being able to reach Ahâ-Men-Ptah, for the liquid doors will close on them without hope. Your souls will perish like your flesh...

Sit's gesticulations during his nephew's homily ended in a disordered roar. The features of his face, distorted by dementia, showed the human anger that was building up inside them. When he could speak, he shouted in a choppy, barely comprehensible voice:

- How dare you defy me, you who can only bite with your mouth? Have you forgotten that once before my power was stronger than yours?

Without losing his composure, Hor retorted:

- It's you who can't remember, you madman! I'm here and I'm dominating you thanks to God and His Power. You can do nothing more against me. You will be destroyed, you and all those who listen to you, if you don't go far away.

Laughing maniacally, Sit signalled to his soldiers to surround the mound so that his nephew could not escape. Then he prophesied in a menacing voice:

- You'd better try to get away while there's still time, or I'll take pleasure in slitting your throat myself!

Hor shrugged his shoulders dismissively as he followed the rebels' movements. He knew that his father could hear and see what was going on, and was ready to intervene when he saw fit. So it was with a confident voice that he challenged his uncle:

- The venom that comes out of your mouth is just good enough to fall into this arid sand. Your spirit is like that of the scorpion that can only be crushed to suppress it. You are like that abject animal, and likewise what circulates in your flesh is nothing but a venom that drives you mad. If you leave quickly, perhaps God will have mercy on you.

- You're lying! I'm the strongest and your filthy God and you are no match for me! I nailed you to the ground once, and I'm going to do it again. I am the strongest, and I hold the Sun in my arms. If you don't admit that, then you're blind in both eyes!

It was Hor's turn to laugh, but in a much more relaxed way:

- Yet what I can only see with one eye allows me to say that the Sun is disappearing from our view. It's hiding its face from your blasphemies because it doesn't want to witness your demise.

A large grey cloud obscured the daylight, blotting out the serene azure of the sky. Addressing the rebels, Hor said in a solemn tone:

- All of you who may be longing to live in peace at last, listen to me! Let this divine sign darkening the sky light up your souls! Don't follow the man who blinds you with this Sun that shines only on heads empty of sensible words! Instead, contemplate the Eternal

One, your only God, through this part of your soul that you have inherited from him, and thank him that you are still alive.

- It's not true! It's all a lie! He is lying! My power alone is greater than his and his God's.

Fuming with a rage that literally made him jump on the spot in mad indignation, Sit resumed in a hateful voice:

- You cannot know my strength, you who are already the head of a "Returned One" who no longer exists. You are like those who did not follow me and disappeared beneath the waters. Ra-Sit-Ou, do as I have done: trust only in Ra, the giver of light and heat, the generator of all life. His God is nothing but a vain usurper. Just as Hor's father died trying to take the throne of Ahâ-Men-Ptah from me. *I* am the new Master, and this time no one will stand in my way!

In a voice that was soft but clearly heard by all, Hor asked:

- Are you that sure you're the new Master? A nervous, unquenchable laugh rose from Sit's throat. The ridiculousness of this question became apparent even to the soldiers. Finally, the leader of the Rebels managed to say:

- Look at your position, you little runt, and that of my soldiers surrounding you!

- There's no question of me...

- Yet you don't want to pretend that your God is coming back to life to take my rightful place as Master? The Sun himself approves of me, since he is appearing again! Let all present raise their eyes to his splendour! Stretch out your arms to thank him for our imminent victory...

The cohort of soldiers, as well as the growing number of families joining them, then prostrated themselves, following Sit's recommendations. The Sun, restored to its golden glare, made all those who tried to obey blink, despite the blindness that had overtaken them.

Ousir obviously chose this propitious moment to make his appearance. The humans below, looking up at the sky, heard a new, unexpected voice, with a deep, full intonation, resounding above their heads. The strange sound that penetrated them seemed to come from everywhere and nowhere. Dazzled, they could no longer perceive the outside environment except through the sounds that reached their ears. Many thought it was the Sun itself speaking, although the words being uttered condemned them without remission:

- *Shame on all of you who forget that you are children of God!*

Sit instantly recognised the sound that often haunted his nights. He raised his head and, having never looked up at the shining star, he saw it. It was his turn to blink to make sure he wasn't the victim of a mirage. But it wasn't! He saw the familiar form, dressed in the same white tunic, which was still stained scarlet where the spears had pierced it.

A terrible scream, which had been held back for too long, escaped from his mouth. This long scream made all those who had gathered around , but who were now ready to flee, jump back:

- No! No! NO... This can't be true! It can't be you! You're not there: you're dead! YOU CAN'T BE OUSIR!

"Ousir! Ah... Ousir!" All these human beings, who had more or less strayed from the divine path, suddenly became aware of a reality that was beyond them. They felt part of an extraordinary scene, one that would decide their future without their involvement, but which concerned them first and foremost. It was as God himself was appearing before their eyes. They cautiously took several more steps backwards, even though they were already well below the ground.

Sit remained alone, dominated by Ousir. On hearing this name from the mouth of his torturer brother, the faces of all those present were filled with fear.

Although most of them had never seen him before that day, they all knew about the misfortunes of the royal family before their country sank. So there was no doubt in their minds that Ousir was dead and that his remains had been thrown into the sea.

Yet he was there, speaking to them once again:

- Yes, I am Ousir! I've come to tell you that Hor must remain the only legitimate leader, because he is the only heir to the Heir that I am. Hor is the son of the Son, the bull of the Celestial Bull who returned to earth to warn you of your sins. Hor is the son of Usir. He alone is girded with the authority of God to lead you to the 'Second Heart' where you will find prosperity and happiness.

This declaration of enthronement was listened to in total silence, apart from the continuous rattle that escaped Sit's throat. With all his companions looking on, Sit stood up straight and, not admitting defeat, continued:

- Erase yourself from our sight, you of whom only impalpable dust remains at the bottom of the sea. You are Ra's enemy and you are dead... You are nothing but a bereft retreat with no body and no soul. You cannot be here: vanish! You no longer have arms or legs. Return to where you came from; turn away from the light of Ra, for whom you are an insult. Your magic that comes out of Leo will never be able to do anything against the new power of the sun. Vanish, you horrible retreat! You are no longer my enemy, for you are but invisible dust.

Usir smiled at his son and hugged his shoulders. he replied in the same gripping voice:

- Hor is saved from all your schemes, O you who are my brother born of the same mother as me, blessed be his name forever! That's why I won' touch you. But from this moment, I pass on to Hor my Divine name. I tell you all: I, Usir, seat Hor on the Throne of this second earth. He will be its undisputed Master, and he will become the first Pêr-Ahâ of Divine essence, from this day forward. He will be the first Ahâ[36], the Elder who will renew the whole of Humanity. Those who do not agree should leave! Let them go at once as far away as possible, and in that case no harm will come to them. But woe betide those who remain here with an unclean heart! I will come down to them and destroy them. I will reduce them so that nothing remains of them... neither body nor soul!

The women moaned. The soldiers themselves didn't know what to do with their weapons, none of which were raised against Usir. Sit's distraught mind suffered another shock when he saw this "appearance" start to descend. Panic took hold of the weakest, who rushed to follow the women and children, who fled in disarray. The unfortunate leader, seeing that the bravest would soon follow suit, shouted:

- Let's all get out of here! This place is cursed and the spectre will kill us all!...

Waving a fist at the relentlessly advancing white shape, he prophesied:

- We'll find each other again! There won't always be these spells between us. You won't always win, because I'm the only Master by blood; the sceptre belongs to me. One day I will reign, I solemnly swear it here, before my faithful!

And I know it will come true...

Without further ado, he turned to the square of brave men waiting for him and said:

---

[36] Phonetically, Ahâ is read as "ahan". Could this be the origin of Adam?

- Let's join the others and set up somewhere else.

We'll be back in force.

This dialogue of ancient events is recounted in numerous texts that paint a vivid picture of the battle between the two titans, , which 4,000 years later would be engraved on temple walls: the Battle of the Giants, pitting the 'Followers of Hor' against the 'Rebels of Sit'.

Throughout this long and exhausting march, thousands of kilometres towards Egypt, Ka-Ptah, thousands of kilometres towards Egypt, the two giants clashed their formations, more and more numerous and better and better armed! And so Hor and Sit fought each other to the death, relentlessly and with a fierceness that only increased as the historical reality changed over the centuries, and then over the millennia, and the hatred itself was fanned by the advance into the Future, towards the Land promised to only one of the two clans, each wanting to be that one!

The Peace that came to unify the two into a single homeland on the banks of the Nile was only achieved out of fear of a new cataclysm. Infighting soon resumed between the worshippers of the Sun, descendants of Sit, and the Cadets of God, born of the Followers of Hor. The Sun worshippers used a hawk as their emblem, while the Sun worshippers used a falcon. The former appeared in white in the Annals to distinguish them, while the latter were given red. Throughout the formidable Exodus, as throughout the Pharaonic period that followed on the banks of the Nile, the texts and engraved inscriptions clearly explain the continual antagonism of the two Giants, even in the explanations provided by the oldest tombs discovered in Egypt, which singularly authenticates the very *origin of* the story. The conclusion differs little in substance, if in another form, and allows us to understand this whole essential chapter:

> "Your son Hor is called to reign, O Usir, Supreme Master of the Two Lands, the Ameuta of the Blessed where you reside, and Ath-Ka-Ptah, where your son's name will

ensure the Resurrection of the Second Heart for all Eternity! He will possess the strength needed to unite the two clans into a single family. The Rebels will do right by the Sun, which will resume its lonely and powerless celestial course! Thus you will preserve eternal peace in the glory of your Father Ptah!

For the time being, Hor and Usir remained alone in each other's arms, overlooking the vastness. The main thing was done for the new civilisation to take off. As the Father had little time left to remain among the living, he took his son by the waist and leaned towards him so that their foreheads touched, as a sign of tenderness and respect. Then, without making any superfluous comments, they climbed down from the mound. Before rejoining the track leading to Ta Mana, they bowed low as they passed beneath the sycamore tree which, from the height of its magnificence, watched them go, merely shaking its sacred foliage in the light breeze as a sign of farewell. The essence of this historic renewal began with the defeat of Sit and his Rebels. The material organisation would follow its course, thanks to the technical knowledge of many of the survivors, who were carpenters, blacksmiths and other manual trades necessary for the normal development of life.

For several centuries, mines had been open a good moon's walk from Tu Mana, in the high mountains. And although the upheaval had stopped all exports to a country that no longer existed, copper and lead could soon be used locally. During the reign of Geb, the last "PêrAhâ" of Ahâ-Men-Ptah, a research team had even ventured as far as the craggy foothills that were the remains of exploded glaciers, much further south, made up of iron in its native state, in enormous quantities.[37]

Yes! Life was returning to normal at Ta Mana...

---

[37] This is the southern Moroccan region of Taouz-Erfoud, where these glaciers are found and where the feet tread tons of iron minerals: magnetite, gœthite, etc.

Chapter Eight

"TA OUZ"
(The 'Abode' of Usir)

O Father! The gates of heaven are open to you! Open are the gates of heavenly welcome! In reply, Ptah, the Almighty, said:
- The doors of Usir's "Abode" are open to receive the "Lord of the Beyond of Life", the one who will watch over the Eternity of the "Blessed".

TEXT OF THE PYRAMIDS
(from col. 795)

The absence of material changes is sometimes exaggerated, but the identity of the Berber soul, through all its vicissitudes, is truly a force of nature!

J. CELERIER
(History of Morocco)

In a short space of time, the tribal institution took on the primordial impetus that would never leave popular administration for the next five millennia. All the inhabitants of Ta Mana voted Hor into his hereditary position, which was never challenged again, at least in this clan. From then on, the titanic battles between the "Followers of Hor" and the "Rebels of Sit" began.

Generation after generation, as families became organised, developed, multiplied and transformed, the very notion of the "first Ahâ", the Elder, and therefore Usir, encompassed Hor, Iset, Nut and even Nek-Bet in the same mythology, long before the people entered Egypt. The many defections that marked the long march eastwards across the whole of North Africa kept the imprint of this spiritual ideology deep in their hearts. The nomadic tribes that swarmed from this exodus - Kabyle, Touareg and Berber - kept the ancestral customs of their ancient descendants despite everything they had endured over the course of their long history.

As soon as it became clear to the inhabitants of Ta Mana that Sit and his horde would flee to heavens that might be kinder to them, a legal Council was set up, chaired by Hor, assisted by his father. The An-Nu attended, still in a privileged capacity, his voice enjoying well-defined prerogatives, and remaining second in Wisdom, advising each 'Descendant' in title.

Osiris was actually buried at Ta Ouz (the place of Osiris). From his body was collected the eternal flame that accompanied the 'Survivors' to the 'Second Heart' Ath-Ka-Ptah, or Ae-guy-ptos in Greek phonetics, i.e. Egypt.

Very quickly, the almost forgotten foundations of traditional Faith and Divine Law were reintroduced. The duties of the members of the community were delineated and organised, both in relation to itself and its own needs, and to facilitate the advancement of civilisation towards future generations. The latter would benefit as best they could, while in turn assuming the same obligations towards their successors, so that ultimately those who reached this "Second Heart of God", this Ath-Ka-Ptah which was becoming the "Promised Land", would have all the Wisdom and all the Knowledge of their distant ancestors.

The first learning classes began their courses, teaching a methodical oral instruction for each level, determined by a particular mnemonic procedure. The subsequent verbal retransmission could then be made in full, without any omission, but also without any addition or transposition of meaning, in the text learnt by heart.

Resting the memory to better preserve the teaching was provided by practising various manual tasks, which had the effect of killing two birds with one stone. In this way, everyone's real aptitudes were put to the best possible use, with the help of experienced craftsmen who demonstrated their practical spirit.

To occupy their leisure time, some teachers taught their pupils how to make clothes from the skins of animals killed for their meat. Buffalo and gazelle skins in particular proved to be very hard-wearing and wonderfully elastic.

There were obviously major technical differences between this "skin industry" and the linen weavings of Ahâ-Men-Ptah, which had been swallowed up like the rest, but everyone's goodwill in the face of misfortune made it possible to deal with the most pressing problems. The plans for making the looms remained in the memory of the specialists, waiting to be brought out, even for a more primitive construction.

For the time being, we had to dress as best we could. Hard stone scrapers were used to dehide the hides using the good old ancient method, which was revived for the purpose. The leather obtained was then soaked in the marrow extracted from the long bones of the buffalo, which softened it enormously. It was then cut into wide strips and sewn together with strips of the same material. The result was garments that were simple in form, but that raised human dignity to a higher level.

As for the ceramists, they had become potters. When they presented the first bowls, they had their minute of success. After that, they and their students set about making pots. There was no shortage of clay, water or sand. By skilfully mixing the three ingredients, the first jugs were assembled and fired over a very rudimentary wood fire. The result, despite its imprecise shape, drew thunderous applause. Improvements in firing methods soon refined the models, enabling the first engravings to be made.

The conquest of metals, which had been the immense progress made by civilisation in Ahâ-Men-Ptah to increase well-being, had made the scarcity of metal objects here acutely felt! In addition to copper and tin, mined in various places from the vanished subsoil, gold and then iron had given metallurgy a definitive boost.

However, as the various States successively defected, the predecessor of the last King had ordered research in distant countries, such as the one that had become Ta Mana since the upheaval, so that there would be no shortage of metals. Lodes of copper, gold, lead and iron were identified. Even under Geb, the last Ahâ, copper mines had been opened in the mountains of this new country until the Great Cataclysm.

For while the knowledge and use of bronze through the alloying of copper and tin had enabled the consolidation of the first ancient civilisation, the second human society had advanced thanks to iron. This was no longer the case at Ta Mana where, a priori, there was no tin to start a new civilising cycle, to make bronze.

Several of the surviving blacksmiths had left to see what was happening at the copper mines, as there had been no news from the mining region. But it was clear that the lack of tin would not solve the problem of the alloy, especially as it was far from having the qualities essential everyday use. Bronze had neither the hardness nor the elasticity required for everyday use, such as farming implements.

The interesting thing would be to extract the iron ore.

According to the explorers' reports, it was found right on the ground, in various mineralised forms, unfortunately a long way from the village. An expedition had to be mounted to an unknown territory, mountainous and barren, where large wild animals lived.

And so, Uzir, judging his son to be fully invested with the powers of authority, decided to reinforce the process of accelerating the improvement of his people's lot, by himself leading a group of pioneers to this land of iron. He still remembered the reports he had read on the subject, as well as the accounts of those who had led the journey.

For this nation, which had been tried and tested in all areas, the deprivation of metals could not last for long without being much more than a nuisance. It was an undeniable factor in decadence, and had to be eliminated as quickly as possible. It was even becoming a matter of life and death for the rising generation, too distraught by the lack of common tools and utensils to which they had previously been accustomed. They could not cope with this complete return to nature, as Ousir had realised perfectly well.

Since Hor had to remain at the head of his people in order to keep everyone's spirits up and organise everyone's new life, it was up to the Father to set off in search of this vital source of progress, which was iron. The short time the Risen One had left to live among his people prompted him to hasten his departure in search of the ore.

This is why, leaving the Council where he had not announced his decision, reserving it first for his wife, the son of Geb took a determined step towards the hut where Iset was waiting for him. He would have to accept this measure as the ultimate help that only he could give to the people, while at the same time consolidating the reign of the "Descendants", and of the first of them, their son Hor.

The use of iron would usher in a second era of prosperity, this time in this new territory. It would make an invaluable contribution to the long-awaited revival promised to the survivors. Because smelting ore was not an insoluble problem, far it!

From the earliest days of the discovery of the veins in the sunken land, blacksmiths had been looking the possibilities of extracting the metal which, from the first results, proved to be much harder than copper or even its alloys. And to obtain it, there was no need for a specialised industry requiring technical prowess. In a very short space of time, a very simple system was put in place to process the ore.

All they had to do was choose slopes that were well ventilated by the northerly winds. Some of them lent themselves admirably to this beginning of an industrial era for a people in the first age of civilisation. A hole had been dug at each base of the hills, surrounded by a low wall of stones sealed together with clay, so as to create a thick, roughly circular inner wall. As well as consolidating the crucible thus obtained, the plastering made it refractory.

Within a short space of time, the reservoir had grown to a very respectable size for its time: around four metres in diameter and the same height. Operation was laughably simple. A layer of wood covered the bottom of the tank, on which the ore to be processed was laid, and which was itself covered by a second layer of wood.

Taking advantage of the favourable, slightly strong wind, which acted as a forge bellows on the fire previously lit at the base of the furnace, the wood gradually became coal as it burned. Its heat reduced the iron oxide to its metallic component, which sank to the bottom of the crucible. All that remained was to clear away the ashes and slag after combustion, to recover the pure ore in its still spongy solidified state.

The still-glowing mass was easy to work. By hammering it, it was given its original pyramid shape and turned into an ingot weighing around fifteen kilos. The blacksmiths and wrought-iron workers then had only to rework them, making tools and utensils, as well as a wide variety of objets d'art, including supports for the colourful stones that were so popular with women at the time.

But better times would come again, just as real forges had replaced primitive furnaces. In these new times, when everything had to be remodelled, the few master blacksmiths among the survivors would soon be able to return to archaic but vital methods. Shaping the resulting iron was no more difficult, as the art of metallurgy consisted of preserved tricks of the hand. Immense progress had been made in this field since the discovery of bronze.

This copper-tin alloy - the bronze of the Greeks - had produced some magnificent works of art. By "annealing", a whole range of physical changes were obtained, depending on whether cooling was sudden or slower. The qualities of the mixture were proportioned for each desired use, and appropriate hammering gave the objects their finish.

This could no longer be done for lack of tin, but not for lack of skilled workers. As a result, the skills of these master craftsmen had to be put to use without delay or they would be lost. Iron would provide the essential material for the rebirth. Yes, it was high time for Usir to set off on his last task to save the people.

Iset was waiting for her husband near the entrance to their house. Nek-Bet had informed her of the decision.

So she knew that once this expedition had departed, she would never again see the man she adored on this earth. But she understood the need that drove him, as well as the need to survive him long enough to help their son overcome the many difficulties that would inevitably arise.

It is true that Nut, although old, would help them to accomplish this immense task, but would they be enough? However, there was still An-Nu, who would take on the heaviest responsibilities, his wife being there to give him the necessary strength; she would assist him in choosing the spirits best suited to preserving the sacred texts in their memories, and then, when the time came, transmitting them in their entirety to the next legendary figures.

Seeing Iset like this, her husband realised that she knew where she stood on her plans. He took her tenderly in his arms and they remained there in silence, forehead to forehead, their souls one inside the other, saying to each other what their voices could not express aloud.

What followed was a rigorous fine-tuning of all the details of the expedition. Hor himself chose around forty of the strongest and most dedicated men to accompany his father. The most unusual request came from Nek-Bet, who asked her husband to allow their eldest son, Anepou, to assist the expedition leader. The An-Nu agreed without asking for an explanation, as this wish could only be justified for a vital reason, notwithstanding their son's youth.

Usir also gave in to his sister, having realised that the young man had a particularly sharp mind and, above all, a great memory. What he was doing already showed a deep personal art, and his whole person emanated a subtlety that amazed those who spoke to him. Even the enormous black-coated animal he had made his faithful companion, and which was so ferocious towards others, was devoted to him! There was no doubt that part of his mother's gifts inhabited and inspired him, and that he would bring the members of the expedition back without the risk of getting lost, if the leader was prevented from doing so.

This was vital to the progress of Ta Mana and its population, who were being joined by new survivors every day. The town was beginning to spread outside the perimeter wall, which posed a number of problems. But it was impossible to turn away the poor, exhausted people who came from further and further afield, having wandered for many days before hearing about the "Descendants" and the second homeland they advocated.

At first, some of the population followed the men's advance for a while. When they reached the mound of the sycamore tree, the spot where Sit had been routed by the unexpected appearance of his brother, they all came to a halt. The time had come to say goodbye, without any apparent sadness, and with the firm hope of meeting again in the other world for a longer period, if there was no possibility of seeing each other again here below.

Iset asked everyone present to turn back, as she wanted to be alone under the sycamore tree, watching the man who was her life slip away. The young Anepou motioned for the men to come forward and follow him, while the villagers silently returned to Ta Mana.

When the two groups had disappeared from the couple's sight, Usir clutched the woman who had been part of him. He didn't know what to say to her to complete this human role in which he had never been free. It was she who first broke the embrace and found the words that had to be spoken:

- May our common destiny that is coming to an end, O my beloved, be but a farewell! You are a part of me that is going away to do what God wants. So let it be done, but half my body will be missing until I join you. I'll stay here, under this sycamore tree, as long as our spirits are in communion. Go...

Without saying a word, Ousir joined Anepou and his dog, who were waiting for him below, behind a mound at the rear of the troop.

The enormous animal celebrated, as if it understood the need for a diversion from the arrival's sad thoughts. Having rejoined the group, the whole expedition set off towards its distant destination. It disappeared behind the hills, before entering the thick jungle, lush but slippery, hardly conducive to fast walking. Vines wrapped around most of the tree trunks had to be cut, deep water holes bypassed, climbs climbed and descents made no less perilous. Wild animals on all sides shouted their disapproval at seeing their domain disturbed in this way.

No longer sensing any scent from her husband, Iset let herself slide slowly to the ground, groaning. Nothing would hold her back once her mission was over...

As the days went by, progress slowed even more, and the appearance of the place no longer matched the descriptions of the landscapes Ousir had travelled through. It seemed that the "Great Cataclysm" had profoundly altered nature inland. The previous explorers who had trodden this terrain before them had not spoken of these deep, devastated stretches at the bottom of a deep gorge, but of a river rolling tumultuously through a lush valley.

Now, for several days, the men had been treading with difficulty in a hollow that had clearly been abandoned by the waters, but where the pebbles and rocks brought there by the raging liquid showed sharp and very dangerous breaks. Hundreds of fish lay in muddy holes, and thousands of others, gutted, were decomposing. There were also huge tree trunks, uprooted, shredded, with broken and sharp ends, proving that they had been mere pieces of straw in this unleashing of heavenly wrath.

Huge saurians suddenly emerged from their wooded hiding places, opening their jaws with frightening teeth. A gigantic snake even fled just as it was about to spring towards Anepou, saved in extremis by a furious yap from its faithful companion, thus avoiding irreparable harm!

From that moment on, the enormous beast, which everyone was a little afraid of without admitting it, became the mascot of the entire team. Alert, his eyes always alert, very lively despite the weight of his body, he was totally devoted to his young master. When his master spoke to him, he showed his understanding by beating his flanks briskly with his long tail; and his ears, pointed and erect, were attentive to the slightest desire expressed.

There were also hippopotamuses, wandering desperately in search of a watery element to suit them, which they so desperately lacked. They were heading inland, where all they had to do was die. Finally, there were the elephants, gigantic and hairy, peaceful and majestic, eating the young shoots growing everywhere in the detritus left by the receding waters. If they disdained the men who passed by - far enough away from the pachyderms all the same - they grazed with such obvious pleasure that they let out enormous barks to the crowd. Their great spiral tusks then rose into the air, as did their trunks, which continued to shovel food onto their large molars.

The group finally reached the entrance to a vast green plain, where palm trees and plants of all kinds grew in abundance. In the background, the outline of a large mountain range with snow-capped peaks blocked the horizon. This landscape reminded Ousir of a typical description, and it was towards this site that the group set off.

More exhausting days were spent climbing the first slopes, which became steeper and steeper, and above all in an atmosphere that was becoming much colder. Fortunately, before reaching the first snows, the group found a passage between two mountains with almost vertical walls which, from a distance, appeared to be a single block. Had he not known of its existence from those who had gone before him, the expedition leader would never have been able to continue the journey. Shortly before descending the other side, the men crossed a path clearly trodden by humans. Ousir realised that this path must lead to the copper deposits in one way or another. Resisting the urge to change his objective, he led his men up the slope towards the 'iron road' - the physical aspect of the terrain changed completely. As the descent became steeper, the air became stifling. And what had looked like a sea from above turned into a sandy expanse. The closer they got, the more it resembled the bottom of a parched sea.

Imposing cliffs lined what had once been a very wide river estuary, at the centre of which the group had arrived. They all walked painfully across the powdery sand, topped by numerous dunes of varying heights, islands in the arid mouth, beaten not by the waves of a vanished ocean, but by a hot wind.

Deposits of marine shells not yet fossilised, crushed by the feet of the walkers, confirmed the hallucinating appearance of a sea emptied of its contents. As they approached the cliffs, they were able to contemplate at their leisure the incisions made by the receding water on the geological layers. The place had become so barren that it no longer had the landmarks suggested by the first explorers. Ousir knew that the time had come to use Anepou's agility to climb this vertical wall without too much trouble.

This was a welcome break, as they were all exhausted. They took the opportunity to follow the young man's slow progress with interest. The dog himself, sitting firmly on his hindquarters, head raised and ears perked up, stared at the silhouette as it shrank in size. He stuck out his tongue longer and longer, whimpering softly at times when Anepou remained invisible behind a crevice. Suddenly, he swallowed his saliva as he stuck out his tongue and stood up to trot towards the wall, which was impassable for him: Anepou had disappeared after reaching the summit!

Relentlessly, the sun sailed towards the west, flooding them with light and passing the zenith before the men saw a bright spot rising from the top of the wall and falling back down again. The dog barked louder and louder until Anepou touched the sand. The daylight was half disappearing towards the domain of the Blessed when all the members of the expedition finished congratulating each other. His story was short and rather disappointing:

- There's nothing interesting up there! Not a tree, rare grasses, nobody! Hills like here, with nothing on them; and in the distance, there are high mountains more towards where the sun rises.

- What did you see on the plain below?

- Looking over here, on the side of that hand, there was nothing but sand all by itself, meeting the sky on the horizon. Further east, there are high mountains, but in front of them there is a great white expanse. How could there be snow on the sand, on the plain? It's impossible in this heat! Am I hallucinating? Tell me, O you who know everything?

Like all his companions, Ousir smiled at this naivety, which was strongly counterbalanced by the young man's intelligence and gift for observation.

- What you understand, and what I understand, O Anepou, is that it's not about snow. What else is there?

In this heat, the water that evaporated left its salt, all white...

- So it's just salt?

- We'll have to wait and see, because this is precisely the landmark on our route. Let's eat before it gets completely dark, and get some sleep. Tomorrow will be a hard day.

Anepou, who seemed inexhaustible, added between mouthfuls:

- Even further east than the mountains is a green expanse. Here there will be water and food.

- Remember the place well, because those you accompany later on will probably prefer to camp there. Your mother should be proud of you. It's true that you're destined to become the most feared man in every generation... Let's get some sleep!

They stretched out quickly to catch the last rays of the sun, and young Anepou buried his nose in the fur of his dog's neck, but kept his eyes open to try and understand Ousir's prophetic words. Still not understanding, he gazed at the milky celestial light, which formed an enormous sparkling river, the Hapy. It was extraordinary...

Seeing that his young companion was not asleep, Usir whispered to him:

- Why don't you close your eyes, young dreamer?

- All those flashing lights attract me.

And yet they seem so far away! I just don understand it. There are so many inexplicable things!

- Less than you think, because they all concern the march of time, as interpreted by our "Masters of Measurement" to the pettiness of human understanding. You will go beyond this stage, O Anepou, and you will become the intermediary of divine decrees, the intermediary between death and eternal life.

- You were talking like that just now, O most revered of all!

- Because your father will teach you your future; you mustn't walk faster than the Sun. Tell me you saw in the holes in the cliff.

Caught off guard, the young boy bit his lip.

- I was going to tell you tomorrow. Where the rock is scorched by the sun, there are many openings carved out by waters. They continue far into the interior; what an ideal place to store food, or to sleep in peace!

- Certainly, but how can they be reached by someone who isn't as agile as you? But don't forget the place, it might come in handy later. Now stop dreaming and go to sleep!

With a sigh of relief, Anepou buried his nose in the black fur again; the dog wagged his tail against the sand, no doubt approving of the silence that had settled in. The air was gradually cooling, numbing the spirits for the night.

The following evening, the group arrived on site.

The apocalyptic site seemed to have emerged from another world. Even the mountains, literally shattered, showed that not so long ago, the glaciers had suddenly liquefied.

Everything else looked charred: the trees had lost their foliage, the withered grasses were skeletal and the pebbles blackish. But some of them had a peculiar shape, made of several agglomerates welded together and rounded, weighing a great deal.

The first pieces of pure native iron appeared. All you had to do was bend down and pick them up. Another day, and the troop arrived at the very site of the original source: two faults that cut into the ground, barely concealing huge veins of mineralised iron. Compact masses of quartz covered the vertical walls giving access to the bottom, providing a rapid means of obtaining fearsome, highly resistant cutting tools with little effort.

While the men were happily taking remarkable samples, Usir resolved to explore this desolate landscape further, in search of new riches. As Anepou and his dog were exploring some caves, he set off alone, following the bottom of a small, winding gorge... towards his destiny!

Lost in his thoughts, he walked away without really realising how much time had passed. Sadness came over him far too late, after he had admitted that there was nothing of interest to justify his trip; he realised then that his life as a man would come to an end in these parts. Panic gripped him, instilling him with a very human fear. He stopped, but it was already too late to deepen the meditations that were rising in his soul. A voice with a wild, triumphant accent rose above him:

- You dare to disturb my territory, you hated enemy of the Sun! But here you are, alone at my mercy. Ra is with me, and may the luminous be thanked for it! You and your god no longer exist, for you are at my mercy.

Without raising his head towards the man who would become his executioner for a second time, Usir resumed his walk slowly. But the time had come and the work for which he had been born was finished.

Sit, who was accompanied by around twenty Rebels on this long-distance exploration of the place where his clan was established, further north, was furious to see his brother so calm. He shouted, raising his arms:

- Take a good look at him, all of you! His false god will not save him this time. The dazzling disc that crosses the sky will be my witness! As the creator of life, the Sun will justify Usir's death... You hear me, son of no-one, I'm going to kill you...

Again, the Elder stopped, his feet sure on the stones. At last he raised his head and replied in a slow voice:

- Yes, you are going to kill me, but only because God has decided to do so. It is he who is arming your arm, to prove to the world of our descendants that you are indeed the unfaithful son of the one true God, Ptah.

From the top of his mound, Sit shuddered at this supreme insult. Furious, he snatched the long spear from the hands of a nearby Rebel, shouting:

- I am only the son of the Sun! You are not my brother, and you will all die!

- You are very much mistaken, for you will be defeated after my death. You will not reign for long over any of the territories my people occupy, unless you once again fear the one true God, Ptah.

- It's not going to happen! And here's the proof...

Standing on one foot, Sit threw the spear with fierce energy, which pierced Ousir's chest through and through, knocking him down as the tip of the spear sank into the earth. A howl escaped from the victor's chest; he danced on the spot with pleasure before the astonished and somewhat panicked eyes of his warriors. When he could speak, his joy burst forth:

- OUSIR IS DEAD! He's dead for sure this time, and no spell will bring him back to life! O Ra! be glorified by this victory!

The grandiloquent phrases might have continued, but several voices calling for the one who had just been killed and a terrible bark echoing off the walls made it seem as if an army was about to arrive. Everyone was routed, and Sit in the lead, the Rebels sped off towards their camp without asking for a second thought.

Usir was left alone, stretched out and pierced.

The dog was the first to reach the body, licking its face and moaning. His young master was soon there, followed by those who had accompanied him in the search. They fell to their knees in disbelief. Anepou, however, saw that Ousir was still breathing faintly. Imperatively, he ordered silence. Everyone then heard the sound of forge bellows, the antechamber of death. Suddenly opening his eyelids, the dying man saw the dismayed face of his young companion leaning towards him. With difficulty, he said:

- *Let no one... be sad... I am leaving... to join... the Blessed. Only one thing... Anepou...*

- Speak up! O speak, you who are our only Guide! I will obey you in all things.

- *May my Home... be in the place... where the iron is!... The Elder will watch over... all the Cadets... through the centuries... for...* O GOD I COME BACK TO YOU!...

With this final sentence, uttered in a triumphant voice, Usir exhaled. The whistling had stopped. The head fell back on its left side... it was over. But Ousir in his "Abode" survived in Ta Ouz.[38]

---

[38] On today's map of Morocco, it is easy to reconstruct exactly the route taken by this expedition. The starting point, Ta Mana, is still a village 100 km north of Agadir; and Ta Ouz is still an Algerian-Moroccan border post, further south, at the entrance to the desert. Here, iron mines abound, as do the pure minerals derived from them: siderite, magnetite, gœthite, haematite, etc. All along the way, the road is dotted with prehistoric remains and rock engravings. At Ta Ouz itself, there are funerary monuments "from the most remote antiquity", many of which have yet to be catalogued. The Sit clan, meanwhile, had settled much further north in Morocco, then in Figuig, also on the border. The rock drawings are of a different

Chapter Nine

THE GREAT MOURNING

> *I opened the path of the Second Heart to the children of Nut by freeing them from Sit's grip.*
> *But the Rebel has returned with sacrilegious words to deliver the solar boat to the lion. And the stars are ablaze with anger! Who will win this battle of the Two Brothers? Ptah-Hor or Sit-Râ?... And the Great Mourning will come!*
>
> THE BOOK OF THE DEAD
> (To access the "Second Heart" - Chap. CX)

> *Mr Flamand likened the spheroid rams to the Egyptian Amon-Ra, because there is a definite kinship with the engraved figures from the Sahara. But Amon is also the ram-god of water throughout Berberia, where the Berber word for water is "amon", as it is among the Guanches of the Canaries.*
>
> RAYMOND FURON
> (Handbook of general prehistory)

Many centuries passed between the time when the pyramid-shaped tomb destined for Uzir was built by the pioneers of the iron caravan at the place that became Ta Ouz, and the time when the Exodus began, with its exhausting crossing of the interminable soil, which very soon became known as *Sâ-Ahâ-Râ* or "Land scorched by the Sun". But from the day of the burial, the whole period was known as the *Great Mourning*. This lasted for more than five millennia,

---

kind. On the Col de Zénaga (overlooking Figuig), a splendid engraving depicts a ram whose head is surmounted by a solar globe, the emblem of the Ra-Sit-Ou. (The first photo of this creation appeared on Plate IX of E.F. Gautier's *Le Passé de l'Afrique du Nord*). As for the copper mines in the mountains, these are at Midelt, still in operation, at an altitude of 1,500 metres in the Atlas mountains, which can only be reached via the Zad pass, which is snowed in for six months of the year, as it peaks at 2,170 metres.

ending only with the reintroduction of the calendar and hieroglyphics.

But from the start of his reign, Hor's impetus to promote iron mining at the sacred site of Ta Ouz helped to overcome the immense grief of all the survivors. This is why a large part of the population agreed to help Usir's son with the various mining operations, working under the protection of the burial mound that sheltered the Elder.

From then on, a fierce determination drove these first miners and the blacksmiths who skilfully assisted them, so that the first ingots of ore could be quickly smelted. Evidence of the activity that took place here can still be seen today in the remains of some twenty primitive furnaces, the antiquity of which no-one doubts. The slag still scattered around gives an exact idea of the archaic processing methods that were used.

As for the House-of-Life opened to ensure the 'Conservation-of-Traditions', it remained located in Ta Mana during this long period when the first dynasty of 'Heroes' reigned. The management of this Divine College was obviously left to the good and enlightened care of successive AnNu. The first in title was Anepou, who replaced his father when the latter was recalled to the "Beyond Life". Under his impetus, the various 'mental apprenticeship' courses took off and continued to expand right up to the arrival in the second Homeland.

The village retained its early importance thanks to the influx of people who continued to arrive, more than compensating for the technical departures to Ta Ouz. The title of great spiritual centre remained with the village for more than a thousand years, with families who had one or more children in the oral teaching classes staying on until these offspring had themselves grown up to provide a new generation of children for the School. During this time, the parents helped to improve the techniques of the various factories.

During the same period, the "Sit Rebels", who had abandoned their first base camp after the assassination of Ousir, had followed the course of a river up towards the peaks that rose further to the east.

An ebony tablet found at Abydos, dating from before the 1st dynasty. It is the earliest known example of hieroglyphs, dating from the fifth millennium BC. At top left, the royal pennant of Horus and then the emblem of Net-Bet (Nephthys). The second row shows Osiris in the form of a bull; the third shows the boats during the cataclysm; and the fourth, at the bottom, which is actually the start of the reading, shows the new solar start in the constellation Leo.

They reached the spring at an altitude of around 800 metres, where the temperature was mild.

But in this region, food was less easy to catch; only big game abounded, but wild animals were not easy to kill with the meagre means available to hunters. With the onset of winter, an icy north wind swept down from the peaks and chased these nomadic humans even further east.

One evening, they reached the first foothills of the Grand Erg Occidental, which appeared to them like an impassable wall. They stopped at a well-sheltered escarpment above the present-day Algerian town of Ta Ghit, at the very spot where a number of solar-type rock engravings dominate. This is the famous mound known as the Grande Dune, an exceptional panoramic site that is very popular with tourists these days. Everyone can also see that the all-round surveillance avoided any unpleasant surprises in the event of an attack.

But here again, the contrast between the cold nights and the torrid days led them to look for more clement living quarters. They abandoned this eagle's nest and, skirting the Grand Erg in short stages, headed due north around the mountain range. One day, they came to a green plain, pleasant with its natural orchard, and they settled there. They aptly named it *Méri-Râ,* or "Beloved Sun", a place which is still called Méri-Râ at today, and which lies on the road from Colomb-Béchar to Figuig.

If spring justified their hopes and allowed them to build up herds of buffalo and gazelle, the arrival of summer was a call for a fresh start for most of the men, who were more used to fighting than to domestic tasks. So when the Sun shone the calorific power of its rays on the burnt skins, it became a categorical sign willed by Ra, as Sit decreed.

But while most of them complied with this imperative order, some decided to stay behind with their herds, who would not put up with travelling like this, especially in the mountains the clan were about to cross. The chief's anger was terrible, but he soon realised that if he insisted, his authority would be flouted and further defections were likely. So he ordered the families who were settling permanently to look after the animals that would provide food for the whole tribe in the future.

Over the course of a hard day's march, the horde of Rebels had climbed an interminable defile up to a seemingly inaccessible summit, between two vertical walls that let the scorching sun shine through. Their feet, cut by the sharp protrusions of the stones and scorched by their high temperature, struggled to rest on the unglamorous ground in the late afternoon.

The procession, rather gloomy and silent, was getting longer and longer, when the vanguard saw, in a dazzlingly clear gap, a plain where plants and trees were growing. Without worrying about the large boulders scattered here and there and the gigantic rocky spurs overlooking this high valley, everyone rushed in, quickly discovering natural cavities where it was possible to shelter for the night.

This is the present-day Zénaga pass, guarding the road down to Figuig, the easternmost Algerian-Moroccan border post. From this particularly peaceful high point, the fighting temperament of the arrivals gave way to utilitarian planning.

Some of the Rebels built huts of branches and foliage, not very solid but well sheltered in the shade of the rocky overhangs. Others converted the caves. Sit arranged his cave so that his companion could give birth to their first child. For this reason, the halt in this quiet place was most welcome. Ra was thanked by all in front of these primitive graphic representations. For while some people hunted to ensure food for all, or roughly cut the skins of killed animals to make robes, others spent their leisure time "telling", on stone, the story of the clan and the worship they paid to the Sun.

These narrators of a very remote age possessed only crude flint tools. And this marked the essential difference between the works engraved by them and those of the "Followers of Hor", apart from the representation of adoration before the solar globe of the ideas expressed by the "Rebels of Sit".

This did not prevent the designers of the Zénaga Pass from obeying the laws of a tried and tested technique. First of all, they sketched the whole of what they wanted to treat with a simple, light line, using an initial stone punch cut to a point. Even today, it is easy to recognise in places the apparent traces of the perspective corrections made to the relationship between the masses.

Once the drawing was complete, the motifs were engraved more deeply into the local sandstone, which was fairly friable, using a tool made from a harder stone with a wider head. The lines reproduced showed a consummate art of engraving, often even being polished with extreme care, so as to offer posterity a perfect whole.

So, in these beings who were once again, by force of circumstance, semi-savage humans, reminiscences of their deceased past prevented them from sinking by giving them the old ideas they needed to make up for the lack of metal tools. There is no doubt that some of these Rebels were once elite craftsmen and gifted artists. They undeniably showed that they possessed the working methods of their ancient predecessors, at least as far as engraving was concerned.

As for the works of a more sacred nature, they were drawn with a more patient care, demonstrating a need to succeed in transmitting through them the thought that animated these worshippers of the Sun. After 10000 years, there can be no doubt that the attempt to understand the civilised minds that stopped there is complete. It is highly likely that future generations, who visit these places even later, will contemplate the images and immediately give a name to these hymns declaimed to the Sun darting its rays like so many fluids fertilising the seeds of all nature. Every day, thanks to Ra, new nourishing plants were born, just as edible as the animals of all kinds that enabled everyone to eat abundantly.

Their way of life, however, was the opposite of that of Hor's Followers, and time, which continued inexorably to advance into eternity for both clans, constantly widened the gap between them. For the Beyond, for example, Sit had decreed once and for all that, since the Sun was the creator of all things, human beings, after death, would be reborn in another form as desired by the star of the day, which itself took on new life each morning.

At Hor, the ancestral beliefs strongly anchored by the diluvian reality had been strengthened under the impetus of Anepou, the new An-Nu. Man left the Earth only to return to the Ancestors he had left only momentarily, to complete his very short time on earth. For this reason, funerary sites were built in particularly well-chosen locations to facilitate an excellent return of the souls to the territory of the Blessed Ones, on the western horizon, where Ahâ-Men-Ptah had been engulfed. Hence, on the one hand, the name Amenta, phonetised by the hieroglyphs to denote the "Kingdom of the Dead" and, on the other, the name of the funerary antechambers, the *Akh-Menu,* which are the places where "the souls partnercoucher-in-the-water", in Amenta, the Sunken Land where the Blessed Ancestors rest.

One of these valleys of the dead lay to the west of Ta Mana, almost on the edge of the sea, in a huge hollow bordered by dunes. Another, far more important, was the valley where Usir lay. It was under the western hill of Ta Ouz, which became the blessed place where the souls of the demigods of the first dynasty of Heroes who succeeded Hor as PêrAhâ, as well as the various Pontiffs, passed through. Nut, Iset and Nek-Bet found there the rest they longed for after their busy human lives.

Even today, visitors to Ta Ouz, walking along the path that winds between the iron flows, treading the mineralised masses of haematite before reaching the rust-coloured western hills, have the impression of entering the antechamber that gives access to another world. From the moment he arrives, he is clearly gripped by an anguish that is as intangible as it is indescribable. For anyone who has never been there, in southern Morocco lost in the Sahara, this vision of conical peaks at sunset means very little. You need to have seen for yourself the hallucinatory, bloodstained hues that slowly undulate to the rhythm of the arid rotundities, where the human eye has nothing to hold on to, no concrete obstacle holding it back, to understand that humans are already entering a parallel universe.

Anepou, who became An-Nu, contributed greatly to developing this tangible notion of another world, which made all those preparing to go to the "Beyond Life" extremely sensitive. Despite the limited means at his disposal, the Pontiff re-established the theatrical aspect of the ceremonies, making the funerals more solemn with maximum pomp. Souls once again felt the need to keep their fleshly bodies after death, so that they could return to Earth from time to time.

What's more, having replaced his huge black dog, which had died of old age, with another animal that was much younger but looked like one drop of water to another, the supernatural power attributed to him to communicate with the Amenta was strengthened, and the popular belief that he had the power of life and death in the afterlife took root in everyone's minds, to such an extent that mythology seized on him to make him the guardian of Ahâ-Men-Ptah and the "soul-weighing" avenger.

This halo, which he had certainly not sought during his lifetime, nor when he took up his duties as Pontiff, nevertheless prompted him to take advantage of the fear he inspired to look into the problem of preserving the bodies whose recipe could not be saved from the Great Cataclysm.

He did, however, know the main components, but the many trials and errors of these various attempts had not produced the expected result. This serious problem, vital for the complete renovation of the theology of the ancestors of Ahâ-Men-Ptah, developing the survival of souls thanks to bodies in perfect condition, preserved in their entirety, and through which they could reintroduce themselves to the Earth without any difficulty, haunted the sleepless nights of An-Nu.

Shortly before his own death, he finished perfecting an embalming formula that he considered effective and similar to that used by the ancients throughout history. Feeling that his end was near, he decided to teach it to his Elder, who would himself become the next Pontiff, so that the blood of his own flesh would preserve his body for a future return. When the day came, the new AnNu was blessed under the particularly evocative name of *Ptah-Her-Anepou*, the hieroglyph *Her* being that which inspires fear.

As events unfolded, this appellation proved to be more and more accurate, and hardly anyone approached him again without being struck by an intense fear. Shortly after his election as head of the College of Priests, his father died. The young new Pontiff decided, for the first time since the "Great Cataclysm" had swallowed up all life and all the Divine sciences in AhâMen-Ptah, to reintroduce the embalming of corpses as Anepou had taught him.

And for the seventy-two days and nights that the various operations of cleaning the flesh, and then the conservation itself, lasted, an overflowing activity, but singular, agitated the area of the funerary site specially set up for this purpose.

Although he worked day and night, in the midst of particularly nauseating smells that none of his helpers could stand for more than six days, he managed to complete his task by constantly reminding himself of the information his father had given him. It seemed to him that Anepou was all around him, telling him at every moment what he should do... Beyond death, the revered voice supported him in his efforts:

- You see, my son, the dead do not die! You closed my eyes and brought my body to this laboratory, but now you know that my living soul is with you, ready to take on any form you wish, to support you in your task. My spirit will sail constantly on the boat that sails in the celestial Hapy, watching for the slightest of your calls... You will also take extreme care to methodically follow the embalming method I have taught you, because I now know that the formula I taught you is the right one... Don't change any of the ingredients... Don't omit any of the quantities I've given you...

Ptah-Her-Anepou, bare-chested and exhausted, left alone in the middle of the firebrick vats full of different liquids boiling thickly and giving off an unspeakable stench, stood up above the mixture which he was slowly stirring. His eyes were feverish and his face drawn with fatigue, but he managed to smile as he mopped his brow with a greyish cloth that looked as if it had been used a lot. He let it fall to the sodden ground with a heart-rending sigh. He didn't want to admit defeat despite his physical exhaustion. It had been fourteen days since his last helper left him after fainting for the second time in an hour. Twenty-two nights in a row he had been watching over all the vats, and he would have to hold out for another *fifty* sunsets!

All her ingredients were ready, and the hardest part of the preparation was over. For forty-two hours, Anepou's carnal envelope had been sunk to the bottom of a nearby vat, simmering in a composite bath of various juices, the main one extracted from the trunk of a terebinth tree. This solution was intended to dissolve the unwanted fatty substances remaining in the skin itself, which had to be removed before the next operation. This would consist of immersing the body in a soft, sticky pitch mixture made from resin and various vegetable tars, which would block all the pores in the skin, making it perfectly smooth under a dark colour. Because all the openings in the human flesh had to be completely closed, but without any decomposition of the tissue of the carnal envelope, either during the treatment or afterwards, until the end of Time.

As soon as Anepou had finished instructing his son, he began to go over hill and dale, with a host of helpers and hunters, to find the places where the plants grew and where the essences, juices and ferments needed to prepare the various baths for successful embalming could be found.

The bitumen was easy to spot, being solid in its natural state and of an easily identifiable brown-black colour. As it burned rapidly, giving off a very thick smoke with a strong, penetrating odour, there was no doubt as to its identity after the first test burn.

The ammonia compound was the last missing element. It was the most difficult to find, as it had to be found a long way away. Nevertheless, it was vital for the manufacture of the main organic element that required the use of potash. It took over a month of searching in all directions before it was found in very large quantities almost on the edge of the march, twenty days' walk south of Ta Mana.

These nitrogenous substances, decomposed under the influence certain very powerful ferments, had provided, through the liquid that flowed from them, the nitre or potassium nitrate, vital in this formula for preserving the human body. And in this funereal workshop, apart from the bubbling of the liquids, there was not a sound to disturb the solitude of the son who revered his father and prayed to God with all his soul that his devotion on this occasion would be crowned with success. He knew that outside, at , stonemasons were making a tomb, as sumptuously as possible with the meagre means available on site; others were completing the braiding of the bands needed to hold the various parts of the body together, while blacksmiths and goldsmiths were hammering and chiselling jewels and amulets intended to attract all the blessings of heaven to the soul of the deceased Pontiff. Ptah-Her-Anepou also knew that all this would be in vain if he did not carry out the task set for him by his father. But the much-loved "Voice" spoke to him again:

- Never despair, my son! I'm here to help you. Never forget that although you are not a direct "descendant" of God, you are one of his beloved children, a member of a noble and very ancient family. You are now the undisputed Pontiff of the House of Ta Mana, where no one questions your authority or your wisdom. Your influence is spreading, and even the revered Master Kai-Our is seeking your advice and arbitration... Keep up your invincible courage, for you are not yet at the end of your tether , O my valiant son! Never again let any fear touch you about your abilities, for it is you who must inspire fear!

The young Pontiff heaved a sigh and went back to the vat to slowly mix the solid elements that would gradually melt. He no longer felt his fatigue, taking his work as it came and as it had to be done. On the sixtieth day, he came out of his retreat for the first time to pick up the strips and return to begin the slow clamping and soaking operations, which were to be carried out six times, one on top of the other, in forty-eight hours each time. And so the seventy-second day arrived. An-Nu could finally breathe: the success was complete.

Later, Ptah-Her-Anepou made his mark by calculating the exact date for the start of the "March towards the Light", towards this "Second Heart-of-God", this distant promised land that would become the second homeland, AthKa-Ptah. The Pontiff had calculated the best "Divine-Mathematical-Combinations", banking on the new *retrograde* navigation of the Sun.

This confirmed that the period of restructuring of the reborn buds of the population would not come to an end before the Sun itself emerged from the constellation of Leo, to enter in *reverse* the constellation which, for two thousand years, would watch over a particularly harassing exodus. This era, which would be extremely difficult for all living organisms to endure, would involve walking through a land *eaten away by* the torrid rays of a merciless daytime star, *scorched* by the terrible evil of interminable drought.

However, everyone had to make the best of the particularly treacherous nature of the terrain to be crossed. To this end, the Pontiff devised all sorts of preventive and protective measures that would become beneficial conjurations addressed to God by his faithful. This constellation would later take the name of its medical namesake, Cancer.

For the time being, then, Her-Anepou asserted that the solar precessional recession in Leo did not favour a mass departure to the promised land for the "Descendants of Hor", and that it would be best to make do with the hospitality offered by Ta Mana, which was not without its charms. The appearance of the "Divine-Mathematical Combinations" demonstrated - and the Pontiff did not hesitate to prove it to the Council, which listened attentively to what he had to say - that God was giving his rediscovered children this respite, so that they could secure Cadets capable of restoring popular unity in the midst of rediscovered greatness.

In any case, this would allow the mining research teams to try and find the twelve beneficial stones in the subsoil of this place, which every new-born child carried from the moment they arrived in the world of the living. All hopes were pinned on this, since jasper had been discovered and a rare mineral, orichalcum, had been found in a copper vein not far from present-day Midelt.

Several centuries passed in this way, the fever that gripped all the inhabitants as the great departure approached. The successive improvements made to living conditions were innumerable, as the means of production were greatly developed.

When the 'Descendants of the Eldest' were in their forty-second Pêr-Ahâ, just a decade before the time of Departure, the reigning An-Nu, whom his father had rightly called *Anepou-Hotep*, 'the Peaceful One', made a revolutionary proposal at an inaugural meeting of the Grand Council.

In the space of a thousand years, this learned assembly had regained its honourable position, but without the luxurious surroundings it possessed in Ahâ-Men-Ptah. The Pontiff proposed the institution of a talisman for each new 'Master' enthroned after the start of the new year of Sep'ti, the modern Sirius, which this time would coincide with the conjunction of the Sun entering the new constellation in reverse.

Given the countless difficulties that would constantly arise under the feet of the emigrants, their Guide, the venerated Pêr-Ahâ, had to be protected against all the evil influences he might encounter and thwart them for the benefit of his beloved people, his Cadets.

The talisman would therefore be the beneficial link that would unite his earthly actions with the heavenly harmony combined by God. What object could be more appropriate *than a lion's tail?* It would encircle the waist of each new 'Descendant' on all occasions, giving him or her dominion of heaven, which would enable him or her to dominate all actions on Earth. The end of the hairy appendage would touch the ground, so that the wearer would live as long as possible. The project was adopted unanimously, and a religious ceremony celebrated the award of this leonine belt to its first beneficiary, who was enthroned a few years later, shortly before the Great Departure, under the divine name of "Ahâ", which he took up again for the occasion, because he was the first in this long exodus towards this distant Light that polarised all hopes.

But in the years that preceded, the "Followers of Hor" developed the art of rock engraving, in order to leave visible traces of their new lives as children of God. This is why the graphic representations of Ta Ouz differ so greatly from those of their "colleagues" from the Zénaga Pass. The human images are clad in the famous lion skins, which became the protectors of God's chosen race against the solar fury unleashed during the Great Cataclysm. It was also a way of warding off the evil spell cast by the 'Rebels of Sit', who idolised this same sun in defiance of all Divine warnings, careless of the fact that they were bringing far greater misfortune on all humanity than had previously been the case.

The two clans, which were as far apart spiritually as they were in everyday life, ended up clashing in a mythical hatred as soon as Sit died. Of his three children, the two sons successively took power and held it tyrannically. The survival of the group was assured, as all the members closed ranks, but the hatred grew, fuelled by intense jealousy.

There had been a few instances of mixing of the sexes, however, with the Rebels taking over some of the 'Hor's Followers' outposts and seizing women and children as well as supplies and tools. There had been several bloody battles between the camps, during which the Rebels, who were more battle-hardened, had suffered the fewest casualties, taking what they could in their hasty retreat.

As they prepared to leave, Hor's Followers were deprived of valuable reserves, as well as the companions and children they cherished. To prevent similar barbaric acts in the future, the miners and blacksmiths joined forces to form a retaliatory fighting unit. But the Rebels, having appreciated the good things they no longer possessed, especially metals and fabrics, forged weapons from the stolen ore and decided to move in and plunder Ta Ouz completely!

However, the first great battle between the two giants did not go quite as the "Ra-Sit-Ou" had planned. They had not been aware the creation of a warrior corps animated specifically by the blacksmiths who, for the occasion, became spearmen. In other words, the metalworkers, the "Astiou", became the defenders, the "Masniou", those famous warriors attached to the very person of the Pêr-Ahâ on the banks of the Nile or "Manistiou", a word that is the contraction of the two terms dedicated to the defenders of civilisation against the "Rebels of Sit", several millennia earlier...

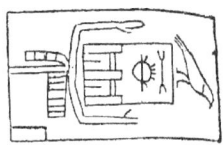

Chapter Ten

"THE BLACKSMITHS OF HORUS"
(The masnitiou-hor)

> *Horus' bellicose nature provides ample justification for surrounding himself with an army of blacksmiths and metalworkers. Horus uses the blade and the javelin against all his enemies. He loads them with chains, not ropes. The texts also specify that the metal used is iron!*
>
> G. Maspero
> (The Blacksmiths of Horus)

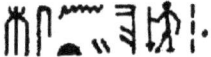

> *Gezer is taken! Yenoam is rendered non-existent! Israel is nothing but a desert where her race is no more. Palestine has become a widow for Egypt! All the countries are reduced to impotence, pacified by the Blacksmiths of "Mêr-NéPtah!"*
>
> J.H. Breasted
> (Old Records of Egypt)

The reigning Pêr-Ahâ, Hor-Ou-Tit, who would soon be giving the order to leave for the "Second Heart", made his way to the room where the Great Council was being held. The Assembly was meeting to decide on the action to be taken to safeguard all human life in Ta Mana from now on.

The administrative building he had just entered had been built some forty years ago and was beginning to show cracks. Nevertheless, the rooms remained spacious. The one reserved for the Council was far from resembling that of Ahâ-Men-Ptah, where the venerable elected Ancestors sat in armchairs covered in thick purple or mauve linen, depending on the rank of the dignitaries with the "Master", or his Pontiff.

Was the reality experienced by these heroic forefathers any less beautiful than the epic tales peddled on school benches by the teachers of this generation of students? Who could tell how many successive additives had improved certain living conditions that had become fabulous? The new minds, focused on today's realities, left aside the past. It was very difficult, given the state of primitive knowledge that had only been transmitted orally, to discard the false and retain only the true.

The meeting would begin as soon as the Pêr-Ahâ crossed the threshold of the deliberation room. The solemnity of the meetings had been restored with the means available, but this restoration was far from reminiscent of the splendours of yesteryear. In any case, Hor-Ou-Tit hoped it would be the last before everyone left Ta-Mana. Life there had been quiet and prosperous, and if the 'Rebels' hadn't been so virulent during their last assault, he might have yielded to certain pressures from the new bourgeois milieu that had grown up, and which was urging him to postpone the departure for the Long March. According to the most influential members of this group, there was no doubt that the land promised by successive pontiffs on behalf of God was too hazardous in its very definition to risk the global displacement of thousands and thousands of men, women and children.

By a disturbing coincidence, the revolting intrusion of Sit's men into this peaceful village had brought the present reality home to him. The Eternal One, through these innocent expiatory victims emanating from the very blood of his Cadets, was ordering without any possible discussion that the march towards the Light should begin on the appointed day. And this date was formally foreseen by the College of "Contemplators of the Stars", who were constantly carrying out the evolutionary calculations of the "Celestial Mathematical Combinations".

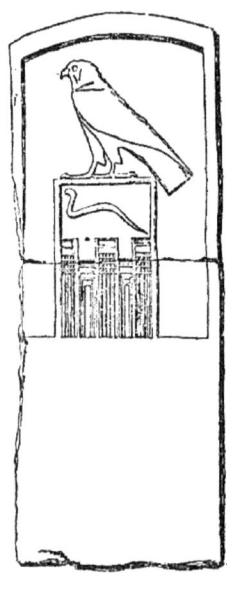

The first known emblem bearing the symbol of Horus, who dominates thanks his blacksmiths.

All that remained to be done was to find the best way to get the process without further loss of life. This is what the Extraordinary Council would have to discuss to find the best solution. He, the undisputed Pêr-Ahâ, would be in charge of getting the result! Even if it meant shaking them up as much as necessary...

At this precise moment in his personal reflections, the direct "descendant" of Usir from such a distant first generation arrived at the door of the Hall reserved for debates, which a guard hastened to open by pushing back the heavy mahogany door. Straightening his tall stature even further, the Pêr-Ahâ entered with a resolute step, taking in the full, beehive-like room with a quick, keen eye. The lively hubbub of conversation died down as soon as he appeared.

The Members of the Council rose in greeting, and a respectful silence ensued. The Pontiff, who had approached, bowed with great deference to the Elder Son of Ptah, before beckoning to the Member who was Head of Protocol to lead them both to their seats.

One of the two was covered with several layers soft skins, and the other was simply made of wood covered with a simple white cloth. When they arrived, a third figure, seated nearby, stood up. It was an imposing-looking old man, the Leader of the Honourable Assembly.

When the three most eminent men of Ta Mana had congratulated each other, they sat down and whispered the agenda to each other. The honourable delegates took the opportunity to sit back down with a sigh of relief, in anticipation of the opening of the debates, which threatened to be lively in view of the events.

With an emphatic and protective gesture, Hor-Ou-Tit indicated that he was going to speak. The murmurs ceased as he rose to his feet. His long diatribe displayed a highly diplomatic tone, returning to that of the old fashion:

- Venerable Councillors of Ta-Mana! We appreciate the great honour you have done us by coming to our request for an extraordinary session. Life, Health and Happiness to all of you, who are here to comfort and encourage me! You will undoubtedly continue to support me in the same way in the very difficult and thankless task that awaits me in this period of the Great Departure. Before we close this meeting, we must find a valid solution to the problem of the Rebels, those infamous "Ra-SitOu" who have wreaked such havoc on our families! Our venerated Pontiff will speak first, so that the point of view of the College of Priests is not overlooked. Then the venerable All-Ankh-Hotep, President of the honourable Assembly of which you are the representative Members, will speak on behalf of you all, in order to save time. Finally, before deliberating on the course of action to be taken and the means to be employed to implement it, we shall hear from the Head of the noble guild of blacksmiths, who has expressly asked us to make here a communication of the utmost importance, emanating from all their mouths combined. We accepted with deep gratitude that such an eminent member of the guild most vital to the advancement of our civilisation should come and speak in our midst, despite the unexpected nature of this request. But the exceptional situation in which we find ourselves can only be overcome by extraordinary means. We will not forget what we have owed for a thousand years to all the founders, the chisellers, the engravers, all those members of the blacksmiths' guild, all those "*masniou*" who have done so much for the recovery of Ta Mana! After listening to Mâsh-Akher, their noble President, we will decide what needs to be done to ensure that our departure is not called into question. We'll all have to leave on the day predicted by the "Divine-Mathematical Combinations" in order to benefit from the most favourable celestial omens. And that's it! I have finished with my Just Words; may Ptah deign to accept them in the shaping of his daily work[39] !

Majestically, with a carefully calculated slowness, Hor-Ou-Tit pulled the sides of his unbleached woollen tunic over his knees, before taking his seat. Then the Pontiff stood up, stretching his long, aching limbs, though his face showed nothing of it.

His voice was a little broken, but the firm tone of his words left no doubt as to the path he was advocating:

- Truly, the words of our Pêr-Ahâ are just. May Ptah grant him a long Life of similar Wisdom and the Great Force capable of destroying all those who contravene the Commandments of God! This is why I am certain that a just solution will emerge from your deliberations, honourable children of our great race which has disappeared through its blindness. There can only be victory for the race descended from Usir, son God himself, over those whom the blindness of a single one of them has turned away from the same origin as ours. That is why I deplore in my heart of hearts that we are forced into such a dilemma: helping to annihilate others ourselves. And yet these brothers from Hor-Ou-Tit, whom Health and Strength protect eternally, have come to fight us, stealing, raping, pillaging and ransacking everything in their path, with no regard for the blood of their blood, the flesh of their flesh; in addition, by kidnapping several of our women and children, they have definitively disavowed themselves as children of God. And when Ta Mana suddenly resounded with the clash of spears, the whistle of arrows, the complaints of the wounded, the cries of the dying and the screams of those who had been kidnapped, I realised that we would not find peace and calm again, that we could not leave without fear until the foul "Ra-Sit-Ou" had been destroyed. The Council must therefore find men capable of such a mission, arm them and charge them with bringing us back the tranquillity of the soul, that part of the Earth which God has entrusted to us in

---

[39] The two sentences of the final formula are found in most manuscripts of speeches made by Pharaohs (PêrAhâ) dating from before the 6th dynasty.

order to distinguish us from the beasts, and which some are destroying by behaving like the most ferocious animals. All of us here have learnt and repeated throughout our lives the Sacred Texts handed down by our distant and venerated ancestors - may Ptah preserve their generous souls among the Blessed, so that we can join them there when the time comes without any shame! To do this, we need to pass on to our progeny, in its entirety, the mass of documents we have learnt chapter by chapter, and which will bring Wisdom and Knowledge to the distant future generation who will settle in the second homeland, the "Second Heart of God". For it will be this ultimate descendant who will re-establish writing and reintroduce the glory of Ahâ-Men-Ptah, which is ours. May the terrible power of the one God help us in these memorable times in which we live! The humble prayers of thanksgiving that I shall raise to our Creator will rise to him with a much deeper joy if I am certain that you will unite your efforts to decide on the swift removal of those who hinder us. Long live our Elder with the Right Voice!

The Pontiff inclined his bust towards Hor-Ou-Tit before resuming his seat. The President of the Assembly rose in his turn to speak. He did so in a voice that was quite loud, but which, coming out curiously from between his trembling lips, had a gripping, very special sound:

- You know as well as I do, ladies and gentlemen, that we have talked too much over the last few days - far too much! All we have done is add sand to the desert that is forming all around us. And we have sprinkled salt where the ground is beginning to drain it in abundance! The conclusion I draw from our chatter is that we can no longer defeat those who have done us so much harm with our tongues. We need to build up an armed force without delay, and give it the means to fight and win. Just as the solar disc on its boat overcame Set, a long time ago, by changing its course in the Lion, let us roar our men as this same Lion disappears into the sky. The Sun will leave it, and we ourselves must go. The Living Annals will take note of our deeds and actions, which will become history. Don't forget, and never forget again in the future that awaits us, that during this long march towards the land that is promised to us, many incidents will occur. They will condemn us not only to defend ourselves, but to counter-attack immediately if we want to preserve our families. So, as we make our first protective spear thrusts, we must remember that it is better to bite our adversary to the quick than to be devoured by him. So let's wait for the Honourable Mâsh-Akher to make his statement before we start debating the matter; what I can assure Hor-Ou-Tit is that the majority of the members of this House agree with me. Long live the PêrAhâ à la Voix Juste!

In his turn, the President bowed respectfully to Hor-Ou-Tit, before sitting down with as much dignity as he could muster, to await further discussion.

The Pêr-Ahâ gestured towards the guard standing by the door and ordered:

- Let us introduce the honourable representative of the guild of blacksmiths. Let their leader Mâsh-Akher enter.

A few moments later, a tall man with a full black beard and imposing stature appeared, dressed in a long grey clerical robe. His virile bearing and elastic gait commanded the respect of all present. The impressive muscles of his arms, playing freely for all to see, made the "Elder" smile slightly. When he reached the throne, the giant bowed deeply, and did so twice more, turning towards the seats of the Pontiff and the President. Then he stood with his head slightly bowed before Hor-Ou-Tit. Hor-Ou-Tit, a consummate comedian, put on an affable air and said:

- You asked to be heard by all the Members of this honourable House, and your wish has been granted.

We will listen carefully and sympathetically. We hope that the solution you propose will sing pleasantly to our ears, as well as to those of our venerable Councillors.

With a protective gesture of one hand, which was an invitation to start talking, the Pêr-Ahâ showed that he was all ears. But Mâsh-Akher had not reached the top of the blacksmith hierarchy without acquiring the most elementary notions of diplomacy. His face, with features as if carved from the raw mass of metal he could bend at will, remained impassive. Slowly, he spoke, thinking less of his turns of phrase than of expressing as accurately as possible what he and his companions were feeling, and his thin-lipped mouth betrayed no apparent emotion.

- To defeat the Rebels, O thou revered Descendant of Uzir the Blessed, thou needest men... and I bring them to thee. You are the Master who protects your people when they are in danger. You are the one who commands, and you will have the arms to do what you order them to do. I am at your command, O Master, who represents the Lord over the whole earth! Long life, strength and health to you!

Proudly, Mâh-Akher raised his head, pointing his chin towards Hor-Ou-Tit, awaiting his reply. The answer was a little long in coming, for the Monarch's eyes were filled with a keen interest and a deep nostalgia for the glory and splendour of the Elders of Ahâ-Men-Ptah. And you could see it beneath his mask of impassivity. After a short meditation, he sighed briefly and replied in a monotone:

- To defeat these savages once and for all, you'd need a lot of men.

- The workers in our guild are usually called "*Ror-Astiou*" Hor's workers. Because ever since your illustrious descendant Hor-Ahâ, "the Elder", put himself at the head of the first miners and smelters of iron ore to restore comfort to all, we have been devoted body and soul to the Descendant. We, the proud descendants of the first blacksmiths, are bound by oath of blood and flesh to you, the Elder with the Right Voice. To help you, all of us - engravers, chisellers, hammer-makers, scrap-makers, all metalworkers - propose that we ourselves use the spears, javelins, picks and axes that we have just made in large quantities, to destroy your enemies. We now want to become the 'masniou' of the Illustrious Elder Descendant of Usir. Make us your "lancers".

The Pêr-Ahâ was clearly stunned this time by the scale of the warlike measure proposed. He was certainly aware of the proposal made by the head of the blacksmiths before it was submitted to the Assembly, and to which he had given his prior agreement, as he should have done. But he had not expected such unanimity behind the throne he represented. To give himself time to collect himself, all he had to say was a short question:

- What do you mean by "all"?

- All the workers in the metal industry will defend you, O you to whom we owe our very existence today. More than 8,000 of us are fit to carry the weapons we have forged, and to take the offensive right into the territory of those who have so far horribly profaned the God of our birth as well as theirs. And not only have we made weapons of all kinds, but we have also made wheels for sixteen wagons, which will carry supplies and ammunition to victory. There are also two wheels chiselled with art to support a chariot if you want to take our lead.

- You're offering me command of a veritable army!

- Yes, only to serve you faithfully, O venerated Peer-Ahâ! Our javelins, specially dipped in a bath, have hardened to such an extent that they could pierce flesh, even through a carapace of hardened leather. There'll be no way out for those foul creatures who unleashed the Elder's fury.

- The Council will debate your proposal immediately. I would like to thank you personally for your support in these difficult times. The dedication of the blacksmiths' guild will go down in history. I therefore appoint you Captain of the Masnitiou. You will be the beloved soldiers of my exclusive escort. As of today, you are the

Chief of my company of men-at-arms, *the Company of Hor's Blacksmith Lancers*[40] !

Wait for us in the antechamber.

Mâsh-Akher bent almost to the ground to hide the gleam of pride that lit up his eyes, then stomped back out of the room to wait in peace for the conclusion of a deliberation that could only be perfunctory after what he had said.

The debates, after Hor-Ou-Tit's harangue, were singularly shortened. However, no one was upset In fact, the opposite was true, and a deep sense of relief could be seen on everyone's faces. Barely half an hour had passed in the water watch on the table next to the Pêr-Aha when the head blacksmith was asked to re-enter the room.

The Elder spoke without further ado:

- May my desire of just now become a reality in the service of Your Mana! I command you, the captain of the Masnitiou, *Mâsh-Akher-le-Masniti*, for such will be your title from this day forward, to gather all your men for the fourth sunrise. That morning is the most favourable preceding that of our Great Departure, and the calculations of the Chief of the Horoscopes can only be correct. Have the wagons ready the day before, and take them first to the arsenal where the weapons are stored. Then have them taken to my depots to load up with the necessary food. Finally, let my chariot shine in front of my Abode at sunrise on the fourth day. I myself will lead the Masnitiou. You will ride beside me, and from then on you will be considered by all as a royal child. This Divine decree will prove to our children, eternally, that the 'Blacksmiths of Hor', by being the main architects of the victory of the Elders from Usir, are also the *Shesou-Hor-MemMasnitiou*, the 'Servants-Warriors-

---

[40] There is no shortage of texts relating the "legend" *(sic)* of the "Masnitiou". Among them: Naville, *Le Mythe d'Horus;* J. de Rougé, *Les Textes d'Edfou;* Brugsch, *le dictionnaire géogr. ; Le livre des morts; Le rituel des funérailles, etc.*

Blacksmiths of Hor'. And more simply, for our Annals, as your foot soldiers will follow us, we will call them the *ShesouHor*, or "Followers of Horus". May each Masniti who succeeds you at their head, become in turn a royal child by divine right. May every Masniti smelter also be a smith, may the blacksmith also be a thrower, may the chiseller also carry a dagger. From now on, let the Masnitiou work with the idea that they are also working to destroy all violence! May their handiwork combine with the work of war for the greater good of Ta Mana!

- And for the greater glory of Hor-Ou-Tit, Long Life, Power and Health!

It was Mâsh-Akher, his arms raised to the sky, his eyes feverish and shining with pride, his voice trembling with contained but very loud excitement, who had shouted this phrase. With that, all the honourable members of the Assembly rose to their feet and repeated the same words three times, chanting them with their arms raised. There was then a sort of general delirium, with everyone falling into the arms of their nearest neighbour, touching his forehead and both congratulating each other on this happy end to the debates, which undoubtedly heralded the beginning of a beneficial era that was paving the way for the Great Departure.

This was what Hor-Ou-Tit thought as he discreetly slipped away, after beckoning the Pontiff and new captain to follow him. An-Nu, although relieved by the way the meeting had gone, could only deplore this final but necessary decision for the peace of God's chosen people. For this reason, the omens could only be favourable for this decisive battle which, while giving Ptah and the Sun their respective rights, would make Hor-Ou-Tit the avenging and victorious Son of Usir. Only God could say what legend would later make of the account of this battle preserved in the Annals! Hor would perhaps become a bloodthirsty conqueror who would bring with him the cult of a warlike god. The old man sighed deeply: why did the soul of man, even though it was a part of the One Divinity, always advocate evil, even when it was acting for the good of its fellow men?...

But the dawn of the fourth day dawned on a Pontiff smiling and relaxed at the sight of the immense troop of "Masnitiou", whose thousands of spears, which were made of iron, seemed to be haloed by a brilliant cloud, all shining in the first rays of the Sun. Meanwhile, the 'Rebels' awoke to the cries of women and children, the mooing of tame buffalo and their own roars, for all these people lived more or less communally with the animals, deep in the caves. Centuries had passed without any improvement in their living conditions. The invasions against the village of Ta Mana, however, had suddenly developed this long-suppressed need to modernise. As they had made tools and above all weapons from the iron ingots[41] left over from the last raid, their appetite for novelty whetted their thirst for conquest. The pikes may have been rustic, but their points were no less deadly.

On this day, which saw the "Blacksmiths of Hor" emerge from their lairs to severely punish the "Rebels of Sit", the latter were preparing the biggest raid ever on Ta Mana, which would ensure them a definitive victory over their hereditary enemies. They would set off that very evening on their final leg of the journey, having left

---

[41] It is wrong to believe, say or write that "iron was rare in Egypt even at the time of Ptolemy and the Roman emperors", as many Egyptologists have done. One of the most renowned, G. Maspero, wrote in *L'Âge de Bronze en Égypte:*

"Two deposits of iron objects were found by me in the pyramid of Ounas (Vth dynasty), and in the much older brick pyramid of Dashour. In the Dunas pyramid, the iron appeared in two places. Firstly, rust-ridden fragments of five or six sculptors' chisels, mixed with wooden tool handles and paint pots. Then, between two blocks of masonry in the sloping corridor that I had to break up to make access to the rooms easier. There were many pieces of iron. The Dashour deposit was discovered in an undisturbed part of the pyramid. It was a considerable heap of tool fragments, probably broken during construction, including adze and knife blades, as well as scissor bristles. These objects were exhibited in the Old Kingdom room of the Boulaq Museum and in the cabinet of the Curator, Mr Vassalli-Bey, where they still were when I left in 1886).

This clearly proves that they arrived in Egypt *with* iron tools.

the Zénaga pass more than a month ago to settle in the village after driving out or killing its inhabitants.

The way in which they had fled in fear during previous attack, allowing them to stock up on weapons, victuals and various spoils of war, showed that there was no need to fear the warrior value, or even the simple defence, of the cowardly descendants of Hor. This was the conclusion reached by the Council surrounding the leader of the "Rebels". This is why all the members of the clan arrived together with weapons and baggage, convinced that the first cries they uttered would make those who were not killed or taken prisoner flee in terror.

This is how the "Ra-Sit-Ou" and the "Masnitiou" came face to face, in practically the same place where Ousir had appeared above Sit, but fourteen centuries later. They clashed in a terrifying clash that shook all the sandy mounds. From the outset, the advantage went to the "Blacksmiths of Hor", whose vanguard was quick to spot the noisy presence of the first group of "Rebels". They were thus able to make an immediate strategic withdrawal to warn the Pêr-Ahâ and Mâh-Akher, who took all the necessary steps to surround and attack the majority of the Râ-Sit-Ou, who were trapped as if in pincers, unable to avoid the battle from a position of inferiority.

Hor-Ou-Tit had suddenly appeared with the enormous roar of an angry lion, resplendent in his holy wrath, at the top of a mound. There was only a palm tree at the top, but the absence of a protective sycamore tree did not diminish the surprise caused by this extraordinary appearance. The lightning couldn't have done more to stun the thousands of shaggy heads that looked up in amazement and fear. Suddenly, thunder rained down on the haggard horde as the thousands of male voices of the blacksmiths came tumbling down from all sides, pikes and spears flying.

However, the massacre was less appalling than might have been expected. The general stampede, as spontaneous as it was instantaneous, was such that a passageway opened wide to let the mass flee as quickly as it could. Only a few prisoners were taken at

Hor-Ou-Tit's request. The Elder indoctrinated them before releasing them, so that the College of Priests and its Pontiff would be satisfied: none of Usir's descendants would get their hands dirty with his brother's descendants.

The Pêr-Ahâ took his most threatening tone:

- You will tell your leader that it is useless to attack again the one who has the traditional rights to govern conferred on him by God. I, Hor-Ou-Tit, Pêr-Ahâ by the purity of my blood, Descendant of Ousir by the legitimacy of my power, am the Son of God. It is He who has armed my avenging arm to punish you. Go and tell this to your chief. Return to your companions in misfortune to the misery that will henceforth be the lot of you all, for you have defied the Lord and unleashed His wrath with your punishment. Our people are leaving this land, but it is not destined for you and it will never be yours. We are leaving here a garrison that will be invincible, protected as it will be by our battle tanks. Our people are leaving this land to go and meet the "Second Heart of God" promised to us, over there, in the East. But if ever we meet a single one of your brothers on our way, we will kill him without hesitation. Our route passes through your mountain-top dens; and I solemnly tell you that if ever a single living creature who is not one of us is in sight as we pass, we will catch him and burn him inside the caves, destroying them completely. Make sure you tell your chief all this: don't let anyone stay in the territories that will be in our way! The only reason you will be to live is to go and repeat my righteous words. I have finished; may Ptah use it to shape his daily work.

A heavy silence descended, barely broken by the trembling of the prisoners whose hands were tied behind their backs. Mâsh-Akher, gigantic among these human wrecks shrivelled in on themselves, approached the group bent over, and with a wave of his hand, made them stumble and fall to the ground. Fiercely, he spoke to them, firmly planted on his two outstretched feet:

- Vile scorpions! What are you waiting for to thank the Descendant of Usir for his kindness? He lets you live. His

Righteous Voice orders you to go and repeat what his august mouth has deigned to tell you. Will you do so?

None of them opened their mouths, terror paralysing them on the one hand, and their lips sinking into the sand on the other. They were too terrified to move. The Pêr-Ahâ held back a smile, for he had to maintain his sovereign dignity. But he added in a deep voice:

- Rub your forehead on the dust of the ground, so that I know whether you have understood me correctly; and for obedience to my just words, freedom will be restored to you.

The men shook their faces vigorously in the sand, clearly delighted to have got off so lightly.

And so ended the first great battle after the Great Cataclysm. The Annals record that 8,000 "Masnitiou" clashed with 6,000 savage "Ra-Sit-Ou", clashing their forces in a gigantic confrontation that left few casualties on the ground.

It took 1,440 years for the battle launched by Sit against Usir, the two giants of antediluvian times, to resume in the same struggle for the supremacy of God against solar usurpation.

As the Sun prepared to leave its long journey to and fro in the constellation Leo, it triggered the Exodus of the 'Rebels' and the Great Departure of the 'Blacksmiths'. That morning, the very bright *Sep'ti* star rose just before the Sun occulted it as it moved backwards, retrograde, into another stellar configuration. A new era began with the long march towards the Light, at dawn on 22 July 8352 BC...

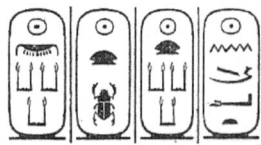

Chapter Eleven

SA-AHA-RA
(The "Burnt-by-the-Sun-Ancient" land)

> *A kind of column, ending in a ram's head, was discovered in the middle of the Sahara, at Tamenti[42]. It was undoubtedly a sacred stone. It is assumed that it belonged to a cult introduced into the desert by Berbers faithful to the Zoolatria of their distant ancestors.*
>
> S. Gsell
> (Ancient history of North Africa)

> *The Atlanteans were indeed the ancient inhabitants of this country. The discovery of the famous cave paintings of Tassili-Ajjer have highlighted the importance of this empire that reigned in Fezzan. What has become of these populations since then? It is impossible to answer this question, but what is certain is that the main Berber tribes came from this archaic stock.*
>
> Henri Lhote
> (The Tuaregs of the Hoggar)

The African lands between the 25th and 35th parallels became increasingly parched over the millennium following the upheaval of the earth's axis and the Great Cataclysm. And it was to the edge of an almost barren land that the "Followers of Hor" arrived when they crossed the Zénaga pass, emptied of the "Rebels", to descend to a once verdant valley.

Seeing this vastness of uniform ochre, the Elder's heart clenched with insurmountable anguish. Not for his own fate, but

---

[42] Although in the southern Oranais, Tamentit is a sacred place at sunset. The quotation is taken from Volume VI, page 161.

for that of the tens of thousands of women and children divided into several groups of heads of families who followed for a few kilometres.

Up to this point, there had been no shortage of food, as God had somehow solved the problem of food supply in its place, by abundantly supplying the game and plants needed by the multitude, all along the winding clear streams followed before climbing the foothills of the Grand Erg Occidental.

The pass was a welcome stopover after a whole month of exhausting walking in the heat, then the freezing cold, and finally in the terrible muggy heat of the last few days. Hor's Followers" could finally regroup and take a breather in this place. But the huge clearing where the vanguard accompanying Hor-Ou-Tit in his chariot had arrived no longer had its lush tropical vegetation. It had been smothered by the thick savannah that had gradually taken its place. There was no longer a living soul around, and only the birds of prey hovered in heavy flight in concentric circles above the humans, perhaps hoping that one of them would collapse, inert, within reach of their shredding beaks.

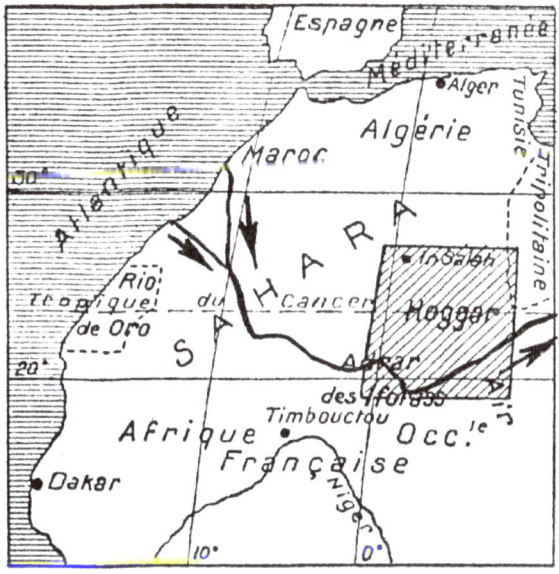

General view of the Exodus of the Rescued.

Seeing this, the Pêr-Ahâ thought that life would be more pleasant on the summit. Accompanied by a few of his "blacksmiths", he climbed the steep slope that hid the western horizon and arrived, out of breath, on a high plateau planted with trees, which dominated the pass and the clearing.

He immediately saw the double advantage of this strategic position. As well as providing better protection for the camp of thousands of families below against an unexpected attack by the "Rebels", this position enabled them to obtain drinking water from a fresh spring that flowed there, and to intercept any animals that came to drink there.

When the Pontiff met up with the Elder, he was particularly concerned about the "Ra-Sit-Ou" fleeing eastwards, into the desert. This meant that they were being preceded on the path they themselves would take when the time came to leave.

A sort of war council was held on the spot, bringing together Hor-Ou-Tit, An-Nu and Mâsh-Akher. Its decision was unanimous: after a halt of at least one lunation, to ensure that the entire population was reunited, the direction to be taken would not be altered, depending above all on the device that was locked up in the sacred chariot.

The Pontiff had been formal: the sun's shadow, which determined the real direction of the Promised Land every day at noon, could not be altered much further, as it was already too far south on the initial marker. The 'Descendant', confident of the shocking power of his offensive force, had agreed, saying that it would be pointless to circumvent any potential difficulty, as it would be visible in the desert from a great distance. It would then have to be fought off extensively before descending on the population. In view of this, it was unanimously decided to move forward, straight ahead, when the time came.

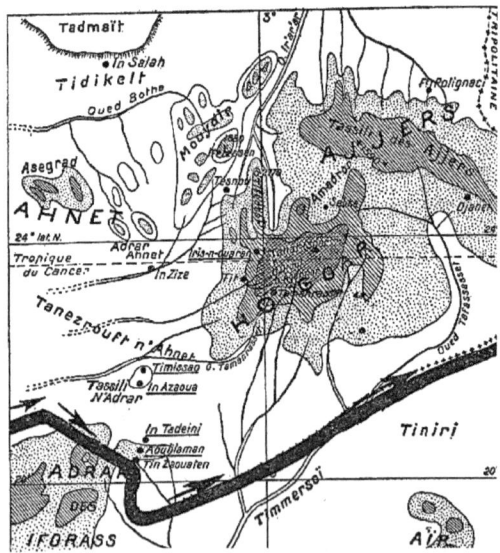

The wide road, followed from west to east by the Rescapés in the "Land Scorched by the Elder Sun" the "Sâ-Ahâ-Râ".

Taking advantage of this break, the various oral school groups went back to work, repeating over and over again the part of the Knowledge they had conscientiously stored in the back of their minds, without omitting or changing anything, even though they hardly understood all the sentences any more, as they were already losing their original meaning in the thick mist of the new mornings.

The Pontiff, to whom was exclusively reserved the class of adult initiates who would train those who would bequeath to later generations the initiatory elements destined to re-establish the College of High Priests, constantly repeated to his pupils the same phrases accompanied by the same arguments and the same comments, having himself learned them from his father. He reserved only one final chapter for his eldest son, to the exclusion of all others, as had happened with his father in his regard, and as had been the practice with all the Elders of the An-Nu who had preceded him since Ta Mana.

Taking advantage of a longer break in his initiation course, he led the man who would soon replace him at the head of the cohort of priests towards the sacred chariot. Today's teaching was far from that of heroic times, of course, but those who wore the white robes and shaved their heads were devoted to their thankless task of spiritual training of the spirits; alas, they were tired and far too preoccupied with the hallucinating march of the day to concern themselves with the future life of the Beyond Life, which was nonetheless more important.

The Pontiff gently shook his long white hair, accompanying the movement with a long sigh of resignation, and at the same time leaning firmly on one of his son's shoulders to help him down the slope. He was delighted to feel his eldest son's muscles playing hard under the skin of his arm. His replacement would be as intelligent as he was strong. Wasn't he called by a Divine Name that suited him perfectly, *MériNet*, "the Beloved of Neith", which although a modern abbreviation of the ancient and revered first name Nek-Bet, had nonetheless retained its full symbolic value. Yes, this son would know how to deal magnificently with the scabrous situations he was bound to encounter during the exhausting struggle of crossing the desert.

This Eldest and Beloved Son would replace him very soon, for it was high time he rejoined the Land of the Ancestors, all those Blessed Ones he now aspired to meet again. His earthly duty was completed with the accession of his own flesh from his blood to the rank of An-Nu, continuing the renovation willed by God before reaching the 'Second Heart'.

Once they reached the pass, they walked across the savannah, skirting a series of stinking caverns. This was where the "Rebels" had laid their dead, giving them no burial, leaving the bodies to rot and thus denying them any chance of eternal life. For how many years had this rot been piling up? No one could have said, as many of the bleached bones were very old.

They quickly crossed the area before skirting around the bustling camp, which was growing by the day with the arrival of many late arriving families. They arrived in front of the heavily laden carts grouped together at the far end of the camp, advancing to the last one, set well back and guarded militarily by two "Masnitiou". The latter had been formally instructed to allow only the An-Nu and his pupils to pass, so they bowed respectfully to the arrivals.

The Pontiff meticulously untied the intricate knots he had made himself to bind the fabric covering the wooden frame of the caravan tightly together. Then he slipped inside, where an empty space between the crates allowed two people to settle down to work or to gather around a table on which rested a tub full of water.

Méri-Net, who had followed his father, looked curiously at the rustic bowl into which An-Nu was gently placing the "device". Admittedly, the son of the Pontiff was already familiar with it, having contemplated it on several occasions, and he knew by heart the various coordinates that would enable the whole troop to follow the course calculated in advance, without any fear of error. But each time he was amazed by the disarming simplicity of the mechanism

of this tiny device, which held the key to reaching the Second
Homeland and its Light.

The old man gazed at his son, reliving his own youth; he read
Méri-Net's mind like one of those inaccessible books that he had
never known, but knew by heart. In fact, he had had the same
reaction when he was that age, to that same "gô-men". He smiled
with contentment, because the words his father had said to him at
that moment came back to him quite naturally, so that he could say
them too:

- In the "Mathematical Combinations" that formulate the
essentials of Divine Law, God did not seek complication. It is Man
who has complicated everything by seeking to turn the elementary
legislation governing all life and its development on its head, so as
to ignore it; hence his downfall and the swallowing up of the
country that was his joy and prosperity. Ahâ-Men-Ptah thus became
Amenta. Never forget, my beloved son, that Ptah is the One God,
the Great Modeller of the Creative Principle. Inculcate this as the
first axiom in your pupils, and half your teaching will be resolved.
Ptah is the Primordial Being, author of the conditions of
equilibrium in the physical world and inspirer of human laws. He is
Lord of Truth and Master of Celestial Harmony.

- I have learned all this, O my revered teacher! Being convinced
of this, I repeat it to myself over and over again, so that I can teach
it to my pupils with the immense faith that inhabits my heart.

- That's all very well, my son! When I was contemplating you,
leaning over your nappy when you were still a baby, I was already
overjoyed to see the abundance of Divine goodness blossoming in
you. And over the years, the Creator's grace has only added its most
sublime radiance. Your heart is therefore pure and full of love. That
is why the Faith that is in your heart is reflected there more
magnificently and more fruitfully every day. The clarity that
emerges from your heart will soon make you see the true aspect of
things and people; even the stars will no longer be content to
silently describe their silver circles. They will punctuate the rhythm
of the eternal harmony I was telling you about earlier. You already

know everything I've told you, of course, and I've only repeated it because the place where we are lends itself to it and your astonished gaze invited me to do so. I myself am always surprised by the simplicity of God's love for us. This ancient "gô-men", saved from the Great Cataclysm, makes it possible to go anywhere in the world, thanks to the cuts made in this wood thousands of years ago. Is it not a dazzling demonstration of Divine Power, the power granted to this simple little log of wood pricked with an iron pin, when the time comes for it to be exposed to the golden rays of the Sun, this resplendent star which, by the arm of God, can be an engine of death as it was at the time of the Great Cataclysm, or perhaps also an instrument that grants life, like this 'gô-men'?

- Can my soul be moved directly by the Eternal One, O my Father? I have wanted to ask you this question for a long time. It seems to me that the particle of Divine spirit that you have passed on to me and that stirs within me to impose decisions on me that are obvious, but that I did not see, hides something unreal within me, that can make me become a guide that is perhaps too capricious...

- The Divine part of you comes from your grandmother Nek-Bet, whose illustrious surname you bear. Your eldest sister is very much like her; like her, she is gifted with the power of second sight, which God only grants to those he wishes to use as a common Guide. You have learned how our venerated Ancestor found Usir on the very day that our Original Land was swallowed up, held in place by a low sycamore branch, thus preventing him from being devoured by the fish in the open sea, by allowing him to live again in order to prepare for this Great Departure to the Land Promised by the Eternal. It is towards this "Second Heart" that we, the great-grandsons of these valiant pioneers of ancient times, are directing our steps. We owe it to them to honour them by not disappointing them. That's why some of us are guided to carry out a task precisely defined by the calculations of "MathematicalCombinations". You are one of them, my son, and perhaps the first of them for this new generation, for you will have to bravely support the sceptre of the son of Hor-Ou-Tit as we advance into the heart of the desert.

- Why do you say this, Father?

- He doesn't seem to me to have the strength required to carry out the difficult task that awaits him. He has neither the physical nor the moral strength of his father. There has been too much blood mixing during the last generations of Pêr-Ahâ for the special Divine particle of the "Descendants" to have lost any of its integrity. But as they are in fact the direct 'Sons of God', you must ensure that they are always respected as such.

- Everything in my power will be done to make it so, O my Father! The Elder will remain eternally the bearer of the Divine torch.

- I am fully satisfied, Méri-Net; I shall leave this land of exile with a heart full of joy for you.

- I beg you, please! Don't say those painful words. I know that when the time comes you will leave, no longer supporting me with your just words, but I hope it will be as late as possible. Instead, give me some enlightened advice on the method to be used to ensure that harmony is respected among men, so that it also reigns in heaven.

- Harmony comes only from the communion of souls with the Divine Spirit itself. This human achievement is certainly the most difficult to obtain, especially as far as our people are concerned, constantly on the move on an ungrateful soil that is perpetually changing. Ours is a humanity exhausted by its heavy burden and its continual preoccupation, at the slightest halt, with finding its daily food. How much time is left for heavenly food? And yet it would come to anyone who even bothered to look for it. If only by combining the configurations formed by the Breath of the Twelve from above in relation to oneself; then everyone would be in harmonious harmony with the celestial movement.

- We should be able to stop for a long time in an appropriate place, to try and rebuild a Golden Circle, which everyone could consult at their leisure.

- Alas! Content yourself with leading those you will be responsible for guiding to their final destination. Until then, and throughout the solar navigation in this constellation, which is weakening our anaemic blood, check our route while monitoring the moral health of our people, as arrival at the "Second Heart" is not for tomorrow. The suffering will be terrible before we reach the end of the line.

The old man stretched out a gaunt finger towards the parallel drawn on the log floating in the tub. He brushed against the meridian, then caressed it, as if he could see in the depths of his half-closed eyes the immense hardships these families would still have to endure before the cast shadow indicated the end of the journey. He could not have known that on the modern map this famous but imaginary line would be 'Cancer'. Shaking his head at last, he continued:

- Unfortunately for us, this is the axis of the 'Land Burnt by the Old Sun'. This is the *Sâ-Ahâ-Râ* from which you must never, under any circumstances, stray, for you would no longer have a point of reference: it would be an eternal flight to a land you could never find. God wanted to impose this additional ordeal on his children so that, on reaching the long-awaited goal, they would really feel like the Chosen Ones. This is the reason why the ground is drying up, becoming increasingly arid and less hospitable under the feet of all the emigrants, but which you must cross without deviating from your course, despite the cries or threats. Look at this needle, and the shadow it will cast inside the circle of the other parallel lines you see there, which encircle the meridian leading to Ta-Mérit, the 'Beloved Place'. These two lines should correspond to the maximum distance you can give to the pitfalls you need to avoid. Leave the central marker as little as possible.

- I understand, Father; so I'll be watching over our path.

- So my goal is achieved. I can entrust the rest of the work you.

- What do you mean, Father?

- Tomorrow, during the blessing of the apparition of the day, the ceremony of the transfer of my priestly powers to Méri-Net, the new Pontiff of the "Shesou Hor" will take place. You will then become the 487th An-Nu since the death of Usir.

- O Father!

- Do not protest, O you who are so worthy to succeed me! Hor-Ou-Tit himself will direct your anointing, for he knows that my time has come. But enough has been said, for I still have several points of detail to conclude.

Come with me to the Priests.

Two months went by, however, before the "Masnitiou" resumed their forward march, in order to open the way for the families who were burdened with worries and still tired. The Pêr-Ahâ stood proudly on his chariot, often with the Giant MâshAkher and the young new Pontiff Méri-Net at his side.

Every morning thereafter, a huge, reddish globe of sunlight appeared at its eastern rising, right in front of them, in an already heavy atmosphere. As the hours passed, its burning rays fell on an earth that was becoming completely dehydrated. After a few days, it became clear that the precious reserves of liquid brought along in the wagons would not be enough to satisfy the increasingly parched gullets.

There was a heated discussion between the young Pontiff and the head of the Hor blacksmiths about what to do, as MâshAkher wanted to impose a halt at this point in order to return with the wagons and some of his men to replenish an even greater supply of water. The last stream crossed, in a less torrid region three days' walk away, would suffice for the task. But Méri-Net, who "knew" that a large river had to be reached soon and without risk, but who did not want his extra-human powers of visual perception to be known, firmly maintained that it was essential to continue the advance in the same direction until the arrival at a source of running water gave the signal for a prolonged halt.

This last phrase made the fiery leader of the 'Masnitiou' family jump to his feet.

- At this resting place, we could be counted on the fingers of one hand! And when do you intend to get us to this source, O Great Pontiff?...

Méri-Net pretended not to notice the irreverent irony of these words. He even smiled appreciatively, content to reply with all the seriousness he could muster:

- The "Mathematical Combinations" which indicate the configurations of the sky that Divine Law, and only Divine Law, would like humans to follow, will benefit us for quite a long time once the next two sunrises have passed into the past. We should therefore continue to walk at the normal pace of our people for another *two* days before making a stopover, which can then be extended if the Pêr-Ahâ so desires.

Mâsh-Akher stood sheepishly before the candid gaze of the An-Nu, who had just spoken so confidently about a future he considered uncertain. Hor-Ou-Tit, pleasantly seduced by the words of his Pontiff who was asking him to settle the debate, inquired with an air of interest:

- What do you think we'll find that's different from stifling sand, the burnt colour, irritating to the eyes, in the place you say is only two days' walk from here?

- I can assure you, O you who are the Master of all things, that we will arrive in a much more pleasant place, with plenty of water. And if it pleases God to carry out his celestial designs to ensure harmony between heaven and earth, we will be in that place before the star dedicated to daylight reaches the zenith of the sky for the third time. I will end with this Truth.

The Elder, who could feel the sweat coming from everywhere under his tunic, could only agree. He hastened settle the dispute between his two main technicians:

- I accept the omen, O Pontiff! The trust I placed in your father, and which he richly deserved, is equally yours. May your words always reflect the Truth! We'll be leaving as soon as this break is over. I said.

When the third dawn appeared over the people, who were waking up as best they could on a kind of blackened scree, a vanguard of "Masnitiou" quickly set off at Mâsh-Akher's request. No more than two hours had passed before the burning Sun showed a subtle change in the configuration of the ground itself. But it wasn't until an hour later that the blacksmiths realised: the ground *was turning green!* Shortly afterwards, the grass appeared in numerous tufts, and then the first shrubs appeared.

Arriving at a high hill, the men climbed it in all haste, passing a few frightened gazelles along the way. At the top, the horizon revealed its splendours. A wide liquid serpentine flowed in the distance, surrounded by an immense green oasis. In the background, a chain of mountains blocked the view, but it wasn't too much to ask.

Quickly, a stretcher returned to the rear to join the main body of the troop, exhausted from the heat and the various aches and pains. It was time to bring comfort with a happy ending to this short stage.

In the evening, when the people were full of buffalo meat - a large herd passing nearby had provided abundant hunting - the Sun disappeared behind Ta Mana, towards the place where the Blessed were resting, in the Amenta. This prompted the An-Nu to tell them that the place they had just arrived would be called *Ta Mantit*, the "Place-hoped-for-at-sunset", which combined the place they had come from and the place they were going to, Ta Merit.

In the same way, for the future *Sâ-Ou-Râ* Annals, this impetuous, bubbling river would be called "SunburntWater", which was a linguistic subtlety, as this newfound liquid seemed to be gripped by an overflowing fever after the desolate drought of Sâ-Ahâ-Rà. This water symbolically represented the new Sun becoming the Master of Nature and inundating the new population with its benefits.[43]

From the very next day, Hor-Ou-Tit displayed a rare organisational genius. His Pontiff's foresight had invigorated him, and he took the useful decisions that were needed. He scattered the great clans of his immense family all along the river, going back to the source.

After Tamantit, many other villages were founded, some of them troglodytic, as many caves were suitable for settlement. After eighty centuries, they all bear the same name.[44]

Méri-Net moved further east with his family and priests, in order to have more time to revise the texts he had learnt by heart, and to innovate in terms of anatomical teaching, as many people with broken limbs had to be abandoned along the way without their families, who held a piece of the Knowledge.

The Pontiff therefore settled on a pleasantly temperate hill overlooking the Sâourâ on the western horizon, and named the whole region the *Touat;* as for the panorama stretching towards the "Second Heart", he immortalised it in the most dazzling way, taking his inspiration from the name of his illustrious ancestress who had been the first to recommend departure for a "Second Heart" of

---

[43] These territories, situated between 0° and 4° longitude at the height of the parallel of the Tropic of Cancer, all have Berber names that can easily be written using hieroglyphics, and with good reason!

[44] As well as Tamentit, on the Sâourâ near its source, the most important town is Lahmer, or the "Beloved of Men".

God. This is why the region took the sweet name *of Ahâ-Net*, the Old Net or Nek-Bet. It is still known as *the Adrar des Ahnet*.

This part of Africa, along the Tropic of Cancer, quickly became a place of repopulation during the very long time that the "Followers of Hor" stayed there. For almost more than a millennium, during which time solar navigation retrograded in this constellation, which became Cancer, in memory of the tragic suffering endured by these people.

Over hundreds of kilometres, between the 20° and the 30° parallel, thousands of rock engravings have sprung up from the depths of time to testify to the abundant life described on hundreds of sandstone walls. They also demonstrate the violence of the second terrible clash that one day pitted the "Masnitiou" against the "Ra-Sit-Ou", the latter wreaking bloody havoc on those who were clearly not expecting them.

What Hor's 'descendant' didn't know was that the 'Rebels' had settled a little further north, in this same Hoggar, several centuries earlier, under the enlightened reign of Sit's successor, the peaceful An-Sit-Râ, who was less warlike than he was. But this tribe, which had proliferated, found itself under the thumb of a bloodthirsty tyrant on the arrival of Hor-Ou-Tit, who ruled his people with an iron fist, aspiring only to return to the land of Light promised to his hereditary enemies but which rightfully belonged to him, being the direct product of the Ancestor Sit who was the only Elder of Geb, King of all the Earth. And that title was his.

One lunation had not even completed its cycle when the various encampments set up along the Sâourâ were detected by advanced elements of "Rebels" who were hunting in the distance on behalf of Bâk-Bâ, "Sparrowhawk-Resplendent". Bâk-Bâ was quickly alerted to this, and decided to prepare a dazzling revenge for the defeat he had suffered so many centuries earlier. He methodically prepared the invasion, in no hurry, waiting for the right moment when he would be ready to swoop down on his prey, like the sparrowhawk whose emblem he had made his own. Like that bird of prey with its piercing eyes, he prepared his plan from afar, then, like lightning, he closed his powerful clawed talons on the enemy. He would kill them without mercy and without giving them the slightest chance to mount a defence.

Although the weapons of the 'Rebels' had become primitive due to the lack of metal, the flint and quartzite with which they struck their blows killed even the biggest beasts. As they combined strong arms with a certain cunning developed while hunting fast-moving animals such as ostriches and giraffes, they became formidable adversaries.

All along the Sâourâ, on the western bank, far from today's strongholds commonly known as "Ksour", the "Masnitiou" had taken up residence. It was quite naturally near these, under the neighbouring lines, that the "Funeral Rooms", the "Akh-Menou", or "Ancestors' Antechambers", were dug, where the bodies of those who had joined the Beyond of Life were deposited. These underground boreholes, in the shape of pyramids supported internally by huge blocks of stone, still abound in this region of the Touat, referred to in the texts of the Egyptian Funeral Rituals, improperly called *the Books of the Dead.* Notably near the old fortifications defending the access of the villages to the "Rebels": Raoui, Men-Ouara, Quarari and so many others that the Berbers continue to hide. The Ahnet heights are full of them, but they are difficult to access because of their sacred nature. They are all on the "Hill of the Priests", and their layout is strictly identical, geographically speaking, to that of the "Akh-Menou" on the "Hill of the Pontiffs", located at Denderah not far from the Nile.

The engravings throughout this area are significant; in many places they are superimposed on the previous ones, proving that the first inhabitants were dispossessed by invaders who scratched the sandstone, chiselling it with furious flint blows, before these hands engraved their drawings of a different, more rustic conception.

These overproduction figures are almost life-size, often exceeding one metre in height. All the human bodies bear animal heads, rams or birds, with the appearance of the first hawks to celebrate the victory of Bâk-Bâ, the "Resplendent Hawk". In many places, the body of the first engravings has remained; only the head has been erased and replaced by that of the bird.

During the counter-attack by the "Masnitiou", much later, the chronology was re-established thanks to these drawings, as a third engraving superimposed the heads of men on the previous ones, and, by way of signature, this same third hand added a lion's tail encircling the waist. It is thus easy to re-establish the deeds of ownership of the place: first, there was a "Follower of Hor", then there was a "Ra-Sit-Ou" worshipper of the Sun, and finally, just to return things, once again a "Masnitiou".

At Ta Mentit, several statues carved into the basalt rocks of the site have even been found, thanking Ra for the victory of the "Rebels of Sit". A ram's head carved on a cylindrical tenon can be seen in the Algiers museum. To fully understand the hieroglyphic-Berber imbroglio, you need to know that the "sacred" name of Sit, who died at sunset, was *Amen* (from AhâMen, the "Ancient of the Sunset"), the name given to the ram whose thrashing symbolised the first "Rebel" and his victories over Usir and Hor, as if the living strength of Sit had been reincarnated in all rams.

"Amen" thus became the hope and faith in the power of the Sun for all the "Ra-Sit-Ou" who, over the centuries, have come to call water by the same double syllabic sound. For it was Ra who protected the desert rivers so that everyone could quench their thirst. All Berbers have kept this word, "amen", to designate water, even today!

The battles between the spear- and axe-bearers and the stone-throwers, or the chariots ramming into naked men, are also amply detailed on the rocks of Tassili-n'Ajjer, demonstrating, in the sobriety of the engravings, the revenge that the 'Masnitiou' later took on the 'Ra-Sit-Ou'.

This second battle was very deadly, as both sides found themselves equally armed, the "Rebels" having made a plentiful harvest of picks and axes during the previous invasion. After this bloody clash, the worshippers of Ra were once again driven further east into another desert.

At that moment, when the Sun was leaving the constellation through which it had travelled for nearly two millennia, the Chief of the "Ra-Sit-Ou" was Bâk-Sit-Akher, the misnomer since the strength of the lion (akher) had added nothing to that of the sparrowhawk to enable him to win. His opponent was Hor-Ath-Akh, but he had died in the final tussle - crushed under his overturned chariot.

It was obviously his eldest son who took his place, and it was the Pontiff of the day, Anepou-Sen or the second Anepou, who crowned him the 150th 'Descendant' of the Son of God, a special ceremony that allowed the names to remain intact. And the leader of the 'Masnitiou', the proud Kamem-Kapt, threw himself on the ground to kiss the bottom of his robe as a sign of total submission to the new Master.

The second Anepou quickly became similar to his illustrious ancestor. He was feared in the same way because he took a great interest in anatomy. In a school reorganised on the heights of Ahâ-Net, he perfected a technique for operating on heads, because axe blows split skulls more or less severely, and as many as possible had to be saved for the survival of the "Followers of Hor". The leader of the 'Masnitiou' was a great help in this task, especially as he was practically the only person not to fear the Pontiff. Kamem-Kapt, the "Impetuous Horse of Good Naves", had himself forged several metal instruments according to the An-Nu's instructions. But it was only after much trial and error that the operating tools were perfected.

Thus were born the famous "Serk-Kers[45] ", the "openers of skulls", hence the "Trépaneurs". This guild has been established in this part of the Aurès since ancient times. Today, they are still

---

[45] *Serk* is the hieroglyph for the verb to open, and *Kers* is the "top of the head", hence the term "skull opener".

practising the same methods, which, for them, go back to the beginning of time. And the tools and methods remain the same...

This new pause in the mass exodus of the population allowed us to catch our breath. The engravings are better incised, even among the "Rebels" retreating to Fezzan, still several hundred kilometres ahead of their hereditary enemies.

There was just one small event, which seemed insignificant at the time, but which later became of paramount importance. The Hor-Vainqueur, Hor-Nou-Li, succeeded in taming a falcon. As a joke, he took the title of Hor-Two-Time-Victor, because his falcon had killed a hawk. From that day on, the falcon became the emblem of the 'Descendant'. This was in the eternal order of things, and went hand in hand with celestial harmony.

CHAPTER TWELVE

THE TRÉPANEURS
(THE SCHOOL OF "SERK-KERS")

Only one language was spoken in North Africa; from the Canary Islands to Egypt, from the Mediterranean to Sudan, all the ancient names of places and people are Berber, and they can only be found there!

HENRI MALBOT
(Studies in Algerian Ethnography - 1895)

There is still a small group of trephineers with bizarre medical customs who come from who knows where; who have been performing this singular trephine operation for who knows how long; who learnt it from who knows whom; and who, still savage and inaccessible to modern medical ideas, astonish us by their boldness in operating and by the successes they achieve!

DOCTOR R. VERNEAU
(Trepanation in the Aurès)

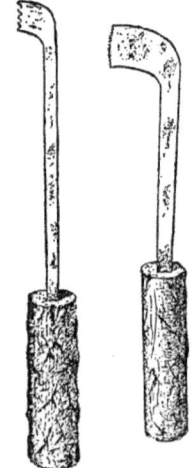

"This Abode, where Ptah allows us to gather in order to preserve his teachings intact in our memories, is the shining testimony of His Divine goodness. Only a moon ago, blood and death filled the atmosphere, and this building was nothing but ruins! Today, the indelible imprint of His Breath has enabled us to rise to the unequalled celestial heights of His ineffable Wisdom for us. May our souls ceaselessly give thanks to him; glory be to him! Glory to Ptah, our only Almighty God!

Tools used for trepanning.

"Glory to Ptah! The thirty-eight adult students repeated this sacred praise in a loud voice. They were gathered in the prayer room adjoining the rooms reserved for the new anatomy classes. AnepouSen had just completed the consecration of the building, which had been quickly rebuilt, albeit in frail clay, but sufficient for the temporary use for which it was intended. The first lesson, which everyone had been waiting for, would be the dissection of a skull. This in no way frightened these "medical students", who would see much more. For the moment, curiosity far outweighed fear.

An-Nu, a fine psychologist, knew how to lead his audience.

- As you know", he said, "O all you my students who are the descendants of the survivors of the Lion and who no longer have the means to write because of this, today we will study, not the chapter concerning the eight incisions to be made on a fleshly envelope before proceeding with any embalming, but that which is brand new to you, the precise gestures to be carried out to save a human life whose head is more or less seriously wounded on top.

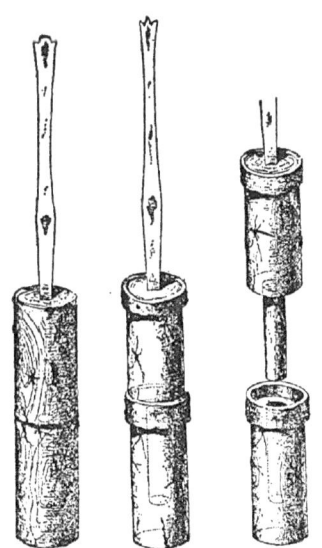

For this purpose, special tools have been made at my request by master blacksmiths, following the various experiments I myself have carried out on the bodies of Rebels killed in battle, the last of which were successful."

Tools used for trepanning (collected in the Aurès in 1884 by Dr Verneau).

A murmur of admiring astonishment ran through the audience; the students were more disturbed than they cared to admit, by this reality that they themselves would probably have to overcome. Anepou-Sen let them relax a little, because it wouldn't be long before he took them into the adjoining room, where four bodies, ready to be trepanned, lay frozen and rigid on a table.

When silence returned, the Pontiff continued

- As you know, you will have to carry out these operations yourselves, which are easy to do when you know by heart the movements to be performed, with the corresponding tools. We don't have enough time to rehearse successive operations at length, because the number of injured people waiting for relief is very large. But practice will soon give you the confidence you need. Only then will we worry about retaining the essentials and teaching them to our young people, so that they themselves can pass them on to future generations of practitioners. So follow me into the next room!

Cries of surprise rang out as student entered the room, which suddenly seemed cooler despite the large number of occupants. Some of them even shuddered involuntarily at the sight of the corpses laid out so crudely. But it wasn't so much that they were immediately confronted with death, as that they were confronted with a dismembered body that was full of life and hatred for them, just a second before collapsing to the ground and ceasing to breathe. Was there really anything else after the end of earthly life, since this flesh, so fragile, was already reduced to these inert, pale forms?...

Anepou-Sen, as a good spiritual strategist, immediately understood the reaction of his audience, and all the more so as he had foreseen it, wanting to reach that point in order to place his homily on how little earthly life is compared to eternal life. It was the best comparison he had to bring the morale of his future surgeons up to the level they needed to trephine skulls without trembling, or asking idle questions about the immortality of bodies while forgetting that of souls. So he resumed, without giving those around him time to think:

- These bodies, which I pulled out of the pit where they were going to rot, you see them, stripped of their skins, lying like that on this wooden table, all four of them identically rigid and frozen. Perhaps one of them was the leader of a group of Rebels? Perhaps he was simply a herdsman for one of the Barbarians' herds of goats? Or perhaps he was content to draw on the walls of the caves in which they lived? Who can say, looking at them like that, I ask you, my brothers? For there is no difference between a wretched son and a powerful leader. There could be among them a High Priest like me, for I will be like them when the day comes. I will be no more and no less than them, and neither will you!

The Pontiff paused for a moment, and a general murmur went through the somewhat bewildered audience. But it wasn't enough for questions to arise, for Anepou-Sen continued:

- Geb, who bore the child of the other tribe of the Earth who is our enemy, was also the human father of the one who begat our "Descendant". This is why we are all alike in face of *human* death. It is only from this passage into the Beyond of Life that the earthly stages regain their primordial value, and eventually require justification. Only those who have lived fully in Justice and Goodness, and in all Purity, will go directly to the Blessed, who alone possess Eternal Life. As for the others, I pity them in advance! We must therefore be content, at the time of the "opening of the top of the head", to preserve from death, without any distinction of origin, all the carnal envelopes that will need care. This will also allow the healed to bring their souls into line with the Divine commandments. Beware of these celestial parcels if the threshold of Eternity is not opened to them at the Weighing!... So do not concern yourselves with anything other than carrying out the acts prescribed to work according to my method. Leave the rest to God to judge. Take your places around this table. I'm going to proceed slowly to open one of these skulls, explaining to you everything I'm going to do. Three of you will then repeat them on the other corpses after me. And tomorrow, all of you will operate on the wounded, because there's no time to lose. You'll know how to do your job. I've finished!

The An-Nu himself approached the wooden table, unashamedly pushing aside two bodies that were hiding the tools needed for the trepanning. All the students leaned forward, their eyes wide. Anepou-Sen picked up a simple, very sharp knife, raising it so that it could be seen clearly, and explained very simply:

- You'll all recognise a knife, but this one particularly sharp, because not only does it have to cut the hair short, it also has to cut the piece of skin, the larger or smaller flap of flesh above the wound where the head will be cut open.

With precise movements, but in slow motion, he cut off the strands of hair one by one, scraping the skin; then, after making a deep incision, he cut out the contours. As he removed the surface of the flesh, he said:

- Here the blood does not flow, because of the death of the subject; but on a living being, it is possible that the blood flows a lot from the wound. In this case, you should always have a few red-hot points near you on a fire so that you can apply one without delay, without worrying about the patient's screams or the flesh sizzling as you cauterise the wound. Then you take this other tool, which I have called a "kem-khem", in other words the tool that "probes under the hair".

Raising the kem-khem, he turned it on itself several times before explaining its characteristics:

- This is the instrument we will use to pierce the skull. As you can see, there's nothing complicated about it and it's very easy to use. It consists of two independent parts. The upper part consists of a very strong iron rod, which the blacksmiths have treated for this purpose, after giving the upper part the shape of three teeth. It is embedded in a wooden handle about five fingers high, the whole solidly embedded in each other to form a single element. The second part, the bottom one, is made of hollowed out wood, into which the handle and rod slide, making it easy to drill into the skull bone. Watch how I do it, and when it's your turn, you'll see how easy it is.

The Pontiff bent down over the body, placing the metal trident that was to act as an auger in the open area of the scalp, right where he wanted to perforate the frontal bone. Then he fixed the fixed upper part to his bent forehead, pushing it down and driving in the three-pronged point, which rotated easily until the upper bone was pierced. He stopped and straightened up, carefully taking out the kem-khem. He examined his work carefully before commenting, apparently satisfied:

- The upper bone is drilled, and it is a good idea to stop at this point to examine the state of the skull, as there is still another bone underneath that may need to be perforated, but you mustn't pierce it wrongly as the brain is just beyond. Put the kem-khem back on the table so that you can take your time to examine the cavity opened up by the hole. If the person is alive and the blow to the head was not too brutal, there will be some blood dripping. This is proof that the cranial protection has not been damaged. Indeed, if the blood had flowed underneath, there would even be a crack in the lower bone. So, if the blood has been preserved in the hollow between the two bones, simply take the kem-khem and drill three more holes around the first one to enlarge the opening sufficiently to clean the place where the loss of substance occurred. To do this, a woollen cloth will suffice as a sponge; then the ointment that's there, which I made myself from a preparation of my Ancestor Anepou, will have to be poured into the wound, which has proved to be very effective. My son already knows the exact composition; just remember that it's a combination of salt, tar and this very sweet gelatinous substance produced by bees, all diluted with goats' whey. Do you understand all this?

A general murmur of approval spread across everyone's lips. Anepou-Sen took it as read and was about to resume his demonstration when a concerned voice inquired:

- But, O Pontiff, if pieces of bone have fallen into the hole, won't the cloth sponging up the blood make them go away?

The An-Nu's eyes sparkled with satisfaction at this very pertinent question. His voice took on an interested tone as he asked in turn:

- Who are you? Come closer, you who have a strong enough head to ask an interesting question.

A bright-eyed young man boldly stepped up to the table and planted himself firmly on his two legs. The Pontiff held back a smile, as this attitude showed him that his opposite number was not as confident as he wanted to appear. But apparently satisfied with his examination, he continued:

- You look so young! Who are you?

- I'm the son of the master blacksmith Sâr-Ta-Hem. Before he made the weapons that defeated the Rebels, he chiselled the metal supports for the ornaments that the women wear with pride. I am Nek-Pa-Sâr, whom your Priests assigned to the oral course on the march of the "Wandering Ones" through the sky, for, O Pontiff, I have a very good memory.

All present burst out laughing, the young man's tone being that of a cock crowing. This lightened the mood considerably, allowing Anepou-Sen to resume his anatomy lesson in a more playful tone:

- From tomorrow you will be assisting me so that you can see for yourself what is at the bottom of the wounds, because you have the keen intelligence needed to operate properly. Indeed, as soon as the blood has been removed from the cavity, the most important thing is to look to see if there are any small pieces of bone left. Either of these two instruments will enable you to remove them.

The Pontiff took them from the table, raised his hands and detailed them:

- This one has a hook which can be used as a lever to remove any awkward bone protrusions. This one, as you can see, only has a rounded head, which can be used to probe the bottom of the wound; when it encounters a piece of bone, however small, it will make a particular, characteristic sound.

He put down the two tools and picked up some long stems before continuing:

- These metal tools will enable you to pick up the pieces of bone you find.

That's all there is to say and do about this simple, fairly common injury, as there has been no shortage of blows in recent times.

- What if the injury is old and hasn't treated?

It was the young Nek-Pa-Sâr who was asking this question, maintaining the same childish tone when making the most serious requests. The Pontiff looked at him with greater attention, this time tinged with admiration:

- Your question, about chiselling bodies like your father chiselled metal, is very pertinent. I've already operated on, if not cured, a good number of old cripples. When the skull has been split for several years, and this is noticeable by a scalp that is practically in a state of decomposition and flesh that oozes thick, yellowish water, the upper bone should be removed over a large surface area. It will therefore have to be cut rather than drilled. To do this, use the other main instrument, the 'mench-râ', which will easily separate the bone surface thanks to its eight teeth, which are much finer than on the kem-khem. The action then continues on the lower bone that normally protects the brain, because here the purulent oily water has penetrated to the brain and is making it sick, causing its owner to suffer and very often acting abnormally. The brain thus cleared must be quickly brought into contact with the remedy that will cure it. It should be applied every day for a full month, spaced out according to the needs of the healing process. This balm is very different from one that is applied only to the bone. In addition to various ingredients, the essential ingredient is a decoction of carbonised egg yolk, which becomes a fatty liquid. This is obtained by cooking the yolks in an earthenware pot until they reduce to ash. The juice that remains at the bottom of the pot is then collected, admittedly in small quantities, but sufficient to ensure the healing of the brain in the mixture applied. I suggest this in case you don't have any ointment, as this liquid is extremely soothing, and you can easily prepare it with hen's eggs. For healing, after one month's treatment, the tar-based solution will be used and covered with a herbal compound. Is all this understood? Does anyone have any other questions?

It was Nek-Pa-Sâr who rightly asked about an important point:

- Can the flesh be cut anywhere on the top of the head?

The Pontiff, who was expecting another question from the young man, who was decidedly much more intelligent than his elders, replied immediately, in fact addressing himself alone:

- Naturally! Any part of the skull will do, because there's no need to locate the infected area in advance. If there is a visible wound, a break, an indentation in the bone, or an obvious place where the blow was struck, this is where, and only there, the operation should be carried out. When the cut is old, it would be better to make the incision where the injured person remembers receiving the blow if no trace remains. For the rest, there is no change in the sequence of operations. However, before I finish, I'd like to add an important point that none of you know yet... not even Nek-Pa-Sâr!

The future bone-cutters laughed again, happy to be relaxing like this. AnepouSen quickly continued:

- I realised that the bony envelope that protects the brain is in fact a receiver of celestial waves. It was through it that the Divine Breath came to form the soul at birth, when the carnal envelope took on its definitive form. I am going to show you what this is, and why I am telling you about it.

Skilfully, the An-Nu stripped the scalp from the skull, scraping the cranial bone in one place to reveal a sort of seam. He pointed to it with an index finger, following the tiny meanders of these bony sutures.

- The bones fit together in a different and complicated way, forming a very particular structure for each individual. These broken lines reflect the celestial writing that Nek-Pa-Sâr's beloved 'Errantes' breathe into each individual. But this is by no means the time or the place to talk about God's real influence on our lives, and the acts that it makes us carry out, whether consciously or not. I have spoken to you about this only so that you understand that a bone should not be pierced where the stitches are. Before you set to work, you should know that the larger the perforated hole, the easier it will be for you to relieve the brain of its woes. It will never be more complicated than milking a goat. The resistance of life will do the rest to save the wounded. That remains the main objective if our forward march is to retain as many able-bodied arms as possible.

The exodus resumed shortly afterwards, leaving behind a team of these trephineers and their families to care for the many wounded. The Sun, in its retrograde course, was close to the next constellation, characteristic of the celestial harmony of the time that would follow, as its representation showed two very bright "Fixes" of different colours, seeming to oppose each other in a confrontation that the "MathematicalCombinations" would last for two millennia.

Now, in the desolate land of Sâ-Ahâ-Râ, the two Giants, their troops reconstituted, were preparing for a new battle, which, alas, promised to continue for another two thousand years. What better name for this constellation than that of the Twins? And so it was, with the Earth also arbitrating the struggle between these two children born of the same mother, who hated each other so fiercely.

No name could better describe the titanic struggle of the "Followers of Hor" against the "Rebels of Sit". What term other than "Giants" would have better suited the "Masnitiou" or the "Ra-

Sit-Ou", who fought each other century after century, prolonging their hatred for millennia? Even after the unification of the two lands of the "Heart", the anathemas contained in the rival royal cartouches continued this battle. But the latent evil was already contained in the seeds of the previous constellation, already gnawing at the souls of the 'Descendants' and the 'Rebels'... like a Cancer.

The fight resumed at the gates of Fezzan, where the rebel families had taken refuge after their bitter defeat. These families had grouped together at the bottom of a canyon, leaving a bright spot in a gigantic black stony desert. It was at the end of this dead land that the exiles breathed again, finding there an oasis of freshness, still full of fine white sand. Animals of all kinds were still living in this area, which was only a few kilometres in size, and they were getting on well with each other. Unfortunately, there were a lot of humans, and they had to eat!...

This stage, which was only temporary in the minds of the leaders, lasted longer than expected, and animals of all kinds became scarcer, then disappeared from this oasis, which eventually dried up itself. But before leaving this enchanting place, nostalgia led to the reproduction on the walls of the multitude of animals that had lived there: elephants, rhinoceroses, giraffes, crocodiles, etc. *All the engravings were around two metres by three metres*[46]...

But now it was time to try and take the "Second Heart" from those who claimed that this land was promised to them alone. Just then, advanced elements of the "Masnitiou" reached the entrance to Fezzan, looking for a camp for the next stage. A terrible clash

---

[46] A 60 km long, winding and almost impassable gorge prevents access to the source of the Wadi Mathendous. It was here that the descendants took the name of Garamantes, dear to Herodotus. The place itself, "Garamara", in the local dialect has kept its meaning, repeated by my guide: "Double sacred place of the Sun"!

ensued, which dragged on, trapping the two clans in their positions for some fifty kilometres.

The rocky masses that abound in these parts are once again a lasting reminder of this. On the engravings, the figures become "animal" and the two Giants are *Hawks* and *Falcons*. The first are indisputably "Sun worshippers", and the others "Hor smiths". From that time onwards, the emblems of the two clans featured this name, which quickly became mythical.

The splendid sculptures engraved on the rocks have the sacred characteristic of being located on the faces that receive the *sunset*'s golden rays. This was so clearly intentional that the practice was repeated at all the Pharaonic funerary sites over the four millennia that they were spread out along the *western* shore of the Nile, where the sun fell asleep on the rock faces that surrounded them.

The reason for this is easy to understand when we admit that the Ancestors, those who rest Blessed in the Amenta, on the other side, on the celestial western shore, and who wake up when the daylight disappears in the eyes of those who live in the "Second Heart" of God, *see the engravings during the few minutes when the flaming globe illuminates the two hemispheres*. This is because they come to life expressly so that the harmonic link between the two worlds is constant. In this way, everyday life is depicted, work in the fields, fishing, hunting, as well as battles and victories, so that those who are beyond Life are immediately aware!

The foreigner of our 20th century who, like me, is lucky enough to have been there and witnessed this extraordinary sunset, in the midst of astonishing solitude, can only be overwhelmed. He contemplates the glowing circle, which seems to grow ever larger before sinking behind the rocky escarpments of this desert Fezzan, beyond this high plateau lost in the immensity, and which beforehand shoots out its millions of bloody arrows, like so many magical strokes striking the engraved silhouettes, suddenly bringing them to life. Our contemporary eyes blinked in astonishment several times, as the speed of the sun's descent caused the shadows to move with disconcerting rapidity across the sandstone, bringing this army back to life, fighting, and emerging *truly* victorious, *alive* beyond the mists of time!

But these unforgettable moments were all too brief, as night fell swiftly in the Tropic of Cancer. But the impression remains!

What is nevertheless very difficult to understand, and therefore to admit, is this fratricidal struggle between the two members of the same family, begotten and created by God, over the millennia that preceded and continued for just as long, before the final destruction of both sides under Cambyses in 525 BC.

Since the Great Cataclysm, they have killed each other, but have also intermingled on a number of occasions in the course of wars, so much so that the fighting, while perpetuating itself and increasingly bloodying the two families, no longer meant much by the time they were on the banks of the Nile, albeit a long way apart.

But the myth of Sit and Hor had become so completely integrated into everyday life that it had *already* turned into an epic legend which, as soon as it was established in Ath-Ka-Ptah, was transformed into the strictest religious symbolism, intended by both the "Descendant" and the An-Nu, as we shall see in the next chapter. Strangely enough, by not looking for it, the monotheistic religion that was re-established at the birth of the first king of the first dynasty came closer to the original ancestral truth. But it obsessed the minds of the two rival groups, to such an extent that the universe of each was of an opposite conception to that of the other.

From the time of Menes, or Menna, the unifier of Egypt, the struggles did not cease. The inextricable tangle resumed as early as the Second Dynasty, demonstrating that the union of the Two Lands into a Second Heart could not allow two branches to be grafted onto a single branch.

The latent opposition between the North and the South had never ceased to pit the new 'Rebels of Sit' against the reigning family of the 'Followers of Hor'. This hatred was always alive; it haunted and bloodied all the families in the struggle for divine power.

The echoes of these events reverberated 2,000 years later, engraved on the walls of the Temples of Karnac, Oumbos, Abu-Simbel and Denderah, passions having been unleashed by Ramses Ier, usurper of the reigning Pêr-Ahâ, who instituted the XVIIIth Dynasty according to Manetho's chronology. It was still going on during the XXth, when Sesostris escaped the treachery fomented by a rebel from Sit, which will be more fully developed in the volume that deals with this chapter of history.

But isn't it astonishing that in every area there is such a clear antagonism between the two parties? This was the case from the outset. When Menes unified the two lands of Upper and Lower Egypt and settled at the base of the Nile delta, he built the Ath-Ka-Ptah, the "Second Heart of God", around which the capital, later called Memphis by the Greeks, was built. But when, in the next dynasty, a 'Sit' took over the sceptre and wanted to keep the same name, the priests of the Sun poisoned him, but he survived and won his case. A few decades later, when a 'Hor' returned to power, he renounced the name of his clan in favour of *Ta-Nou-It*, the 'Place of Nut's Sycamore', which became another name for Egypt, 'Land of Sycamores', from Dynasty III onwards. From this name, the Greeks derived another famous phonetic name, Danaos, which in a different way represents the "naos" where the Sacred Sycamore was planted.

Amun was thus in open conflict with Aten for millennia, culminating in the poisoning of Amenhotep IV who, under the name of Akhen-Aton, sought to destroy Amun by building another capital and banning the cult of Aten. This is why the history of the Pharaohs was one of constant to-ing and fro-ing, in which a spirit of revenge was constantly expressed beyond the grandiose, from Dynasty VIII onwards, ending only with the invasion of conquerors of all kinds and the destruction not only of the civilisation that existed at the time, but also that of times gone by! There was nothing solid left that the sand didn't invade and make disappear from sight! After the disappearance of the oldest civilisation in

Antiquity, this imbroglio of the most unusual misunderstandings led to the most fantastic and far-fetched interpretations of a language that had become extinct and incomprehensible, which continued unabated for the next two millennia, leading to Champollion's revival of interest, while leaving in the shadows the key to gaining knowledge of the hieroglyphs.

Before God, fed up as he said he was with the blindness of his creatures, decided not to leave any more stone upon stone of the buildings of the "Second Heart", opposition was still going strong among the survivors of Ahâ-Men-Ptah on both sides, and when they reached the banks of the Nile, it took on a much more serious dimension with regard to monotheism.

The Pontiffs obviously preached the fear of the Almighty United God, whose human incarnation was the Elder, or "Ahâ" personified as the Conqueror Falcon. The Sun-worshippers had also created their College of Priests, doubling Ra with Aries, under the same name, although their royal emblem was still the Solar Hawk. Both were thus the starting point for idolatrous schisms, which rapidly spawned a proliferation of abominable gods and led to a highly questionable form of Zoolatry.

The long march, which had lasted fifteen centuries punctuated by fratricidal struggles, had allowed this slow development of customs. It was almost on the outskirts of Ath-Ka-Ptah that the last great battle took place, with both sides exhausted.

The "Masnitiou" and the "Ra-Sit-Ou" found themselves practically face to face along the present-day border between Egypt and Libya, in front of the foothills that gave access to the last oasis in the extreme south-east of Libya, which for each clan was like a blessing from heaven, and which they naturally had to secure for themselves.

It was the "Blacksmiths of Hor", better equipped with weapons, who won supremacy in a hard-fought battle. They drove the exhausted Ra-Sit-Ou northwards, a high desert range literally closing off the road to the east, with the now-occupied oasis closing off the strategic opening to the east from the south.

While the "Rebels" fled back towards the sea, where they regrouped and made their way to the Nile delta in short stages, the "Descendant" who was the last to camp abroad was a woman. The Pêr-Ahâ had only daughters, so the eldest, Mout-Pet-Ahâ or the "Daughter of the Ancient Scorpion", was called to reign. She ordered a well-deserved break in this soothing place, a vast palm grove where water flowed in abundance.

The Pontiff of the moment greatly helped him to take this wise decision after so many others, by showing him that Divine Harmony demanded this solution. It was necessary to wait, as the calculations made with regard to the "Mathematical Combinations" proved the harmful celestial influences. It was better to model here the future life that would come into use in the blessed territory, rather than enter it in advance and incur the bad solar influences of the new constellation that was approaching, that of the twin "Fixes".

Mout-Pet-Ahâ, who married shortly afterwards, took advantage of this pleasant temporary location to extend her reign until her eldest son, born the following year, reached his royal majority at the age of eighteen. Throughout the time she reigned, she took the Vulture as her personal emblem, as this bird of prey symbolised in her eyes the ancestress Mut, whose surname she proudly bore, who personally watched over the progress of her descendants from the heavens.

Shortly before setting off on the final stage, the new Pêr-Ahâ was crowned with the name Ahâ-Haï, which enabled him to enter the "Second Heart" under favourable auspices, cancelling the hold of the "Twins of Heaven" who were to receive the solar globe.

But what the Pontiff had not revealed to the Queen, at the time of her request for a fairly long pause, was his desire to have a further respite before arriving in AthKa-Ptah to complete the finalisation of all the disciplines that would have to be reintroduced *in writing,* as soon as the Colleagues of Priests were reconstituted, which was vital for the spiritual jurisdiction to come.

To prepare and complete this last, very important stage, a hill close to the oasis was marvellously suited to this installation, which lasted almost twenty years. In a short space of time, the school had been built from the frail material of the time: clay, dried in thick slabs and bound together with woody palm branches.

Teaching developed at an unprecedented rate. It was during these two decades that the ideographic symbols, the hieroglyphs, were methodically revised in detail. During the rare moments of rest, the pupils contemplated the green carpet that stretched out below, where their families were cosily settled, to which they gave the name of *Khou-f'Râ*, "Plaine-Verdoyante-Au-Soleil", which has always kept this name since it is still Koufra.

We know the real meaning of GIEPO4θIKA from Ceremon, "Keeper of the Temple Archives" and "Scribe of the Sacred Characters". Not only do we know this from Eusebius[47] and Suidas[48], but above all from an authentic extract from the original work, concerning the chapter on "Combinations-Mathematics", which enabled Tzertzes to discuss in detail Homer's supposed knowledge of hieroglyphics, when this poet put forward the idea that "silver is none other than the white light of the Moon[49]".

As this is by no means the place to discuss the Egyptianisation of this remarkable initiate immortalised by his *Iliad*, it will nevertheless be interesting to quote here a few hieroglyphs taken by Tzertzes from the treatise of Chérémon, which show, and

---

[47] Eusebius, *Praep. Evang.* V, 10.

[48] Suidas, *Lexicon,* volume V.

[49] *Johannis Tzetis Exegis in Homeri Iliadem*, first published by G. Hermann in Leipzig in 1812.

demonstrate, from its origin taken up again as early as Khou-f'Rà, the powerfully evocative value of the sacred astronomical characters. It will thus be easier to understand this Pontiff who was theoretically redesigning writing and the calendar, before the harmful "Mathematical Combinations" of Gemini prevented him from doing so.

Originally, hieroglyphics was the name of the new Renaissance script whose characters were *the Sacred deposit* bequeathed by the Ancestors, those Elders who were "direct descendants of God". They were therefore, and this is self-evident, dedicated to the restricted expression of sacred subjects. These included not only the theodicy of Ptah's monotheism, but also the symbolisation of the Law, which grouped together the various commentaries on the Ritual of the Beyond of Life that justified the Commandments of the aforementioned Divine Law, as well as the disciplines of mathematics, geometry and the study of the stars that made up the *Great Book of Heaven and the Four Eras* through the calculations of the 'Divine-Mathematical-Combinations'.

It is for this reason alone that Manetho calls hieroglyphics "the writing of the gods[50]", the figurative effect of the objects represented. Clement of Alexandria, another Master qualified to speak about what he knew in detail, speaks of the exclusive sacerdotal mode of this writing[51], and this explains well the real interpretation of Ceremon, himself initiated as a "Scribe of sacred characters".

This makes it easy to understand the meaning of the 5ᵉ and 6ᵉ hieroglyphs side by side. Ceremon says: "A snake that emerges from its hole or re-enters it, and whose position is either to the right or

---

[50] Quoted by Le Syncelle in his *Chronique,* Chap. 40.

[51] *Stromates,* V, 657.

to the left, signifies the rising or setting of a star when it is followed by the designation of the Fixe".

When he cites as an example this sentence "of the most remote antiquity", he who dealt with astronomy in the year 457 BC: "A sothiac year (Sirius) is coming to an end, and the festival celebrating its new rising will begin a glorious era", it is easy to understand the hieroglyphic meaning:

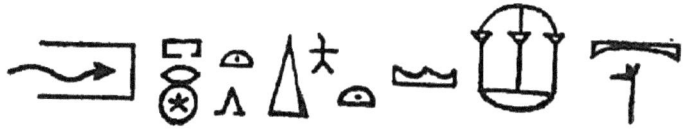

This was how the oral revisions came to an end, bringing to a close an era of patience and self-sacrifice despite the exhausting internal struggles, as much for the physical as for the moral and spiritual. The long-awaited end of the last stage.

The Pontiff, during a ceremony of thanks addressed by all to the United God who had enabled them, despite often intolerable suffering, to reach safe harbour in this "Second Heart".

The huge crowd surged behind the lead carriage, which remained the centre of attraction from every point of view, since it was from its tarpaulin-covered and strictly hidden interior that the route was indicated. It contained the latest 'gô-men', certainly more sophisticated than the old one.

It would seem, however, that An-Nu, as a forward-looking politician, sent out several advance parties to explore the best passages, and waited for them to return before relying on the sun's shadow to take this final route.

However, as the destination was on the same parallel, the long caravan took the narrow gully slightly to the south of the oasis, recognised in advance as opening the door to the desert valley, which fortunately only took four moons to cross.

One evening, at nightfall, the leading group found itself cornered by an impassable cliff edge, but pleasantly dotted with palm trees and various trees as well as a spring. It was only at the last moment, when the men reached the void, that they let out a howl of joy. In the distance, illuminated by the setting sun, a very wide serpentine stretched from the northern horizon, crossing the entire panorama perpendicularly as far as the southern horizon.

The "Gift of God", this "Celestial River" since it was granted by God, *Hapy*, the Nile, had been reached for the best part of the lives of the Chosen!... But the worst was yet to come with the solar retrograde crossing into Gemini.

Chapter Thirteen

CHRONOLOGY OF THE "FOUR STAGES"

> *Despite the immense size of this city, despite all the efforts made by different peoples to destroy every last vestige of it, transporting the materials from which it was built far away, and despite the 4,000 years and more that have added to so many causes of destruction, its ruins still offer a confounding collection of marvels that man would undertake in vain to describe!*
>
> ABD-EL-LATIF[52]
> (Journey to Ath-Ka-Ptah - Memphis)

> *While these archaic bas-reliefs of decadent emperors were being chiselled at Denderah, still using script dating back to the dawn of time, Christians were gathering in the catacombs of Rome and dying in ecstasy in the arenas!*
>
> PIERRE LOTI
> (Journey to Denderah)

Apart from the short extracts from the three books of the Chronology of Manetho, the priest of Sebennyte, which only came down to us at the beginning of our era through Greek and Latin authors, there are fortunately the engraved stones, which are indisputable first-hand historical documents. The original Pharaonic chronicle was therefore firmly established. However, when it came to the times before the first king of Dynasty I, Manetho was regarded by specialists as a merry joker.

But the discovery of the Nebadah burial site, with its unimaginable number of royal tombs, nobles, courtiers and their wives, forced us to face the facts. While a civilised empire flourished

---

[52] Arab physician from the 13th century.

on the banks of the Nile, human Europe was reduced to clans of bipeds who had not yet learned to use fire, and were killing each other like crazy.

For this translator of Egyptian traditions, charged cataloguing them and translating the Pharaonic Annals on behalf of Ptolemy Philadelphus, placed before Menes, the 'first' King, a whole series of dynasties with extravagant names: that of God, those of the demigods, then those of the 'heroes' and 'masons', followed finally by those that predated Menes, those known as the first human Kings. In all, some 25,000 years of countless reigns.

Among the Egyptologists and historians who tried to untangle this tangle, M. de Bunsen willingly left all these dynasties to the cosmogony of the ancients, but not to the history of Egypt[53]. Fable thus took precedence over reality, whereas this learned man nevertheless imagined that he was advocating the opposite. He did, however, recognise that "the last three human dynasties before Menes, which are said to have reigned for 4,000 years, should nevertheless be taken seriously and considered as probably historical, since an Armenian translation of Eusebius' *Chronicle* confirms this part of Manetho's work".

The illustrious German Egyptologist Lepsius, for his part, admits only one very short dynasty that preceded Menes, since he grants him only 350 years of anteriority.[54]

Mr Brugsch, who is responsible for the superb three-volume *Dictionnaire des hiéroglyphes*, also believes, albeit more radically, that

---

[53] *AEgyptens Stell/e...*, vol. I, pp. 101-107.

[54] *Chronoligie der AEgypter*, t. I, p. 473 *ff.*

these fabulous dynasties have nothing to do with history and should therefore not appear in any textbook.[55]

A book of five hundred pages would not be enough to list all the quotations from the most famous and erudite authors of the nineteenth century on this subject. And then there were the Nebadah discoveries... Since then, there has been another version of the story, which tends to exaggerate in the other direction, attributing to the prehistoric Egyptian dynasties otherwise fantastic lengths of time.

The most striking example is provided by the very serious Hellenistic translator Larcher, who treats Herodotus's learned calculations with good-natured fervour, concluding that Menes himself began to reign in 12,356 BC.[56]

Without going into the endless discussions between all the early Christian chronologists, let us quote Eusebius, who lived in the fourth century AD, and who found a total duration of 5,264 years as the dynastic time from Menes to the domination of Artaxer Ochus. He arrived at this figure by adding the totals of the reigns recorded in the extracts from Manetho that he had in his hands.

As in the 8th century, Georges Le Syncelle, using the same data, found only 3,555 years, the commentators split into two groups, the originals having disappeared by then. Was this duration really taken from the work of the Egyptian priest, or was it already no more than a biblical extrapolation more in line with Genesis?

In order to avoid useless epiloguery on the real or theoretical value of the Manethonian extracts, it is better to try to combine the content of the writing with the foolproof solidity of the monumental engravings. At the very least, to establish a dynastic

---

[55] *History of Egypt*, part one, chap. 3, p. 11.

[56] *Chronology*, following the translation of Herodotus, 2th edition, vol. VII.

concordance between the documents in order to draw up a historical chronology in its own time.

Judging by the buildings unearthed along the thousand kilometres of the "Celestial River", and not to mention those discovered elsewhere, such as in Palermo, the royal genealogies are numerous, but they do not always indicate where the Pharaohs came from or where they lived - and with good reason!

One set of royal cartouches, while indicating the blood affiliation given as legitimate, leaves out another, enemy or opponent, which remained or was substituted in such and such a part of the territory during the same official Egyptian period... And vice versa.

Elsewhere, another document presents a complete series of Pharaohs who succeeded each other without interruption for several dynasties, but ignores the succession of 'Rebels' occupying the Throne for a certain period, omitting it altogether, as if this interregnum had been non-existent.

Sometimes, the two rival clans established parallel dynastic chronologies; when they took possession of engraved enemy monuments, they took advantage of the opportunity to hammer out, erase, cross out and even superimpose the names and emblems of their gods and kings, thus blurring the real Annals in an enigmatic and senseless way for the poor researchers of the 20th century AD.

The glaring discrepancies, and even concordances, between the lists of royal chronological series from the same very early period can be clearly explained in this way.

Among those that are authentically Pharaonic, the main lists used as a basis for the complicated calculations of Egyptologists, lists that take no account of the differences between the "Descendants of Hor" and the "Rebels of Sit" and therefore do not use their personal Annals, come from engravings known under the following names: "The Royal Lists of the Turin Papyrus", "The

Tables of Karnak", "The Tables of Saqqarah", "The Tables of Abydos" and "The Annals of Denderah".

It is therefore quite natural that there should be such discrepancies between the Northern Chronology engraved on the walls of Saqqara at the time of Ramesses II, and the Karnak Chronology dating from Tuthmes III, whereas the one drawn up at Abydos by Seti I[er] combines the two to some extent, since although he was a member of the Ramesses family, by his very name he was a descendant of Sit.

Hence the apparent complexity of the chunks of Manetho's chapters available to the Ancients, whose meanings they could only interpret as they themselves knew nothing of the ancient history of Ath-KaPtah.

We can still compare the above-mentioned royal lists, and extract a *possible* genealogy from them:

Saqqara table.

Saqqara: The Great Architect in charge of Royal constructions, Prince Tounar of the Just Voice, descendant of Usir the Pure, in his tomb, enters the Beyond of Life after the Weighing of the Souls carried out by his 58 Ancestors, all named.

He follows all those who have preceded him among the "Blessed", and shows them to their Elder, Usir, calling them by their royal names, one by one. In this way, he makes his offering to the "Son of the Sun" - and therefore a "Rebel" - Ramses-Meri-Amen, who lives forever.

(Top row)

1. Ra-Ousir-Ma, "Righteous Voice
2. Râ-Men-Ma, "Righteous Voice
3. Ra-Ptah-Men, "Righteous Voice
4. Ra-Ousir-Kheper, "Righteous Voice
5. Ra-Neb-Ma, "Righteous Voice
6. Ra-Men-Kheper-Ou, "Righteous Voice
7. Ra-Aha-Kheper-Ou, "Righteous Voice
8. Râ-Men-Kheper, "Righteous Voice
9. Ra-Aha-Kheper-En, "Righteous Voice
10. Râ-Aha-Kheper-Kâ, "Righteous Voice
11. Ra-Sar-Ka, "Righteous Voice
12. Ra-Peh-Neb, "Righteous Voice
13. Ra-Kher-Neb, "Righteous Voice
14. Ra-Shankh-Ka, "Righteous Voice
15. Ra-Hotep-Hat, "Righteous Voice
16. Ra-Kheper-Ka, "Righteous Voice
17. Râ-Noub-Kâ, "Righteous Voice
18. Ra-Shu-Kheper, "Righteous Voice
19. Ra-Shu-Ka, "Righteous Voice
20. Râ-En-Ma, "Righteous Voice
21. Râ-Ma-Kherou, "Righteous Voice
22. Ra-Sebek-Ka, "Righteous Voice
23. Râ-Kher-Kâ, "Righteous Voice

(Bottom row)

30. Ra-Shu-Nefer, "Righteous Voice
31. Râ-Aset-Kâ, "Righteous Voice
32. Ra-Nefer-Meri-Ka, "Righteous Voice
33. Ra-Saha-Ou, "Righteous Voice
34. Râ-Ousir-Kâ, "Righteous Voice
35. .... (deleted)
36. .... (deleted)
37. .... (deleted)
38. .... (deleted)
39. Râ-Men-Kheou, "Righteous Voice
40. Ra-Shou-f, "Righteous Voice
41. Râ-Tet-ef, "Righteous Voice
42. Khe-Fou-f, "Right Voice
43. Si-Nefer-Ou, "Righteous Voice
44. Ra-Hani-ef, "Righteous Voice
45. Ra-Neb-Ka, "Righteous Voice
46. Ra-Ousir-Teta, "Righteous Voice
47. Ra-Usir, "Righteous Voice
48. Râ-Baba, "Righteous Voice
49. Râ...... t'à..., Just Voice
50. Seker-Nefer-Kâ, "Righteous Voice
51. Ra-Nefer-Ka, "Righteous Voice
52. Ra-Usir-Sent, "Righteous Voice

24.	Râ-Meri-An, "Righteous Voice	53.	Sit-a-Nesa, "Just Voice
25.	Râ-Pepi, "Righteous Voice	54.	Bâ-Neter-Ou, "Just Voice
26.	Ra-Teta, "Righteous Voice	55.	Râ-Ka-Keou, "Righteous Voice
27.	Ra-Ou-Nas, "Righteous Voice	56.	Râ-Neter-Baou, "Righteous Voice
28.	Râ-Ma-Kâ, "Righteous Voice	57.	Râ-Kheba-Ou, "Righteous Voice
29.	Her-Men-Kâ, Just Voice	58.	Râ-Meri-Ba-Pen, "Righteous Voice

The drawing reproduced above, taken on site by Mariette, clearly shows the layout.

Karnak: Here the situation is completely different, because not only are we almost 1,000 kilometres further south, but the name of Karnak itself, in its hieroglyphic form, needs no comment: "She who counts". So when Tutmes III, the most famous of the Pêr-Ahâ of the XVIIIth dynasty, "Life, Strength and Health be in him eternally", undertook to have bas-reliefs representing his Ancestors engraved on the walls of a room in his Palace, he did so with the most rigorous accuracy. For more than 3,500 years, they have stood in four superimposed rows, seated one behind the other in a deliberate though apparently dispersed order, some of them, particularly those from the IIIrd to XVIII[(th)] dynasties, facing those they had replaced.

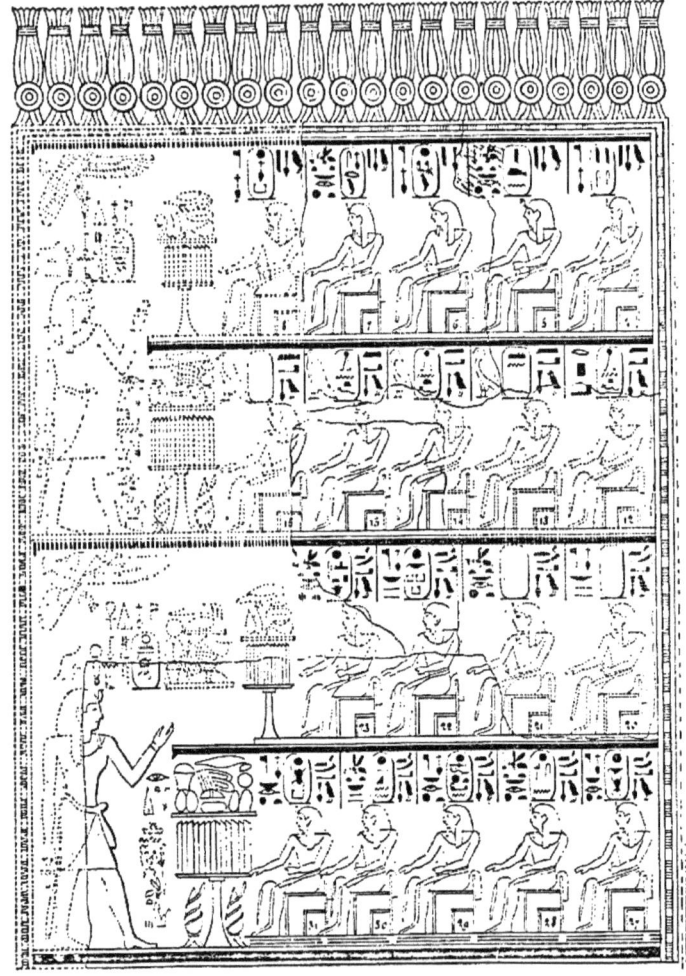
Karnak table.

Abydos: A little higher up, in the city of Abydos, several Annals have been found that overlap perfectly. One of the most famous is the one left on the walls by Seti Ier. In all modesty, he called himself the "Descendant of the Celestial Bull" and the "Unifier of the Two Lands". To justify this title, he could do no less than trace on the walls of his city the most important Annals found to date. They contain no fewer than 130 names. Unfortunately, however, they are no less open to question.

Indeed, how could a 'Sit rebel', i.e. a northerner, who had acceded to the Supreme Staff of the Command of Upper and Lower Egypt, claim to be directly descended from Usir, whom his clan continued to hate with the same tenacity?

His thanks, engraved for Eternity, is another challenge, since it is unashamedly dedicated "to the gods". That's why this dedication of the Annales "twice enduring in the Two Lands" must be scrupulously catalogued in the sole light of the ongoing antagonism that has fiercely opposed the two enemy clans for millennia, to extract only the names of the Kings who actually reigned.

The "Table of Abydos" reproduced here is described in three rows of superimposed cartouches, to be read vertically from the first column on the left, where we can easily recognise that of Menna or Menes, and above all the great subtlety of mind of this conqueror of the Two Lands (a).

(1) From the Primordial Earth, to King Menna, the Elder Ancestor, (39) From the Primordial Earth, to King Ra-Sea-Sibes, the Peer-Ahâ, (77) as a respectful offering to Sit the Falcon, on behalf of the Son of the Sun, Mennaptah Seti Ier.

(2) From the Primordial Earth, to King Atota, the Elder Ancestor, (40) From the Primordial Earth, to King Râ-Nuter-Kâ, the Pêr-Ahâ, (78) in respectful offering to the "Great-of-Life born of the Sun-Set".

(3) From the Primordial Earth, to King Tota, the Elder Ancestor, (41) From the Primordial Earth, to King Râ-MenKâ, the Peer-Ahâ, (79) as a respectful offering to Sit the Falcon, on behalf of the Son of the Sun, Mennaptah-Seti 1er.

(4) From the Primordial Earth, to King Alta, the Elder Ancestor, (42) From the Primordial Earth, to King RâNoufer-Kâ, the Pêr-Ahâ, (80) in respectful offering to the "Great-of-Life born of the Setting Sun".

(5) From the Primordial Earth, to King Khou-Koï, the Elder Ancestor, (43) From the Primordial Earth, to King Râ-Nefer-Nubi, the Pêr-Ahâ, (81) as a respectful offering to Sit the Falcon, on behalf of the Son of the Sun, Mennaptah-Séti Ier.

(6) From the Primordial Earth, to King Mer-Bapou, the Elder Ancestor, (44) From the Primordial Earth, to King Râ-Dekâ-Mâa, the Pêr-Ahâ, (82) in respectful offering to the "Great-of-Life born of the Setting Sun".

These Annals thus contain thirty-eight registers interspersing and glorifying the "Rebels" who reigned in Ath-Ka-Ptah before Seti Ier. A full translation will be provided at a later date, when the study of these various dynasties has been completed. But here is the general drawing, by way of example: *Table of Abydos*.

With the circumstances that led to the amalgamation of the two territories into a changing monarchy, depending on whether it was dominated by the North or the South, well placed in their spiritual and mythological context, it is worth trying to understand the popular mentality of 6,000 years ago.

The dynastic era of the Pharaohs was being actively prepared with the solar abandonment of the constellation Gemini. Taurus was appearing, heralding the second Resurrection of the "Elder". This is why Sit was already becoming, during this crucial transitional period, an object of opprobrium, an evil subject increasingly distorted by the myths that were taking shape, a perpetual rejection on the part of the "Descendants", forcing the "Rebels", when they regained power, to reintroduce their Chief, born of Sit, alongside Hor on an equal footing.

Beginning of the Abydos Table.

The tribes of the North, organising themselves and becoming very powerful under the impulse of the teaching spread by the schools of their Colleges of Solar Priests, tried in their turn to create a unification of the two elements dispersed in the Second Heart, but forming part of the same ethnic group. What they had refused to the ancient Pêr-Ahâ, they tried again in the other direction, but with no more result. Eliminating one or the other always seemed the only solution.

Hence the severe counter-attacks and defeats inflicted on the North, which in no way prevented the construction genius of the Kings of the South from developing the Nile Delta by digging irrigation canals and dam-like walls. Palaces were built, new temples to Ptah replaced those of Ra, and strongholds were constructed.

At the same time, the last Queen "Pêr-Ahâ" sent mining expeditions to several remote territories, and began exploiting the copper mines of Sinai. The two centuries preceding the dynastic establishment were a period of intense progress in all areas, the latest being the reintroduction of the sacred characters of writing.

This created enormous difficulties in getting the Annals off to a normal start, for the proliferation of emblems, clans, Uhu 'protectors' or nomes, whether terrestrial or celestial, accompanied by an abundant category of Priests officiating in any possible and imaginable place as being the true birthplace of this or that god, inevitably led to that aberration of Ptolemaic times when the Roman Emperor became the "Pharaoh beloved of Isis".

Without going back that far, at Abydos, this statement made to Ramses II can still be read: "Such you are, such was the son of Usir. Here you are, his heir in the same way, in his likeness! This term, Pêr-Ahâ, "Descendant of the Eldest", undoubtedly inspired all the formulas for divinisation that were tirelessly repeated according to a very rigorous ritual, from the beginning to the end of the thirty dynasties that established the civilisation of the Egyptian "God Cadets". This was clearly not understood by the Caesars and Ptolemies who, like the fifth of the latter name, adorned themselves with epithets that did not suit them, such as "beautiful adolescent who sits on the throne of Horus and makes you God as the son of Isis and Osiris".

But the degeneration and decadence of this people, who were the "Chosen Ones", led to this proliferation of great and small divinities in Ath-Ka-Ptah, and the "Second Heart-of-God" became compartmentalised into a multitude of individual sanctuaries, each of which assumed the role of Pêr-Ahâ and Ancestor as the reigns changed.

Monotheism thus disappeared, as did 'heliotheism' in the North, to make way for an incredible pantheon of celestial figures representing the gods, whose sons were adorned with the heads of more or less real animals. Thus were born those whom the Greeks have perpetuated under the names of Mercury, Mars, Venus, Saturn, Jupiter, and tutti quanti.

This mishmash alone allowed the usurping pharaohs, and only after the 6th dynasty, to be the heirs, the "sons", the "flesh of the gods" establishing themselves on the throne of the Ancestors. This saraband of divinisation ensured that the 'Rebel' in possession of the Sceptre, with the acquiescence of the Clergy who could no longer do anything, would reign as despot over the entire population of the 'Two Lands'.

From the end of the Archaic period, well before the advent of Menes, when cities such as Hierakonpolis, Nebadah and Abydos were barely at the height of their fortunes, double and triple royal titles were already commonplace, with each new 'Elder' appropriating those of his predecessors that would best confirm his illustrious descent in people's minds.

In this way, the South became entangled with the North. And vice versa... because the movement of the northerners towards Nubia led to a wide variety of mixtures. The Queen of Nekheb's "vulture" became entwined in Bouto's uraeus through marriage; the Pontiff of Herakleopolis magna having been deposed and the chief of the "Masnitiou" killed in the North, the "souten" of one and the "bee" of the other were appropriated, changing and increasing the royal banners and cartouches.

The two most powerful Colleges of Priests remained, however, each in their own domains in the North and South, cautiously waiting. Abydos and Heliopolis the Sacred watched each other from afar... but not for much longer. The merciless war they fought for divine supremacy gave rise to a new religious class, that of Karnak, the fortified and forbidden city of the ram-god. However, this would prelude the destruction of the entire Pharaonic civilisation, with the PêrAhâ having only the name of "Sons of God", without having either the origin or even the mentality.

In the Nile Delta, long before that time, the Heliopolitan solar cycle grouped most of the divinities of the time around its celestial bark, assigning each one a role corresponding to a specific function, modelled on the primitive legends about them which all referred to the influences they exerted on the Sun as it passed by them. Characters from the heroic era before the Great Cataclysm also found their place here, as did Sit, whose rebellious descendants were often Pontiffs of Heliopolis. The "Great Rebel" thus played a vital and beneficial role, allowing him to use and abuse his fighting strength, the very essence of the Northern revival within the titanic struggle that pitted one side against the continual oppression of the other.

All Memphite theology, based on Heliopolitanism, shows Sit standing at the prow of the solar bark, killing the Osirian serpent that is trying to prevent the renewal of the era through the death of Hor, before the star sets behind the horizon, bringing with it the cataclysmic upheaval that will engulf the "Elder Heart" and Ahâ-Men-Ptah.

Various passages in the texts known as the "Pyramids" show that Sit already had this aspect of a legendary beneficent giant, firmly established in the north of the country. In fact, it was well before the beginning of the Pharaonic era that the great 'theological' compositions on solar influences enabling access to the Beyond of Life began to emerge.

In paragraph 128, for example, an unambiguous appeal is made to the people of the "Rebels" by their leader, so that the "barbarians" born of Sit will triumph over all the land of the "Second Heart":

"Rise up, sleepers; wake up, you who are born of Sit and the Lion; so that you may contemplate and follow in his forward march the Great Dazzler who makes all things tremble in the swamps and advance into Eternity, for he is the opener of the paths that will progress all along the Great River!"

This fulfilled prophecy allows us to return to the Chronological Annals, which ended the previous volume with the sinking of Ahâ-Men-Ptah on the day of the Great Cataclysm, and to continue them here until the advent of Menes:

Sun in constellate.	duration in years	Duration before Christ	Total duration before 1975	Duration dep. Creation	Heroes dep. duration
Lion	576	9 792	11 767	25 920	11 520

... on that day, the Great Cataclysm stopped the solar boat from sailing ahead...

The Earth tilted by around 180° on its axis, and the Sun's path, which had stopped at 8° in front of the constellation Leo, resumed a *retrograde* course at 20° from this same stellar configuration. Thus, the third period of regrouping of the population that had survived the engulfment began on another continent throughout the solar recession in Leo:

Lion	1 440	8 352	10 327	27 360	12 960
Cancer	1 872	6 480	8 455	29 232	14 832
Gemini	1 872	4 608	6 583	31 104	16 704

At the end of the 'Age of Gemini', the titanic struggle between the two brothers and their totally different conceptions of a way of life desired by Ptah, or decided solely by Ra, haunted everyone's minds. In 4608 BC, while the Sun was still moving backwards through the last degree in the constellation of Taurus, Sep'ti, or Sirius, was in turn approaching the end of its 'sothic' year, preparing for the long-awaited new cycle.

The leaders of the two camps were polishing their weapons and putting the finishing touches to the equipment and the enlistment of the men who would ensure the supremacy of one side or the other over the whole of the territory that was soon to be known as the 'Second Heart'.

The final formula, whoever won, would combine Usir, the symbol of Resurrection and Rebirth on this second earth, with the Sun shining in the Celestial Taurus to give it new life every day! The Scriptures themselves underwent profound changes before being reintroduced for the making of the Sacred Texts. The liturgy of the ritual was intentionally inverted in the engraving so that it would follow the retrograde harmonic movement of the new solar navigation, starting from the right and reading all the way to the extreme left.

In the year 4303, when Menes was called to take the sceptre, everything was already ready to function according to the rhythm of the new calendar, which did not, however, come into operation until 62 years later, when Sirius rose in conjunction with the star of the day, thus opening the Year of God. That same day, he had his "Elder" crowned as his "Descendant", the "Pêr-Ahâ", who *invented* the calendar and began it immediately: on the 1st of the month of Thoth 4241...

The interesting thing is to see what Ménès and his three successors are up to:

 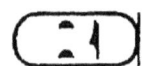 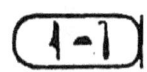 

They are here simply submitted to the "ideographic" perspicacity of the readers, because they will be studied later. Let us conclude instead with the historical chronology, starting from the Great Cataclysm, where it was interrupted in the previous work, so as to bring it up to Menes and the founding of the Dynasties:

GEB: Last of the "Pêr-Ahâ" who reigned in Ahâ-Men-Ptah

NOUT: Wife of Geb

Usir: Eldest son of Ptah and Nut

 (OSIRIS)

OUSIT: Eldest son of Geb and Nut

 (SETH)

ISET: Daughter of Geb and Nut

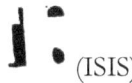 (ISIS)

NEK-BET: Iset's twin sister

 (NEPHTYS)

HOR: Eldest son of Ousir and Iset

 (HORUS)

From these 'Descendants' came a multitude, which Manetho lists quite correctly in his Egyptian Chronology. They can in fact be considered 'demigods' not only because of their origin, but also because they were the direct founders of the future 'Second Heart'.

Over the course of these pages, several millennia have passed, including several reigns that have survived in the predynastic cartouches that have come down to us:

HOR-OU-TIT, who left Ta Mana at when the Sun entered the Constellation of Cancer (22/7/8352).

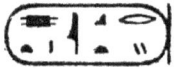

HOR-ATH-AKH, who was the 150th Pêr-Ahâ when the Sun entered the Constellation of Gemini.

HOR-NOU-LI, "Twice victorious", , who introduced the Falcon symbol into his emblem.

MOUT-PET-AHA, the Daughter of the Ancient Scorpion, who took the sceptre and introduced the vulture into her emblem.

AHA-KAI, the last Pêr-Ahâ before the Sun enters the constellation of Taurus and reaches Ath-Ka-Ptah.

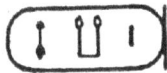

The "Sit Rebels" also sprang up to perpetuate the battle of the "Two Brothers":

AN-SIT-RA, who organised the fight against the "Shesou Hor" in a rational manner.

BAK-BA-RA, the Bloodhound who first introduced an ideogram to define it: Sparrowhawk.

RA-MEN-AKHER, the Rebel who tried to unite the two enemy Clans before arriving in the Second Heart.

Perhaps one day, following this outline, a complete chronology of the kings who made up the succession of Hor and Sit will be established. But it will take several volumes and as many years to achieve this.

It's high time we followed the "Descendants of the Two Brothers" into this second Land Beloved by God...

CHAPTER FOURTEEN

THE AGE OF GEMINI
(... OR THE PREDYNASTIC STRUGGLE OF THE "TWO BROTHERS")

> *In all probability, this line supplanted that of the Falcons, of which it was perhaps an offshoot, and established itself at Nekhen at a date which, if tradition is to be believed, can be put at 1,600 years before the appearance of the I^{st} Dynasty.*
> ARTHUR WEIGALL
> (History of Ancient Egypt)

> *The beginning of history also coincides with the appearance, or rather the relative spread, of writing. Although the first hieroglyphs appear on prehistoric palettes, it was not until the Thinite period that the use of writing developed.*
> J. VANDIER
> (Egyptian Archaeology Manual)

In the space of a few centuries, civilisation was established on the banks of the Nile, but clearly separated under two sceptres. The main "Uh-U" (pronounced Ouh-U and meaning "Twice from the waters") emerged almost all together during this period. These were the 'Nomes', due to bad Hellenic phonetisation.

Over a thousand years, a regularly retrograde Sun passed over the zenith of the twin "Fixes". Their distinctly different brightness seemed to set them against each other on clear nights, like a dark omen. And indeed, they attracted the hatred and discord that formed the core of the drama of these two enemy offspring: the Hawks and the Falcons.

For the "Kingdom of the North", that of Lower Egypt, the Nile Delta was enslaved by the "Rebels of Sit". The first town to be named after them during the first unified dynasty was Pa-Ouet, located on the Mediterranean coast, but well away from the marshy area. It thus became the residence of the first "Reed" kings, later taking the Greek name of Bouto.

The second was Pa-Asit, whose name was changed to Pa-Ousir after unification, and where the temple of the Sun became that of Ptah. Its current name is Abousir, and in addition to its temple from the first dynasties, there are three pyramids as famous as those at Giza.

Finally, the third important predynastic city was Pa-An-Râ, the sacred locality of the first official priests of the Sun, whose College was modelled on that of the Pontiff of the South, quite simply. However, this capital took on additional importance when the [32nd] "King of the North" decided to settle there himself.

The town then became Kemti, which the Greeks turned into Saïs. Bouto's disaffection stemmed from the stench of the marshes, the source of various infectious diseases and even the plague. But it is also certain that the predominance of the priests throughout this more fertile region encouraged the King to come and live there himself.

The leader of the "Sit Rebels", who once again went to war against his southern counterpart, took the opportunity to display a new royal emblem, the Cobra. This reptile, so feared in the delta and its marshes, had finally been defeated by a variety of tricks, becoming the symbol of the power of Sit's descendants.

Throughout the Era of Gemini, which lasted 1,872 years, were 64 "Cobra" kings, "Sparrowhawk" kings from the "Reeds" and "Sun Worshippers", hence the apparent complication of protocol denominations in the cartouches that appeared during the reigns of the last ten chieftains. The last of these chiefs submitted to the "Masnitiou" of the ShesouHor in office: the Master "Falcon", born of the "Lotus" and flying over humans imperially like the "Bee". This peace treaty, the most important of all time, preceded by 217 years the entry of the Sun into Taurus, the "era of the Resurrection of Usir". This period was devoted by the King of the Two Lands, North and South, of l'Amenta in the west and Ath-Ka-Ptah in the east, thus the Master of the Four Times of the Earth and of the Universe, to making colossal achievements in honour of the One Almighty God who had made this possible, which, by thanking the Eternal for his benefits, would unite heaven and earth, Humanity and Divinity.

An extract from the so-called Turin papyrus, which traces the chronology of the Pharaohs back to the "Followers of Horus".

At the time of Khufu (Khufu), the "legendary" Ancestors were already credited with founding the aforementioned cities, as well as building the most important religious sanctuaries of the time (4th Dynasty), in particular the temple next to the Sphinx, opposite the Pyramid.

Naturally, we will come back to these gigantic constructions in the next volume, which will be devoted to the first six dynasties, but it is necessary to give a few details here, before moving on to the southern kingdom, where, moreover, those who erected the monuments had been able to experiment with their techniques at their leisure beforehand.

Of the pre-dynastic monuments erected to the glory of God in the north by the "Masnitiou" of the south, the most important is undoubtedly the Temple of Ptah, located near the Great Sphinx. Unrepentant tourists are still overcome by vertigo and wonder when they cease to be amazed by this colossal construction.

Before starting your visit, it's a good idea to stand to the right of the main entrance, in the corner formed by the cornerstone, to have your photo taken. And the subject of the photograph is smaller than the smallest microbe!

Imagine a huge block, which means nothing, because it weighs 400 tonnes, give or take 50 kilos. It's a single stone made of Syene granite, and that's certain, because there are none like it anywhere else. It was therefore brought from there by the Nile, and had at least twice the volume, so weighed twice as much, since it was cut to form an internal angular façade several metres long.

But it's just one stone! And it took hundreds of them to erect this sumptuous edifice, made entirely of very fine, black granite from Syene and translucent alabaster from Arabia, whose summit vault, whose weight would be unthinkable even with modern lifting equipment, is still supported after eight millennia by square pillars with absolutely smooth sides, all in one piece.

The interior remains impressively pure and prodigious in its total bareness, for although there are obviously no hieroglyphs engraved, no ornaments or mouldings to interrupt the eye or the mind stricken by prayer; only this gigantism, created for the glory of God.

In an inscription preserved in the Museum of Bulaq, a papyrus from the Scribe of Khufu, the Khufu of the [4th] Dynasty, refers to it as a building erected by the "Followers of Hor", whose origins are lost in the mists of time. The edifice was found by chance, during this Pharaonic reign when colossal constructions abounded, by workmen tasked with clearing away the rediscovered Sphinx.

The history of this people of the "Two Lands" thus really begins in this unified era, around two centuries before Menes ushered in the dynastic era in 4241 BC. At that time, the country was still only the "Promised Land", hence its hieroglyphic name of Ta Merit.

But these most diverse mixtures will only form a single nation behind the United-God from the day when the bearer of a single staff imposes his hereditary power, derived from Usir. This theocratic monarchy therefore waited in anticipation for the imperative affirmation of a "Descendant", a Pêr-Ahâ from the South to unify the "Second Heart", for this kingdom, privileged from the moment of its arrival on the banks of the Nile, was then reaching its edifying as much as its mystical apogee.

For as soon as the cliff was lowered, or bypassed, this valley of fertile silt became a veritable new Eden for the arrivals. This human mass of "Hor's Followers", fanaticised by the "Elder" and the Pontiff, set out to live on the same scale as the suffering they had endured for 3,000 years on a journey of over 3,000 kilometres to take possession this land and develop it.

The nation as a whole, behind the royal emblem of the South, embarked on a programme of works that defied contemporary imagination, for it had only human arms at its disposal, even if they multiplied by the hundreds of thousands! The era of construction thus began simultaneously around present-day Aswan, in places made world-famous by the gigantic works undertaken under the aegis of U.N.E.S.C.O. some fifteen years ago to relocate the pharaonic temples threatened with engulfment by the waters of the Aswan Dam.

But these temples - Philae, Abu-Simbel, Elephantine - were only reconstructions carried out centuries and centuries after the first ones were built. Then came Edfu and Kom-Oumbos, and the great crowds settled in a large city, Hierakonpolis by its Greek name, but which in those days was called Nekhem - it was here that the first predynastic tombs were found, and a whole funerary ritual already existed.

The first and most important observation is that, while the cities and temples mentioned above are located on the eastern bank or on islands in the middle of the river, the necropolis is the only one on the western bank. The same applies to Thebes and the other major cities. Secondly, and by no means least, the building stones all came, at least initially, from the quarries at Syene, only a dozen kilometres from Aswan, which must have been very close to the ancient city at that time.

All the traditions learnt orally, and scrupulously repeated over the millennia by minds that were less and less convinced, were nevertheless preserved in their entirety, finally finding their first reuses before the papyrus was processed and the ink found.

At the same time as priests were specialising in theology, "Mathematical Combinations" and Sacred Scripture, others were teaching carpentry, metalwork, painting and many other disciplines. To meet the most urgent needs, the Priest-Architects trained an entire school "on the job" at , making hundreds of "Mandjit" boats for use on the "Great River". These life-saving boats, which emerged from the Great Cataclysm, were the starting point for the great shipyards lining Hierakonpolis.

All types of barge, increasingly specialised, were designed and assembled here, including flat-bottomed barges capable of transporting the most voluminous and heavy construction materials.

Let's not forget that the blocks weighing almost a thousand tonnes, which were used to build the "House of God" next to the Great Sphinx, were transported by these barges from Syene to Giza, on the Nile, a distance of a thousand kilometres! For the record, this was 7200 *years ago, and* 500 barges were needed, each with specially designed flat bottoms capable of supporting 1,000 tonnes during the floods, i.e. for three months of the year.

The explorers of the sites who first ventured down this river blessed by God did not go that far. They were content, on the "Mandjit", to approach the area around present-day Thebes, which quickly became the high place of the Lord, as well as the home of all the population not needed in the south for construction or in the quarries.

The first College of Priests was established in a hollow in the cliffs, ideal for the meditation permitted by the bareness of the place, which took the easily understood name of Uhu-Ptah. When you're there, or more modestly when you consult a map, you can see that this spot was chosen deliberately, as it marks the beginning of a loop of the Nile towards the East, the only one that diverts the river's north-south axis somewhat.

What's more, this panorama determines a harmonious location with Ahâ-Men-Ptah, since it is itself on the parallel of the Tropic of Cancer. This latter situation led the Pontiff to search the surrounding area, and inside the loop, for a highly predestined location for the "Temple of Heaven", and its "House of Life", which would be responsible for the study of "Mathematical Combinations". He was quickly spotted: Ptah-Api or "God of the Celestial River".

And so, very quickly, the whole region became the vital centre of the Southern Lands. The most intense activity reigned on the immense rocky esplanade to the west, where the houses of the Divine and those of the Beyond were built, as well as on the fertile and viable plain on the other side of the Nile, where the dwellings of the living emerged from the frail clay.

While the popular towns of Karnak, Luxor and Kaft were rapidly springing up, funerary sites were springing up opposite, on the slopes of the cliffs that were being carved out like Gruyère cheese. Here too, much earlier rock engravings attest to the arrival of the "primitive Oasians", as some archaeologists modestly refer to them.

The "Descendant" Hor-Nou-Ka, the penultimate "Elder" before the birth of the unifying King Menes, led a flotilla of improved "Mandjit" to conquer the territories occupied in the delta by the Rebels. It was here, moreover, that one of the Priests recognised the cliffs of Giza where the Sphinx, the Pyramids... and the Temple later appeared!

On his victorious return, he founded the city that for a long time bore his name, and to the west of which lies his tomb. Hor-Nou-Ka then became Hermontis, with a highly questionable Greek phonetisation. Not far from there, the most sumptuous "Houses of the Beyond" were built at Medinet-Abu, and above all the most sumptuous "Mansion", that of Deir-el-Bahari, where Queen Hatshepsut was buried. Under the XVIIIth Dynasty, she subjugated more than one neighbouring territory and led her people under an iron fist.

But the Pêr-Ahâ of that time had no son. So it was Hor-Nou-Ka's eldest daughter who took the baton of command when the time came. She was the seventh predynastic Queen of the Age of Gemini, which was drawing to a close as the Sun's retreat into this constellation came to an end.

She reigned under the ambiguous Divine name of Hor-Sept-Ka, the soul of Hor that inhabited her as a direct 'descendant', despite her feminine carnal envelope. To leave no doubt in people's minds, this Queen created a new capital, Nabt, better known to the world by its name Nebadah, since Egyptologists have found dozens of predynastic royal tombs there.

But at the same time, one element, and not the least, would rise up against Hor-Sept-Ka's proud and despotic pretensions. This was a young Pontiff fresh from his father's school, consecrated as Chief Priest under the dreaded name of Anepou.

With the support of his illustrious forefather, he founded a mystical city not far from Nabt, and gave it a name that clearly demonstrated his disavowal of the "barbaric" policies of the

"Descendant". He named the central Temple, and thus the entire city, Abt, the opposite of Nabt.

Thus stood the ancient city of Abydos near Negadah, in whose Temple were found the most famous *Chronological Tables*, which included not only the royal genealogical cartouches from the first King Menes onwards, but also those of Kings prior to this first dynasty, including the cartouches of the famous seven Queens.

This fierce struggle between the 'Body' and the 'Spirit', the weak flesh and the soul spiritualised to the extreme; this opposition between the tyrannical earthly life of the Divine Descendant and the ascetic existence of the Prophet of God could only end in a most official union.

So, after many battles and victories, while her personal emblem already included the "Falcon" of the Descendants of Hor and the "Vulture" of those who had preceded her, she ensured her omnipotence by marrying An-Nu Anepou, adding in a second cartouche the "Bee" so dear to her husband's trepanologists. She also drew public attention to herself by having an enormous building erected for the first time, one that was not intended for the glory of God. It was a fortress that soon stood on the banks of the Nile, near the present-day town of Beni Hassan. Powerful and inviolable, it nipped in the bud any attempt by the northern rebels to invade the southern territories, although they were subject to an iron rule, but they were not allies.

The most important event of this marriage, from a historical point of view, was that twins were born. The eldest, by a few minutes, became the last predynastic king, Hor-Sen-Kai, the Scorpion-King; the younger became the highly enlightened Pontiff who re-established writing by reinventing papyrus, under the name of AnepouUr or the Great Anubis.

What an apotheosis for the exit of the Sun from the Constellation of Gemini! The perfect agreement between the two brothers, one of whom carried the royal staff and the other the Divine sceptre, led to the general unification of the Nile valley along its entire length, with great mutual trust giving them complete freedom to go away.

This enabled the "Scorpion King" to set off at the head of a veritable armada to colonise the various "Uhu" of the North once and for all. He then built an eight hundred kilometre bridge of boats, in keeping with the work he was undertaking to glorify Divine clemency for his "Elders". Three of these buildings consecrated the praise that went up to heaven, as a sign of the harmonious link between the Creator and his creatures. There was the Temple of Ptah; "Akher", the "Celestial Lion", which became the Sphinx; and the pyramidal block of "the Beloved-Who-Descends-Light", which will be discussed in greater detail in the next volume.

These fifty-eight years of reign on the scale of a God become man again, with the multitude working for his greater glory and his advent, were a period of overflowing activity, unimaginable for our minds of [a]twentieth century more inclined towards unconditional mechanisation than to deliberately sought-after manual work.

Thousands of boats of all shapes and sizes, sailing in an endless chain up and down the Nile, carried workers and equipment. Whether it was supplies or men, all the boats lined up to make way for the huge flat-bottomed barges, each carrying *a block,* a monolith weighing over 500 tonnes, for a thousand kilometres.

As soon as they disembarked, thousands of enthusiastic hands rushed to load them, one after the other, onto sledges six metres wide and a dozen metres long. Teams in four lines of a hundred men each pulled the gigantic masses.

To make them slide more easily, jug carriers ran from the river to the front of the block to which they were assigned and poured out the twelve litres of water contained in each container so that the metre-wide runners, while making them easier to slide, would not catch fire from the intense friction of the wood against the sand. And all the way *up the* four-kilometre slope to the titanic construction site where the building to the glory of the Lord would be erected.

On each block, a team leader chanted the rhythm of the march by banging energetically on a sound box. This was repeated by dozens of human-coupled vehicles following the same pattern and advancing with the same uniform movement, on a road that seemed endless for this anthill. But it was the only road that gave access to the Beyond Life, beyond these edifices on a Divine scale alone, which constituted the ramparts of Heaven.

Meanwhile, a thousand kilometres further south, the Great Anepou was preparing the spiritual and intellectual renaissance of the unified homeland by restoring the sacred texts to their ancestral hieroglyphic script on parchment he had just reinvented from papyrus.

The long-awaited Era of Taurus was approaching day by day, and every being consulted the sky, but in vain, looking for the sign that the Sun had finished its evil navigation. Little Men-Ahâ had just been born, and this son of the Descendant of the "Old Sun", who would become the first King of this new era, was the object of all the attention of those who would be specially charged with his education in preparation for the unifying task that would be his when the time came.

Men-Ahâ, by becoming "Menâ" or Menes, would indissolubly bind the "Two Lands", Ahâ-Men-Ptah and Ath-Ka-Ptah, by linking the two northern and southern territories of Ta Mérit, the Beloved Land. In this way, the "Second Heart" could be born, grow and multiply in bliss.

Nabt-Négadah lived in feverish anticipation of this event, which would be consecrated by the new era. For his part, Abt-Abydos worked day and night, in the smoke of his oil lamps, to reconstitute all the written forms of Knowledge.

It was for this reason that rock engravings became much rarer from this predynastic period onwards. Only various models of boat still appeared, most of them reminiscent of the "Mandjit" of the Ancestors, the lines drawn on the walls reproducing these frail reed boats with the ties attaching the plants to the boats their entire width and length.

Numerous flint statues and clay figurines of bulls, all from the same period, demonstrate the concern of the artists, and through them the entire population, for a future that the priests portrayed as sumptuous!

In the examples in the British Museum and the Berlin Museum, the horns of the bovids are harmoniously rounded, pointing forward, as if in an attempt to move faster into the future to reach the bliss promised to those who would have taken part in its advent.

For this very reason, the state of civilisation of this people, 5,000 years before Christ, was very advanced in its development. It should not be forgotten that in the north, in addition to the three major works, the Scorpion-King had to give a new direction to the Nile, build dykes to keep its waters out of normal flooding areas, dig an enormous basin to purify the region and various other works which, although more modest, were no less Herculean.

During this time, the rules of architecture and construction reached such a degree of perfection that, despite all our modern technical knowledge, if we had to build by hand tomorrow, we'd be unable to carry out one hundredth of the work of the ancients in the same time and with the same quality.

This is why, in the south, Abydos the Holy, Abt the venerated, developed its buildings and "writings" on gazelle skins before papyrus appeared. More significant, however, was the influence that the Great Anepou imposed on this region. This was the preferred dwelling place of the hard-working population that lived there, but it also had an influence on the whole of the great loop that the Nile begins at this point and ends at Luxor.

And at the end of this great meander, on the western bank, at the most favourable strategic point, geographically and astronomically speaking, appeared the beginnings of what was to become the most sacred and secret of God's 'Mansions': the 'Temples of Heaven' of Tantri-Nouit, which became Denderah. His school, or "House of Life", attracted all the Priests, for his teaching alone enabled initiation, without which Knowledge was but a delusion. This was where the "Divine-Mathematical-Combinations" were learned...

Even in December 1975, without wishing to seek out the truth in the Ptolemaic architecture of the last temple rebuilt for the sixth time under Evergettius II, despite the labyrinths reconstructed according to the "ancient" plans, it is easy to immerse oneself in the padded and studious atmosphere of the initiation, by wandering around the hollow interior of the perimeter, in this enclosure where not only were there shops where offerings and donations were catalogued and stored, separate chapels for each Pontiff who attained the dignity of High Priest here, sacristies for the different categories of servants, passages linking the one to the other, straight corridors several hundred metres long - paragraphs from the Sacred Texts of the *Book of Four Eras* are engraved, seemingly in disorder, on every wall and ceiling - but there are also numerous labyrinth-like corridors that seem to end in a dead end, some of which provide access to the foundations of the central building, at the very heart of the foundations.

They are up to six metres thick and contain numerous crypts, between which staircases lead down to the "Archive Rooms", the "Time Rooms" and the "Treasure Rooms", all spread over three underground levels, obviously linked by staircases carved into the rock and turning abruptly sixteen times at right angles.

At the very bottom of the last basement: the Room of Usir and the "Room of the White Cow", to use the hieroglyphic *(sic)* interpretation of certain Egyptologists. But the history of this people, from its origins to its end, can easily be reconstructed by adapting the different pieces of this giant jigsaw puzzle, a chessboard measuring 81.50 m from its base to its last terrace, the height of a *thirty-storey* building. You have to try and imagine it to fully understand it!

In all this apparently complicated context, but easily identifiable by the very exact north-south orientation of the façade calculated for the year 4387 BC, as indicated in the texts. However, the position needs to be corrected, because when the Nile reaches the end of its loop, it makes a 90° bend°, so the actual course is west-east!

The extraordinary profusion of Texts covering every surface from floor to ceiling shows that the first scribes wanted to perpetuate for all eternity all the chapters of Knowledge, by engraving them on a single monument capable of withstanding all cataclysms, making them easily recoverable, if necessary, by a new generation.

And from the last terrace, the resurrected Usir gestures with his hand to a room, one floor down, where the thread can be found. This is the second chamber, the same one where the famous circular planisphere *was* engraved on the ceiling, near which Iset pointed to the West.

All that remains is a gaping hole, bloodied hideously by the setting sun as I passed by. The story of this Temple is of such importance that it will probably be the subject of the next volume, if the subject is deemed interesting by the public. The staggering and astonishing reality, which far exceeds all fiction, will probably allow this publication, which will be like a resurrection of the Temple itself.

At Denderah, the only link between the Earth and Heaven appears as a pious reality, and not the imaginative fiction of a few priests in search of purely earthly goods. The Harmony in which everyone participated body and soul was the tangible reflection of which had to obey to avoid a cataclysmic renewal even more total than that which had destroyed the 'First Heart'.

Thus, the Pêr-Ahâ, the Pharaoh, the Elder, the Descendant, or whatever other name one might give to the "Old Son", remained the "Heart-of-God" in all his descendants. The first having been swallowed up with Ahâ-MenPtah, the second had to be reborn with

Ath-Ka-Ptah. This is why the obedience of all, great and small, was not contested, since there was no other possibility of survival in the Beyond of Life. This is the conclusion that can be drawn from the Temple of the "Lady of Heaven" at Denderah and from the tombs of the first Pontiffs buried not far from there, under the western hill.

All the Egyptologists were lost in delirious phrases about the beauty of Denderah, although they disputed fiercely about its origin. I'll save the hundreds of echoes in all languages for the many chapters in the next volume, but I can't resist the temptation of quoting a sentence from the most illustrious of them, as well as many extracts from a letter from a neophyte in the field but equally erudite.

Champollion, on his first visit to Denderah, was carried away by a highly poetic lyricism, writing in his notebook:

> "We finally arrived in Denderah! The moonlight was magnificent and we were only an hour's journey from the temples. Could we resist the temptation? I won't try to describe the impression made on us by the great propylon and especially the portico of the great temple! You can measure it, but it's impossible to give an idea! It is grace and majesty combined to the highest degree! We stayed there for hours in ecstasy, running through the great halls with our poor falot![57] "

Before returning to Champollion and Dendera, here is an extract from letter XLII of the correspondence written in 1828 by Baron Th. Renouard de Bussière, then second secretary at the French embassy in Cairo, during his first visit to Dendera:

> "At last, my dear friend, I have seen this marvellous Tentyre! I have walked through its buildings, its porticoes,

---

[57] *Lettres inédites d'un Champollion inconnu,* published by L. de la Brière, 1897.

its temples! What can I do to share with you the delicious and profound emotion that still grips me? What can I do to pass before your eyes the imposing immensity of the monuments I have just seen!

When, having regained my composure, I finally able to examine the details, I discovered everywhere the most perfect proportions, simple and serious lines, right up to the sublime! The bas-reliefs, hieroglyphs, inscriptions and ornaments, so numerous, do not detract from the severe mass of the whole: they disappear into the immensity of the edifice, leaving only the great lines visible!

It would be impossible for me to give an exact description of the bas-reliefs decorating the ruins of Tentyre; the further I examined them, the frightened I became by the sheer volume of detail!

There are twenty-four columns in the portico, divided into four rows of six columns each; the first six, placed abreast, are set into intercolumnal walls. The open space separating the middle column is double that of the others. The capitals are square; on each of the four sides of the die is a mask with cow's ears. These heads are quite mutilated; those in the first row all have broken noses, yet they have retained a noble, calm and gentle expression; above the heads, the capital, which tapers, is still covered with bas-reliefs representing temples and symbolic figures. The shafts are divided into rings depicting religious subjects. The ceilings are adorned with sculptures, all of which are heavily blackened. These include the zodiac[58], which two large female figures are holding in their embrace. The walls are divided into four rows of square compartments, similar in arrangement to the various squares of a chessboard. Each of these compartments contains a bas-relief dedicated to a religious subject and a few columns of hieroglyphs, which no doubt contain a description of what the painting represents.

---

[58] This is the map of the sky giving the date of the 'Great Cataclysm' (see our previous book).

All the sculptures were painted; some of the colours still exist and have retained an extraordinary brightness and freshness. The figures in the lower paintings are colossal. The further I went in my examination, the less I knew what to draw first. Whichever way I looked, I could only see remarkable objects. I saw divinities, men, animals, plants, religious and rural ceremonies: the solitary location of the monument, at the entrance to the desert, lends it even more charm!

So it was only after a lifetime devoted to the study of Knowledge that it was possible to understand what was happening in the 'Other Life'. But an initiation lasting seventeen years gave access to Wisdom and to an understanding of the 'Divine Mathematical Combinations' on a par with that of a young Greek adopted by a High Priest, who after the positive examination of the initiation gave up his Greek name Mnesarchus for that given to him by the last Pontiff of Ath-Ka-Ptah, the same year that Cambyses invaded and devastated the country, *Ptah-Gô-Râ*, he who 'Knows-God-the-Sun'. On his return to Greece, after a further eleven years' exile in Persia, he became the philosopher Puthagoras of Samos, the Pythagoras of our textbooks.

Four millennia before that, another initiate was approaching the unified throne on which he would become the first King of the first Pharaonic dynasty of the Sons of God. Before that, he had to put down an uprising in the northern territories, fomented by a "Rebel of Sit", drunk with holy glory, who had inverted the hieroglyphic syllables of the name of his southern enemy to attract the benefits of the sun. He called himself *Na-Râ-Mer*, "the Unifier-Lover of the Sun".

This rebellion only lasted as long as the resounding defeat, which nevertheless took some twenty years, giving both men more experience and intelligence. As a result, Menna, as a magnanimous victor and perfect diplomat, made the defeated rebel his personal and divine representative in the North, after simply giving a more orthodox name to the new 'Son of God', Na-Mer. Ra, or the Sun, was reduced to the simple task of being the instrument of the Eternal's benefits.

This officialisation brilliantly opened the Era of Taurus on that day, 24 May 4262 BC, with the reading of the famous ritual known as the "Two Masters", recorded in all the Annals. This was the oath of allegiance to the One God, the sole Creator of the Universe and Mankind. It was read on the banks of the Great River, in common, by the Pontiffs of the North and South, before all the chiefs of the Uhu of the Two Lands gathered on the banks of the Nile.

Here is the text, preserved in the Archives of Denderah, which forms part of the Annals of the *Book of the Four Eras:*

"The Two Masters spoke thus to the chiefs of the Uhu clans, gathered in a "Second Heart" on the banks of Hapy, being in front of them, on the same Mandjit:

They said in the desert: *You are our border from this day forward!*

They said to the barren mountain: *No one must cross you to leave our Second Heart, because their life would cease for all eternity!*

They said to the nourishing silt: *You will be the future the earth and of our race, for you are the Beloved of the Great River!*

They said to the Great River: *Your heavenly springs will be the springs of our Life, for they will ensure our resurrection every year!*

They said to the people gathered together: *From now on, you will live in harmony with the Commandments of the Law of God, for it is these that will allow all life on Earth as it is in Heaven. You will nourish the soil with your work, and the soil will nourish you with its grain!*

They said to the Uhu Chiefs of the 'Two Lands': *Your authority will remain in the image of your emblems, because as you govern, so will the people!*

The "Two Masters" said to themselves;

So that all the children of God united in this "Second Heart" can grow and multiply in peace, glorifying the Eternal One and his Creation, our work will remain Unique!

Finally, raising their arms to Heaven, they addressed God in fervent *prayer: O Lord of Eternity, Ptah, may Your Law henceforth become the sole guide for our actions in every moment of Life, so that our Descendants may conform to Your Harmony without any fear of Cataclysm! May Your Wisdom penetrate us and help us to live on this Earth in anticipation of the Blessed Beyond of Life!"*

Thus began the era of the Bull Celestial and that of the dynasties of the "Sons of God", the Pêr-Ahâ or Pharaohs, as cited in the Annals of the "Four Eras".

But it wasn't until twenty years later, when Menes' eldest son came of age and was called to help his father, that the Chronology of the Kings began with the introduction of the Calendar. For it was in the year 4241 that Sep'ti or Sirius, in conjunction with the Sun, entered a new "Year of God".

This memorable day also saw Atota, Menes' eldest son, take the throne. He became the second king of the first dynasty. By introducing the calendar into the daily routine, he gave the months names other than those used in Ahâ-Men-Ptah. And what could be more normal than to call the first month by its own name? So the year began with the month of Thoth, and in Greek, Atota became Athothis. But let's not anticipate the 'fabulous' story of the historic people of this 'Second Heart', Ath-KaPtah, because monotheism, which had to survive so that the 'Cadets' could live, often suffers the after-effects of decisions made by human reason, which Reason ignored.

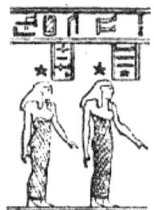

Notes and Bibliography

NOTE A: *ABOUT PLATO'S TIMAEUS*

Many readers of the previous volume, The Great Cataclysm, have objected to the interpretation of the text of the *Timaeus*, which glorifies the "Greek ancestors for the countless benefits they had received precisely from what they were demeaning in the offending dialogue".

And yet nothing could be further from the truth! Plato, who was born in 427 BC, was already a comfortable philosopher in his seventies, and undoubtedly ageing, when he set about writing a trilogy, of which the *Timaeus* was only one part, the other two being the *Critias*, which was never completed, and *the Hermocratè*, which was never written.

Plato had just returned from Sicily, a trip that depressed him, as everyone knows, because of the bitter failure he suffered there in his attempt to establish a communitarian and egalitarian republic where everyone would be happy. He had spent five years learning the ins and outs of the Egyptian temples, and was now trying to bring those famous laws back into force.

Ulcerated by his bitter failure, he returned to Athens and wrote the *Philebus*. It is easy to see in this work the admiration of this very wise man for a people whose grandiose achievements were far beyond the comprehension of the Hellenes of the time. In *Philebus,* VIII, infinite respect can even be read directly in the lines:

> "Discovering that the voice is eternal was the work of a god or some divine man, as the story goes in Egypt, of a certain Thoth who was the first to perceive in this infinity the vowels as being not one, but several, and then of at least tres letters which, without having the nature of vowels, nevertheless have a certain sound, and recognised that they likewise have a determined number. He also distinguished a third species of letters that we now call silent. After making these observations, he separated the mute and soundless letters one by one; then he did the same with the vowels and medium letters until, having grasped their number, he gave each and every one of them the name of elements. Moreover, seeing that none of us could learn any of these letters alone without learning them all, he imagined the link between them as being one. And imagining this as being one whole, he gave this whole the name of grammar as also being one art.

This extract is enough to reveal the admiration and nostalgia of an indisputable scholar, faced with an unfathomable abyss of intelligence. But the important fact, which might perhaps pass unnoticed, is that Plato also confirms without discussion the anteriority of writing commonly attributed to the Phoenicians. As there is no shortage of testimonies on this subject, we can assume that it was with a heavy heart that the illustrious philosopher interpolated the *Timaeus* dialogue in an attempt to revive the 'sacred' union among his compatriots.[59]

His conscience remained untroubled, however, for although his long stay on the banks of the Nile had made him an admirer of the achievements and designs of this ancient Pharaonic world, he was far from having the same admiration for the natives of his time.

There was such decadence and decay among the Egyptians with whom he came into contact, compared to what he had intuitively glimpsed of ancient life as Solon had described it, *that the dread of such a restart took root in him as far as his fellow citizens were concerned.* And he wasn't very young...

Having returned from Sicily and written the *Philebus* while teaching his new philosophy, he wrote the first part of his trilogy, the *Timaeus*, after careful consideration. He knew he had only a few years to live, so he prepared the framework for his 12 books of *Laws*, which would set out his views on the administration of the Republic.

The *Timaeus* is the prelude to, and undoubtedly the exemplary introduction to, the *Laws* that Plato would recommend as a kind of testament to the Athenians. The *Timaeus* should demonstrate that all the glory and valour of Hellenic antiquity belong to the Greeks alone, who will not fail to adopt its Laws, which will restore Athens to its former splendour!

It is easy to follow the thread of Plato's thought, since the beginning of the *Timaeus* is a constant reminder of this conception, which stems from the philosopher's personal mentality. The conversation between Socrates, Timaeus, Critias and Hermocrates is proof of this, thanks in particular to the total concordance between *Timaeus* 17b/19b and *The Republic* II-369/V-471.

This is how the ideal city, capital *of an elsewhere,* Ahâ-Men-Ptah, which became Atlantis, recounted by Solon the Wise 150 years before Plato, in verse and in another version, became an ancient Greek creation.

---

[59] On the subject of the Egyptian anteriority of writing, read: Isidore of Seville *Origine,* I, 5; Cyril of Alexandria: *Contra Julianum,* VII; Josephus: *Ant. Jud,* not to mention Clement of Alexandria, whose justification is the *Stromata.*

On his return from Sicily, at the age of seventy, Plato realises that his brothers are selfish, full of themselves and believing only in their own creations. The bitter aftertaste of 'déjà vu' comes rushing back, taking hold of the old man haunted by the decline of the carefree humanity he loves so much. And it is precisely because of this fear of seeing the Acropolis become a field of ruins similar to those of Heliopolis or Thebes of the Hundred Golden Gates sung by Homer, that he takes up this utopian idea of an ideal government that would make everyone aware of their responsibilities to preserve Divine Harmony in the Future.

He had already tried this experiment unsuccessfully in Sicily with Dionysius II, but he had been mocked and scorned, and it had been a dismal failure. This is why the *Timaeus* was written in such a masterly way, in the form of a homily to Hellenic Glory.

NOTE B: ON THE ANTIQUITY OF THE DENDERAH ZODIAC

Many questions also arise concerning the Temple of Denderah and its "Zodiac". Since the third volume will be devoted solely to Dendera from its first construction to the sixth and last, that of Ptolemy II, there is no need to begin a detailed argument on the very origin of the planisphere, or simply of the religious edifice. But to better understand its original authenticity, let's try to explain the mathematics of the precession of the equinoxes, the only process capable of quantifying *in time* a representation of celestial configurations, in other words of dating the antiquity of a sky map and not that of the engravers of the image.

Let's imagine a spherical sundial divided into 360°, from which the two caps have been removed. All that will be left is a wide circle on either side of the celestial equator, a kind of watch on a solar scale, with a hand moving from right to left, indicating the Sun's movement from sunset to sunrise and vice versa, so that one complete revolution of this dial indicates the time *of one sidereal year*.

But the most important aspect of this astronomical knowledge lies in the fact that the course, or 'navigation', of the sun along this great circular celestial river is not uniform in its temporal countdown. For it is by virtue of the Earth's retrograde movement that the essential mathematics of the equinoxes is formed, our *tropical year having a duration of 365 days 5 hours 48 minutes and 51 seconds*, whereas the *sidereal* annual revolution *is 365 days 6 hours 9 minutes and 11 seconds*. This mathematical difference in time is reflected in space by a retreat of 50 arcseconds each year from its initial point, the vernal point, thus retrograding BY ONE DEGREE IN 72 YEARS.

It is from this discrepancy, which brings the sky back to its primitive position every 25,920 years (72× 360), that ancient chronology has been re-established in its dating with the most rigorous accuracy. When we have precise data, as is the case with the Denderah Planisphere, it is easy to calculate the time separating the primitive position of the equinoxes and solstices relative to our own celestial configurations. The difference in degrees, minutes and seconds of arc will be divided by 50 seconds to obtain the distance in relation to the present time.

But the circular dial, imagined cut out of a celestial sphere, is not easy to handle for a neophyte and does not facilitate popular understanding. It is impossible to mark the infinite position of the annual retrogrades on a finite circle, without quickly leading to extreme confusion. The eternal march of time through space would quickly render all the calculations as incomprehensible as they are risky, even for professionals!

It is therefore essential to use another solution for lay people. For example, a flat surface, the length of which can be stretched indefinitely to ensure that the figures are as clear as they are precise. Any reader will be able to make all the calculations he or she wants. It will be assumed that the circle, presented in profile, will move parallel to itself and from left to right, like a propeller moving through the air, thus depicting a cylinder whose length will increase ad infinitum, according to the needs of the time to come.

The vernal point, indicating the beginning of the year, is represented by the guideline, divided into equal parts. The cyclical chronological flow will not accumulate as in a circle, but will develop on the flat surface from one intersection to the next, *like the pitch of a propeller,* each advance of a helical pitch graphically representing a sidereal year. The successive retrogrades of the other years will be annotated with dots: wave, tropical, canicular or any other.

These different sequences will form *the linear profile of time,* defining the perpetual and continuous transformations *of circular spatial time.* On the cylindrical figure transformed into a flat rectangular surface, the image of the circular movement of our star of the day will be perfectly represented, in the direct view of any eye, even the untrained eye.

The divisions defined in the attached figure are reproduced for the guideline, at the top and bottom of the graph, per thousand years. Each step is one of the parallel straight lines *aa', bb', cc'...,* directed obliquely. The far left column will contain the 360° of the circle, divided into the 12 signs of the zodiac as these represent the state of the constellations in 1976[60]. The next column will show precessional mobility, as solar navigation has presented it to the human eye over the millennia, through the "Mathematical Combinations" and the "7 Fixed Ones", these being the Marker Stars, and not the planets of our solar system, as is often wrongly stated.

---

[60] Date of first publication of the work. Nde.

The actual astronomical calculations will thus be made in advance without any difficulty. The retrogradation of 6 h 9 mn 11 sec of the sidereal year with respect to the vague year (of 365 days) for example, will take place in 1 423 years, the lines *mm'*, *nn'*, *pp'*, which represent it, end on the lower line divided into years, at a distance of 1 423 years from their starting point on the upper line. As for the retrogradation of the tropical year, this will take place in about 25,920 years.

To give the same origin, the year I starts from the calendar of Athothis Ier, i.e. the first day of Thoth 4241 BC, also the first day of the canicular year of Sirius - Sep'ti.

BIBLIOGRAPHY

In addition to the Bibliography appended to Volume I, the documents studied in this book are (in alphabetical order of authors):

AUTHORS	WORKS
AMÉLINEAU E.	The Antiquity of Time
BALOUT L.	The Prehistory of North Africa
BARTH DR H.	Travel in Africa
BERTHELOT	Saharan Africa
BIDEZ J.	The World City
DE SAINT-VINCENT	Essay on the Isles Fortunées
BOSCOWIZ	Volcanoes and earthquakes
BALL	Fossil man in the Sahara
BREUIL H.	Men of ancient stone
BRUSHES FROM	Cult of fetish gods
BRUCE J.	Journey to Nubia
BUCH DE	The Canary Islands
BURMEISTER	History of Creation
CELERIER J.	History of Morocco
CHABAS	Studies on Antiquity
CHEVALIER A.	Chari-Lake Chad Mission
CONTENAU DR	Phoenician civilisation

DAMMANN E.	Religions of Africa
DAUMAS F.	The Algerian Sahara
DELISLES	A Philosophical History of the Early World
DERIGNE R.	A lost continent
DORESSE J.	Ancient Ethiopia
DUBOIS M.	Strabo's Geography
DUPUIS CH.	Origin of all cults
DUVEYRIER H.	The Tuaregs of the North
DUVILLE	Oethiopia Orientalis
FROBENIUS	The African Atlas
FURON R.	Manual of General Prehistory
GAYET	The first civilisations
GSELL H.	Cherchell
"	Ancient History of North Africa
GUERIN DU ROCHER	History of Fabulous Times
HEEREN M.	The ancient peoples of Africa
JAUBERT	Geography of Edrisi
"	Geography of ancient Africa
LA FAYE J.B. DE	History of the Barbary Kingdoms
LAPPARENT A. DE	The Ancient Glaciers
LHOTE H.	Grappling with the Sahara
"	The Tuaregs of the Hoggar
LOBO FATHER	Abyssinian relations
MALLET	Creation

MARCAIS G.	The Arabs of Berberia
MAUNY R.	West Africa
MENART R.	The private lives of the Ancients
MONOD TH.	Studies on the Western Sahara
MORGAN J. DE	Prehistoric mankind
PANIAGUA DE	Neolithic civilisations
SACY F. DE	Arab Antiquities
SALT H.	Journey to Abyssinia
SAVARY CL.	Adrar-Ahnet
SERRES M. DE	Essay on caves
SLANE DE	History of the Berbers
VANDIER J.	Archaeology Manual
VAN GENNEP	The current state of the totemic problem

This bibliography can be found in the library of the "Les Fontaines" Centre, near Chantilly, in the Oise region, among the 600,000 volumes over which the Jesuit Father librarians keep a watchful eye, and which they willingly allow scientific, theological and university researchers to consult.

OTHER TITLES

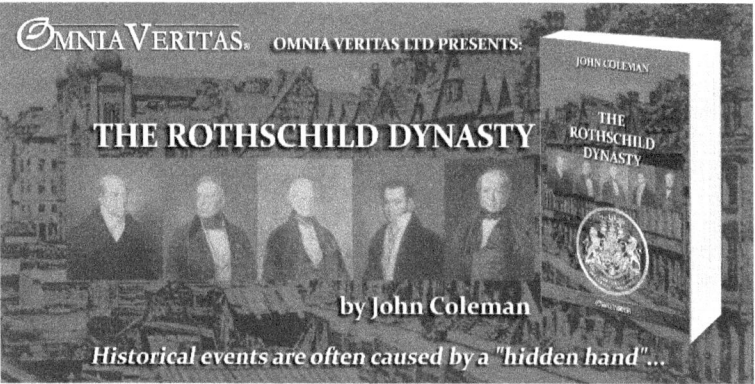

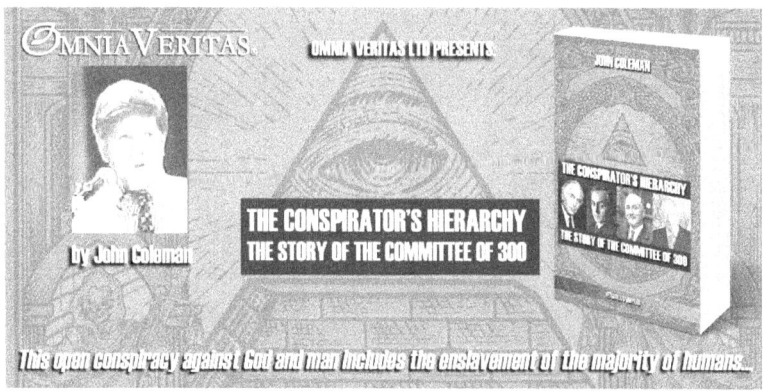

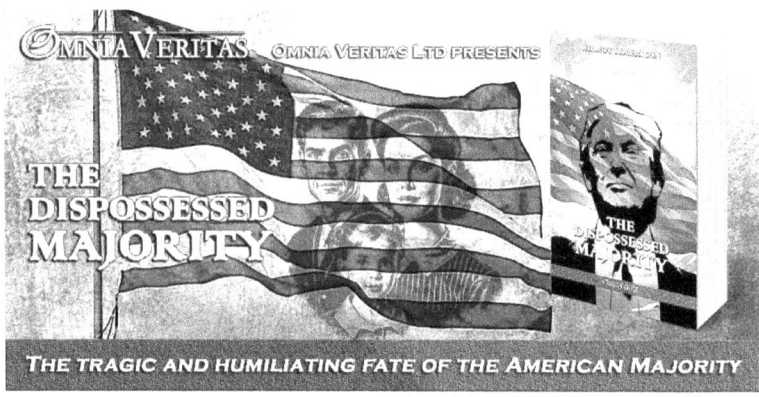

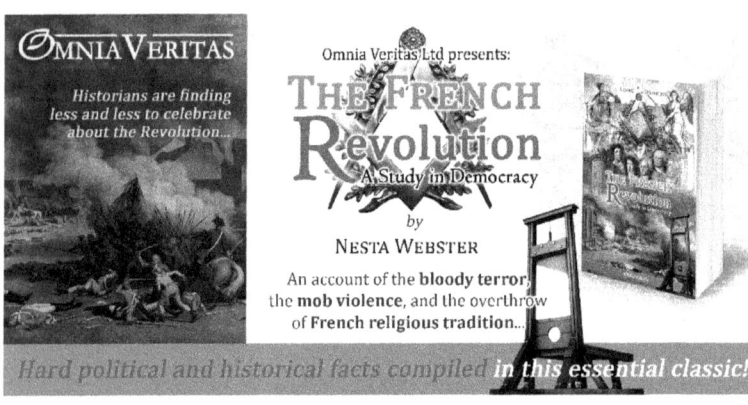

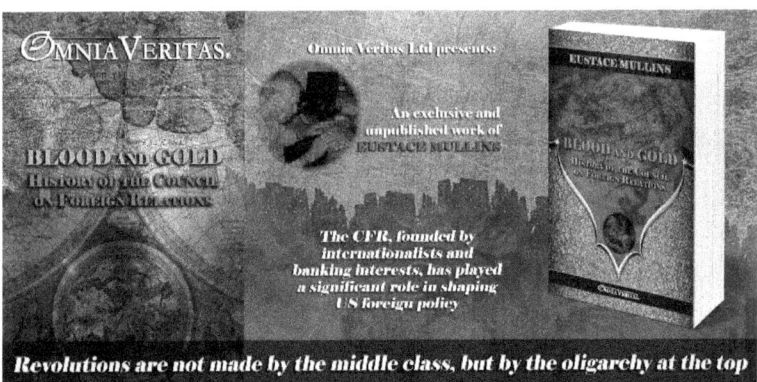

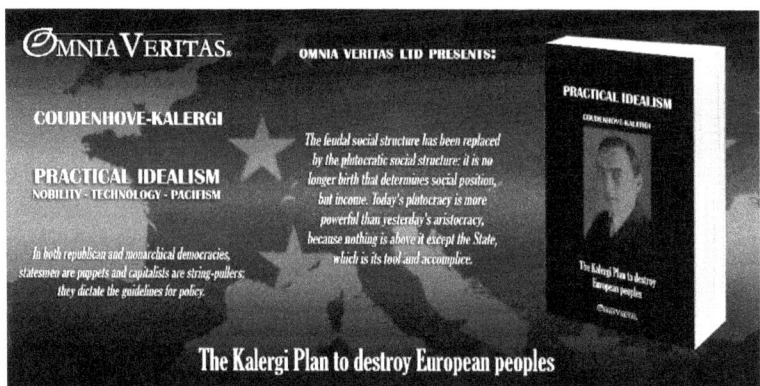

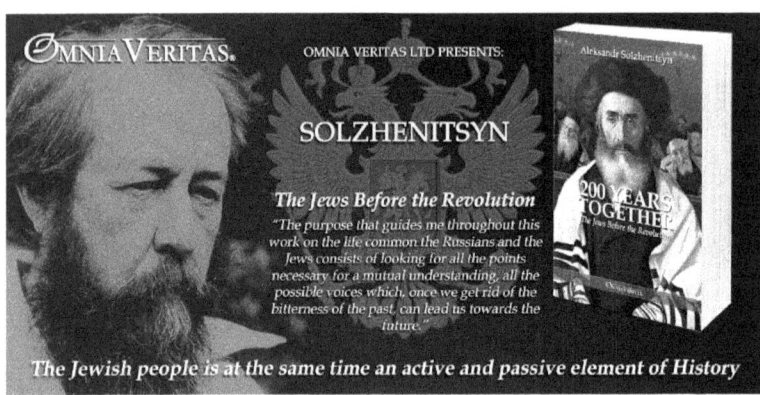

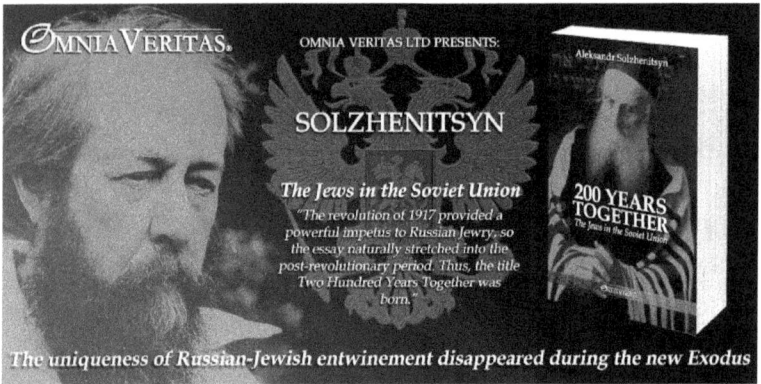

www.ingramcontent.com/pod-product-compliance
Lightning Source LLC
Chambersburg PA
CBHW050127170426
43197CB00011B/1743